NEURAL PLASTICITY ACROSS THE LIFESPAN

Neural Plasticity Across the Lifespan reviews the recent scientific developments that are transforming our understanding of the human brain. The book provides an integrated overview of contemporary research on neural plasticity – the process by which the brain can change in structure and function to cope with new experiences and react to the effects of acquired damage or sensory deprivation. It reviews data on plasticity in the developing brain, looking at both typical and atypical development, alongside clinical and observational research on the adult population. It covers a number of key topics, including:

- different forms of neural plasticity.
- factors affecting neural plasticity (aging and gender).
- neural plasticity in language acquisition, memory and bodily self-consciousness.
- mechanisms of repair – plasticity following sensory deprivation and acquired brain damage.

This is an accessible overview of an emerging field of research that has fundamental implications for how we perceive our potential to change throughout our lives. It will be essential reading for all students of cognitive development, cognitive neuroscience and lifespan development.

Gianfranco Denes is a Neurologist. He has been Director of the Neurological Unit at City Hospital, Venice, Italy, and taught Neuropsychology and Neurolinguistics at the Universities of Padova and Venice.

NEURAL PLASTICITY ACROSS THE LIFESPAN

How the brain can change

Gianfranco Denes

LONDON AND NEW YORK

First published 2016
by Routledge
2 Park Square, Milton Park, Abingdon, Oxon, OX14 4RN

and by Routledge
711 Third Avenue, New York, NY 10017

*Routledge is an imprint of the Taylor & Francis Group,
an informa business*

© 2016 Gianfranco Denes

The right of Gianfranco Denes to be identified as the author of this Work has been asserted by him/her in accordance with sections 77 and 78 of the Copyright, Designs and Patents Act 1988.

All rights reserved. No part of this book may be reprinted or reproduced or utilised in any form or by any electronic, mechanical, or other means, now known or hereafter invented, including photocopying and recording, or in any information storage or retrieval system, without permission in writing from the publishers.

Trademark notice: Product or corporate names may be trademarks or registered trademarks, and are used only for identification and explanation without intent to infringe.

British Library Cataloguing-in-Publication Data
A catalogue record for this book is available from the British Library

Library of Congress Cataloging-in-Publication Data
Denes, G., author.
  Neural plasticity across the lifespan : how the brain can change / Gianfranco Denes.
    p. ; cm.
  Includes bibliographical references and index.
  I. Title. [DNLM: 1. Neuronal Plasticity—physiology.
2. Age Factors. 3. Sensory Deprivation—physiology.
  WL 102] QM575
  612.8'2—dc23
  2015011714

ISBN: 978-1-84872-280-4 (hbk)
ISBN: 978-1-84872-281-1 (pbk)
ISBN: 978-1-315-84946-1 (ebk)

Typeset in Bembo
by Apex CoVantage, LLC

For Elena, Anna and Nicholas

CONTENTS

Foreword   *xi*
Preface   *xiii*

SECTION 1
Introducing plasticity   1

1 Plasticity: a tentative definition   3

2 Neural plasticity: general principles   9
   Brain evolution and development   10
      Introduction   10
      Genetics and brain development   11
      Epigenetics, brain development and plasticity   12
      The process of brain development   13
      The development of the cerebral cortex   15
   The making of the mind   18
      Cultural recycling of cortical maps   19
   Defining neuroplasticity   21
      The emergence and shaping of the notion of neural plasticity:
         some historical remarks   22
      Structural and functional plasticity   26
      Structural plasticity   27
      The dynamics of dendritic spines   27

Neurotrophins	28
Neurogenesis	29
Grey and white matter changes: neuroimaging studies	30
Neuroimaging and neural plasticity	30
Grey matter changes	31
White matter changes	33
Functional plasticity	35
Synaptic functional plasticity	35
The remapping of cortical space	35
The effect of training	36
Large scale remapping following brain injury	36
Structural and functional plasticity: two distinct processes?	37
Spatial and temporal characteristics of neural plasticity	38
Fast motor skill learning	39
Slow motor skill learning	39
Structural plasticity associated with slow learning	40
Unimodal and cross-modal brain plasticity	40
Maladaptive plasticity	43
Focal dystonias: writer's cramp musician's dystonia	43
Writer's cramp	44
Musician's dystonia	44
Chronic pain	45

SECTION 2
The role of specific factors on neural plasticity   59

3	The impact of demographic factors in shaping neural plasticity	61
	The influence of age on neural plasticity: development and aging	61
	The critical period	61
	Brain changes following injury in the sensitive period	64
	Anatomical and functional changes in the aging brain	65
	Age-related neuronal changes	67
	The cognitive functions in the aging brain	68
	Compensatory strategies	69
	Normal and pathological aging	71
	Living aging	72
	Neural plasticity and individual and gender differences	73
	Inter-individual differences	73
	Neural plasticity and sex/gender differences	77

A right brain for the left hand: similarities and differences in the left brain   80
Language representation   82
Handedness and praxis   82

SECTION 3
Specific skills   93

4   Language and neural plasticity   95
    Functional and structural processes of language: typical and atypical development   95
      The anatomo-functional basis of language   96
      The neurological basis of language development   98
      The acquisition of language beyond the critical period and the role of the right hemisphere   99
        Social isolation and development of language: the case of Genie   100
        The missing left hemisphere and language development   102
    Culturally acquired language modalities: reading and writing   104
    Many languages, one brain   107
      Cross-linguistic differences   107
      Cross-linguistic differences in processing written language   108
      The bilingual brain   109
        Individual differences in L2 learning   111
      The neural basis of signed language   113
      Reading by hand: the Braille system   114

5   Memory systems and brain plasticity   122
    Distinctions among memory systems   122
    Processes and plasticity in memory   124
    The effect of sleep deprivation on memory plasticity   126
    Declining memory in aging   128

6   The self and its brain   131
    The strange case of the phantom limb   132
    The changing-body representation   134
    Xenomelia   135

SECTION 4
The mechanisms of repair — 139

7 Sensory deprivation and neural plasticity — 141
   Cross-modal and unimodal plasticity in sensory impaired
       subjects — 142
     Unimodal plasticity — 142
     Multimodal restorative plasticity — 143
     Mechanisms of multimodal plasticity — 144
   Preverbal deafness, cochlear implants and speech and language
       development — 145
     Preverbal deafness — 145
     Cochlear implants and auditory plasticity — 147
   The mechanisms of neural plasticity in congenitally
       blind subjects — 149
     Visual substitution sensory devices in blindness — 150

8 Plasticity and recovery of brain damage — 155
   Factors influencing recovery — 156
     Age — 156
     Nature, extent and site of lesion — 158
   The mechanisms of recovery — 160
     Spontaneous recovery — 160
     Late stage recovery — 162
   The restoration of lost functions: the effect of therapy — 163
     Neural plasticity underlying rehabilitation of motor function
         after stroke — 164
     The effects of speech therapy — 165
   Non-invasive methods for enhancing plasticity in the human
       cortex: uses and limitations — 167
     The use of NIBS to promote functional recovery after stroke — 169

Glossary — 177
Author Index — 183
Subject Index — 191

FOREWORD

In the world of contemporary neuroscience, *plasticity* is one of the magic words. Just use it, and observe the smiles and approving nods in the attentive audience, indicating a widespread, gratifying social consensus about the wonderful concept. One of the possible reasons for this general appreciation is that plasticity is cool. Just say the word, and we all feel like up-to-date, positive-thinking neuroscientists. We are not among the sad people who believe in old stories, such as the one that we are born with a fixed allotment of brain tissue, and that's it. The latter is a dismal concept: basically, if you are lucky enough to become old, you can expect to continuously lose those precious neurons. The concept of a fixed, unchanging brain (made up of "perennial elements", in Bizzozero's terminology) is evocative of rigidity, asociality, lack of interest in others – even predestination, genetic determinism and other unpalatable ends. Plasticity is politically correct, and we all love it.

In order to get the true facts about plasticity, however, you need to acquaint yourself with a large mass of experimental data, ranging from synaptic trafficking to bilingualism, which is not an easy job for anyone. Gianfranco Denes has done this for us, and we cannot be but grateful. This book covers an impressive amount of information and displays an amazing level of scholarship. He guides us through multiple levels of analysis with a masterful touch, and uncovers for us the bright side of plasticity, as well as the darker aspects of maladaptive changes.

Not surprisingly, given his background, the coverage of neurological and neuropsychological aspects as related to recovery and compensation gets the lion's share, but there is practically no aspect of the subject that is neglected, from mRNA to the nature-nurture debate. There is plenty of food for thought in this book, which will be of great interest to specialists in the medical and psychological professions and also to a more general readership, curious to understand the hard data upon which the magic word rests.

Stefano Cappa
Professor of Neuroscience IUSS Pavia
President of the Federation of the European
Societies of Neuropsychology

PREFACE

In his book *Language and Learning: The Debate between Jean Piaget and Noam Chomsky* (1980), Massimo Piattelli-Palmarini reported on what types of mental structures affect the way in which environmental stimuli are processed and cognitive skills, language par excellence, develop. Chomsky argued that man is born with a genetically determined language facility. Faculty, on the other hand, maintained that one's linguistic structures are not defined by the genome but, instead, are 'constructed' by 'assimilating' (organizing) things in the environment.

According to Piattelli-Palmarini, innate models are similar to *crystals*, reflecting an image of invariance and regularity of specific structures. On the other hand, Piaget's empiricist or interactionist position refers to the *flame*, which remains constant in its global form, in spite of endless internal changes. Just as Chomsky was not interested in the neural organization of the mental processes, Piaget wasn't interested in the process of neural recording and processing of information in the environment. Nor did he investigate how elementary and cognitive skills are implemented in the brain and how they evolve through the lifespan.

Although the notion that the brain can adapt to environmental changes had been developed since the seminal works of William James and corroborated, among others, by the anatomical studies of Ramon y Cajal, it was only after the introduction of neurophysiological (mostly in animal studies) and neuroimaging techniques that the concept of neural plasticity gained popularity among scientists and among a general public, often with the intent of finding a method to enhance (or keep intact) cognitive skills.

The human brain – and, in particular, the cerebral cortex – has been found to be a flexible structure, which can adapt and modify with age and with the acquisition of new motor and cognitive skills. While excellent and recent reviews on developmental cognitive neurosciences are available, this book illustrates and discusses the results of experimental and clinical research on human neural plasticity both in the developing and in the adult brain.

The bulk of this book consists of reporting results from neural studies in normally developing children and adults, as well as supplying observations of patients whose brains, in spite of acquired injuries, show remarkable capacities of reorganization in order to reacquire the lost cognitive functions. This book's final purpose is, therefore, to fill the gap between developmental and adult neurosciences and reinforce the concept of the brain as an open, adapting and modifying system throughout the lifespan.

The two initial chapters focus on the notion of plasticity in general and neural plasticity in particular. Plasticity is, by default, intermixed with the process of development: succinct chapters devoted to this topic follow. These chapters outline factors influencing, either positively or negatively, the outcome of the process of plasticity. In particular, they review factors such as gender, handedness and inter-individual characteristics that shape neural plasticity.

The following chapters cover the role of plasticity in shaping specific cognitive faculties, such as memory and self-cognition. Particular attention is devoted to the neural and functional aspects of language, a species-specific ability. Language development, the process of learning a second language, and the recovery following sensory deprivation (preverbal deafness) or brain damage are highlighted. The acquisition of written language, unlike that of spoken language, is not universal and requires a specific learning process; parts of chapter 4 describe the neural and functional emergence and consolidation of the process of acquiring reading and writing skills.

Man, as opposed to other animal species, is a *cultural animal*, and memory process is essential in acquiring, storing and retrieving the mental thesaurus within the brain. Memory processes are dependent upon the type of memorandum and require specific processes and neural loci. Chapter 5 provides a brief review of the plastic processes involved in ten memory systems.

The brain, like all biological systems, can be damaged by various causes. Quite surprisingly, given its near-inability to update and renew its physical substrate, the brain shows a remarkably amount of functional recovery. This is the focus of the final chapters of the book.

Many friends and colleagues have revised and commented on the various chapters with patience and competence. A warm thanks to Giovanni Berlucchi, Alessandro Minelli, Raffaella Rumiati, Franco Piccione, Luigi Pizzamiglio, Pietro Scimemi, Maria Tallandini and three anonymous reviewers chosen by Routledge.

Maria Denes Rosser "translated" for the readers my occasionally unintelligible English. Last, but not least, thanks to Marta Peretto for her secretarial work, coupled with big smiles.

SECTION 1
Introducing plasticity

1
PLASTICITY: A TENTATIVE DEFINITION

Biological existence is an iterative reciprocal process that takes place among genes, individuals and the environment. Genes provide a menu of developmental possibilities, but the phenotypic outcome results from the expression of the genes of an organism, as well as from the influence of environmental factors to which the organism is exposed during its life and random events (stochasticism) – for example, the process of mutation or the genetic rearrangement associated with the development of the immune system (Cashmore, 2010).

The awareness of phenotypic plasticity began to emerge in antiquity, when the notion that a person's physical performance could be improved by physical training became widespread: exercised muscles responded to the stimulation and remodeled to improve performance. In the intervening years, scientists have characterized many physiological aspects of this phenomenon across a range of tissues and biological systems. With the introduction of advanced technical tools, ranging from molecular biology to neuroimaging, it has proved possible to uncover some of the mechanisms that underpin postnatal functional and anatomical changes as well as the factors responsible for such changes.

According to Bateson and Gluckman (2011), every organism is the product of two apparently separate processes: robustness and plasticity. Robustness can be defined as the process that leads to an invariant outcome, making a phenotype insensitive or resistant to genetic variations or environmental perturbations (the constitutive trait). This mechanism can work at different levels, from molecular to behavioral, ensuring that all members of the same species share the same traits (Masel and Siegal, 2009). This trait might have evolved as an adaptation mechanism to reduce the effect of mutations, or as a process to avoid environmental variation, or perhaps as an intrinsic property of biological systems. Different mechanisms work together to maintain the constancy of the phenotype; these include the lack of detection of environmental changes, elasticity (see below in this chapter), and the presence of repair mechanisms. Robustness is not, however, an all-or-nothing phenomenon that acts in the same way in all the life stages: a trait that is robust at one stage may lose its property at a different stage. Bateson and Martin (1999), for example, have shown that some behavioral traits, such as smiling, present in the first months of life, are greatly modified in the subsequent months following social interaction.

In contrast, phenotypic plasticity (the set of inducible traits) refers to the ability of species or single individual phenotypes to exhibit alternative morphological, behavioral and physiological characteristics in response to unpredictable environmental conditions (West-Eberhard, 1989; Garland Jr. and Kelly, 2006) or to developmental or acquired body damage. Such phenotype plasticity, or malleability, is universal among living things: well-known examples of plastic development are seasonal polyphenism (the phenomenon where two or more distinct phenotypes are expressed by the same gene) in butterflies, as well as phenotypic changes like acclimation, learning and immune system adaptation (for a review, see Gilbert and Epel, 2009).

The distinction between robustness and plasticity-induced changes can reflect the distinction between gene-induced developmental processes and the ability of a single individual to change its performance in response to environmental changes.

Plasticity and robustness are not, however, mutually excluding processes. Several lines of evidence lead us to view them as interdependent components of the process that generates individual variation. As stressed by Minelli and Fusco (2010), there is no biological criterion for such distinction because the evolution of alternative developmental pathways for distinct environmental settings may share significant similarities with the evolution of physiological adaptations (Arenas-Mena, 2010).

Plasticity must be distinguished from elasticity, a property in bodies by which they recover their former shape or dimensions after the removal of external pressure or of an altering force, as happens with rubber bands. Examples include the elasticity of the skin, the process of repairing a wound, or catch-up growth after starvation.

Plasticity phenomena can be classified in different ways, based on the nature of the interested trait (morphological, physiological, behavioral), the nature of the environmental cue (e.g. diet, specific learning), the phase of sensitivity of the organism to the environment (early on in development or in adult life) or a change of strategy in processing information. A striking example of these latter mechanisms comes from the studies comparing face-processing strategies between typically developed subjects (TD) and subjects affected by Autism Spectrum Disorders (ASD). ASD is characterized by severe social and communication difficulties. A striking qualitative difference between ASD and TD lies in the ways in which ASD and TD observers process faces. Whereas TD individuals rely primarily on information around eyes and eyebrows for face identification, several studies reported that ASD subjects used different strategies, relying mostly on information around the mouth/lower face region (Rutherford et al., 2007). At a closer view, however, other important differences were recently found between the two groups by Nagai et al. (2013): while all TD observers showed the identical strategy in face processing, using the eye/brow regions, the strategies used by ASD observers were not uniform: some of them used a typical mouth/lower face recognition strategy and others used the same strategy used by TD observers, relying on information concentrated in the forehead region. This intergroup difference could be interpreted as an effect of some ASD subjects compensating for the innate atypical strategy used in childhood by learning to discriminate faces relying on the same type of information used by TD children.

On the other hand, plastic changes can involve anatomical modifications of specific anatomical systems over the lifespan and allow cortical processing to adjust and adapt to experience or to the effects of sensory deprivation or acquired brain damage and provide a mechanism for improving functioning in an adaptive manner. The adjustment processes can extend to different fields; it is possible, for example, to adjust to different temperatures or to cope with the effects of a body part injury due to a mutation or acquired postnatal damage. For example, blind people can learn to use their hands and fingers for reading, through the Braille system; similarly, pre-verbal deaf children can develop an efficient way of expressing language through hand signs (see chapter 7). Another example is the immune system, within which antibodies are formed in response to foreign proteins that have not previously been encountered by the individual.

Several factors can enhance or limit an organism's plasticity: the time scale over which a plastic response is expressed can be almost immediate, as in the case of some physiological or behavioral responses in animals (West-Eberhard, 2003). Alternatively, plastic responses can be comparatively slow, such as the morphological alterations exhibited by animals in response to diet (Wainwright et al., 1991; Price, 2006).

The organism, however, does not possess equipotentiality, nor do its structures conform to the same plasticity principles and constraints. Striated muscle tissue demonstrates a remarkable malleability and can adjust its metabolic and contractile make-up in response to alterations in functional demands, such as following prolonged training. In contrast, it has long been thought that neural plasticity would be possible only in early life and be restricted to specific regions (see chapter 3).

One of the most important variables in determining the degree of plasticity is the time period; there is often a critical or sensitive period during which an organism has heightened sensitivity in order to acquire information from exogenous stimuli, to develop normally, to acquire a particular skill or to be particularly sensitive to noxious stimuli. Exposure to toxins or drugs during specific stages of development can have dramatic effects: the assumption by pregnant women of thalidomide, a mild sedative, caused an enormous risk of limb abnormalities i(phocomelia) in the newborns.

Conversely, a common trait of aging is a reduction in an organism's plasticity. The gathering of crucial information in the sensitive period can influence later learning or, as detailed in the following chapters, the impact of anomalous sensory experiences may constrain the organism's future plasticity. Visual deprivation in early life, for instance, can impair the development of the visual cortex (Hubel and Wiesel, 1970; Hubel, Wiesel and Levay, 1977).

Although it is generally acknowledged that phenotypic plasticity is an important property of all biological systems, allowing the organism to cope with environmental unpredictability and/or heterogeneity, the effects of the changes are not always beneficial. When, for example, lowland animals are exposed to high altitude, an environment where the oxygen concentration is low, they develop an increase of hematocrit (Ht, the proportion of blood that is expressed as a percentage of the red blood cells [erythrocytes] to the rest of the blood constituent) and hemoglobin (Hb, the protein in red blood cells that carries oxygen). However, it is not clear whether the acclimatization response to environmental hypoxia can be regarded generally as a beneficial mechanism of adaptive phenotypic plasticity, or whether it might sometimes represent a misdirected response that acts as a hindrance to adaptation; the excessive number of red blood cells limits exercise performance and pulmonary function, leading the process of adaptation away from the apparent phenotypic optimum under chronic hypoxia. In the following chapters, examples of neural maladaptive plasticity will be reviewed.

In conclusion, increasing our understanding of phenotype plasticity, from molecules to behavior, can help us improve and repair human skills at different levels of anatomical, physiological and cognitive complexity.[1]

Note

1 *Excusatio non petita*: Although, plasticity is a widespread phenomenon across all biological systems, this review will focus only on the nervous system, and almost exclusively on the human brain cortex, the most useful tool in trying to adapt to our ever-changing environment.

Bibliography

Arenas-Mena C. (2010), Indirect development, transdifferentiation and the macro regulatory evolution metazoans. *Philosophical Transactions of the Royal Society B, Biological Sciences, 365*: 653–669.

Bateson P. and Gluckman P. (2011), *Plasticity, Robustness, Development and Evolution*, Cambridge (MA), Cambridge University Press.

Bateson P. and Martin P. (1999), *Design for a Life: How Behaviour Develops*, London, Jonathan Cape.

Cashmore A.R. (2010), The Lucretian swerve: The biological basis of human behavior and the criminal justice system. *Proceedings of the National Academy of Sciences USA, 107*: 4499–4504.

Garland T. Jr. and Kelly S.A. (2006), Phenotypic plasticity and experimental evolution. *Journal of Experimental Biology, 209*: 2344–2361.

Gilbert S.F. and Epel D. (2009), *Ecological Developmental Biology: Integrating Epigenetics, Medicine, and Evolution*, Sunderland (MA), Sinauer Associates.

Hubel D.H. and Wiesel T.N. (1970), The period of susceptibility to the physiological effects of unilateral eye closure in kittens. *Journal of Physiology, 206*(2): 419–436.

Hubel D.H., Wiesel T.N., Levay S. (1977), Plasticity of ocular dominance columns in monkey striate cortex. *Philosophical Transactions of the Royal Society B, Biological Sciences, 278*(961): 377–409.

Masel J. and Siegal M.L. (2009), Robustness: Mechanism and consequences. *Trends in Genetics, 25*(9): 395–403.

Minelli A. and Fusco G. (2010), Developmental plasticity and the evolution of animal complex life cycles. *Philosophical Transactions of the Royal Society B, Biological Sciences, 365*: 631–640.

Nagai M., Bennett P.J., Rutherford M.D., Gaspar C.M., Kumada T., Sekuler A.B. (2013), Comparing face processing strategies between typically-developed observers and observers with autism using sub-sampled-pixels presentation in response classification technique. *Vision Research, 79*: 27–35.

Price T.D. (2006), Phenotypic plasticity, sexual selection, and the evolution of colour patterns. *Journal of Experimental Biology, 209*: 2368–2376.

Rutherford M.D., Clements K.A., Sekuler A.B. (2007), Differences in discrimination of eye and mouth displacement in autism spectrum disorders. *Vision Research, 47*: 2099–2110.

Wainwright P.C., Osenberg C.W., Mittelbach G.G. (1991), Trophic polymorphism in the pumpkinseed sunfish (Lepomis gibbosus Linnaeus): effects of environment on ontogeny. *Functional Ecology, 5*: 40–55.

West-Eberhard M.J. (1989), Phenotypic plasticity and the origins of diversity. *Annual Review of Ecology and Systematics, 20*: 249–278.

West-Eberhard M.J. (2003), *Developmental Plasticity and Evolution*, New York, Oxford University Press.

2
NEURAL PLASTICITY
General principles

The search for the nature of the knowledge that characterizes the human species, allowing it to achieve its outstanding level of cognition, can be traced back to classical Greek philosophy. Since the fifth century BC, there have been two opposite views: the first emphasizing the innate structure of knowledge (Plato) and the second supporting the idea that human knowledge is a consequence of postnatal processes of learning and memory (Aristotle). The dialogue between nativists and empiricists, or on the nature-versus-nurture[1] origin of the human mind, continued and was enriched in the following centuries, although it was mostly considered a theoretical subject, more pertinent to philosophy than science.

It was only in the last two centuries, when the notion that the nature of cognitive skills and their development throughout the lifespan could be experimentally tackled, that the debate between empiricists and nativists acquired a scientific status (for a short review, see Cashmore, 2010).

In more recent times, the massive entrance of biology into the field of cognition entirely reshaped the research field. Genetics, comparative and developmental neuroanatomy and the advent of neuroimaging techniques took over the discipline and, at the same time, enriched the philosophical debate with opportunities for mind-enriching, interdisciplinary collaborations.

At first, the meaning of the terms *nature* and *nurture* did not seem quite adequate and needed further specification: instead of *inborn* (versus *acquired knowledge*), *nature* was defined as a set of characteristics of a given organism, and the term did not carry implications about the characteristics' development. On the other hand, *nurture* stood for the processes by which such characteristics develop (Bateson and Gluckman, 2011). From a more neurophysiological perspective, Wiesel (1981), in his Nobel lecture, proposed the following distinction: "innate mechanisms endow the visual system with highly specific connections, but visual experience early in life is necessary for their maintenance and full development".

It soon became apparent that human cognition could be considered the final result of two interwoven processes that shape the anatomy and functional characteristics of the brain: evolution and development. The time scale of these processes is incomparably different: millions of years for evolution; years, months and possibly even minutes for development and skill learning (Greenough and Chang, 1989). In both cases, however, the final end point is the production of diversity. Evolution proceeds by modulating development: in particular, it allows the environment to develop and differentiate specific neural structures responsible for species-specific and individual neural and cognitive traits. It follows that some characteristics of an organism are explained by the organism's intrinsic nature and shared by the entire species while others reflect the influence of the environmental traits that vary among populations and individuals (Innocenti, 2011).

This chapter will be centered on the functional and neural mechanisms that shape the brain architecture following postnatal experience (neural plasticity). These mechanisms are linked to, and in some way shaped by, innate skills. In particular, we will describe the processes according to which developing and adult brains interact and adapt to environmental stimuli, physiological changes, learning, sensory deprivation and brain damage.

Neural plasticity is enhanced in the developing brain follows that the postnatal and adult plastic changes cannot be understood without reference to the evolutional and developmental processes; the first section of this chapter will therefore outline the neural and functional processes linked to brain evolution and development, while the subsequent pages will describe brain plasticity across the lifespan, as well as its advantages and its limits.

Brain evolution and development

Introduction

The increasing interest (*The Decade of the Brain 1990–1999*, a program launched by former president G. W. Bush; Alivisatos et al., 2013) and the availability of new technologies in the study of healthy and damaged brains have fostered an interdisciplinary approach within the field of brain evolution and development: evolutionary developmental biology. Evo–devo (Müller, 2007) explores the mechanistic relationships between the processes of individual development and phenotypic change during evolution. As a result of this merging, our understanding of how the development of organisms evolved has been considerably improved, and so has our knowledge of how evolutionary developmental interactions relate to environmental conditions.

Genetics and brain development

The decoding of humans' and other primates' genomes (International Human Genome Sequencing Consortium, 2004) seemed to offer, a decade ago, the most valuable opportunity to understand how changes in DNA resulted in the evolution of human cognitive features. Unfortunately, however, the discovery that the genetic distance between humans and our closest primates, chimpanzees and bonobos, is of the order of 1%–5.2% (Chen and Li, 2001) shows only quantitative differences. It soon became evident that the spin-off of such findings was in some way lacking in its explanation of the nature and development of human cognitive skills. Most of these genetic changes do not provide significant contributions to the peculiarities of the human phenotype and are therefore evolutionarily neutral (Vallender et al., 2008). Only a strategy aimed at screening the genome for regions that contain a large number of specific DNA sequence changes (suggesting adaptive evolution in such loci) seemed to be particularly fruitful in the search for the specific molecular bases of the human brain. Charrier et al. (2012) described the evolutionary history and function of the human gene SRGAP2, providing evidence for molecular and cellular mechanisms that may link this gene's evolution with that of the human brain. SRGAP2 is involved in brain development, and humans have at least three similar copies of the gene, whereas non-human primates carry only one. Such duplication gives rise to a gene that may have helped to make human brains bigger and more adaptable than those of our ancestors (Geschwind and Konopka, 2012). In addition, it has been proposed that the amino acid composition in the human variant of the FOXP2 gene has undergone an accelerated evolution that could have occurred around the time of language emergence in humans (Konopka et al., 2009). Other gene changes, associated with reduced brain size (microcephalia) and affecting neural development (for a review, see Somel et al., 2013), have also been mapped.

The next step following the discovery of gene sequencing has been the comparative study of gene expression – that is, the mechanism that transfers the genetic information from the DNA sequence to the organismal phenotype. This approach allows a comparison between the biosynthesis of mRNA (RNA transcription) across different species. It also allows to explore similarities and differences of gene expression within the human-specific mRNA abundance profile across brain regions with specific functions such as Broca's area and the dorsolateral prefrontal cortex, regions deeply involved in human-specific cognitive skills (Khaitovich et al., 2004). Quite surprisingly, no substantial difference was found across different primate species or among different cortical regions of the human brain. This lack of difference seems to indicate that specific cognitive functions can emerge without large-scale genomic changes (Somel et al., 2013).

Possibly the most important result signaling the interaction between genetic and environmental factors is the finding that 70% of genes expressed in primate and human brains undergo changes in mRNA abundance in early postnatal development, although with different time schedules among the species (heterochrony, Gould, 1977). In addition, most changes in the shape of developmental trajectories of mRNA abundance are mainly restricted to the human species. These changes are more prominent in the prefrontal cortex and affect genes associated with the development and functioning of synapses (the junction between axon terminus and adjacent neuron, across which nervous impulses are transmitted). Most importantly in the present context, the peak expression of synaptogenesis is reached around 5 years after birth and extends up to 10 years later than has been observed in other primates, whose synaptogenesis peak does not exceed a few months after birth (Huttenlocher and Dabholkar, 1997, Liu et al., 2012).

Epigenetics, brain development and plasticity

Mention must be finally given to the role of *epigenetics* in the process of brain development and plasticity. The term *epigenetic* refers to functionally relevant changes to the genome that do not involve a change in the nucleotide sequence. Examples of mechanisms that produce such changes are DNA methylation and histone (proteins found in cell nuclei that package and order the DNA into structural units called nucleosome) modification, each of which alters how genes are expressed without altering the underlying DNA sequence. There is increasing evidence for the role of epigenetic factors in mediating the relationship between prenatal and postnatal experiences and long-term outcomes. Exposure to stress during the early stages of prenatal development may involve disregulation of placental gene expression. Nutritional environment during fetal development has also been demonstrated to influence growth, metabolism and brain development.

In postnatal development, epigenetics can influence the process of synaptic plasticity and memory consolidation. High levels of maternal care and exposure to juvenile environmental enrichment (EE) have been demonstrated to improve capacity for learning and memory associated with long term potentiation (see section 2.5.1 of this chapter) enhancement. Moreover, recent evidence suggests that EE modulates signaling pathways in the hippocampus and improves contextual fear memory formation across generations such that offspring of enriched mothers likewise benefit (for a review, see Fagiolini et al., 2009).

The process of brain development

In the course of evolution, specific phenotypes and flexible developmental mechanisms that shape the size and form of the human brain have been selected.

Brain development is guided by innate mechanisms, some of them similar in all mammals, but some events during the course of evolution led to specific qualitative and quantitative changes in the human species (for a review, see Preuss, 2009).

Johnson (2001, 2011) proposed three accounts of how the neural basis supports the process of cognitive development. A first mechanism postulates a process of postnatal development of dedicated neural regions, which allows the emergence of specific skills; a second is based on the establishment and reinforcement of the connections among several cortical regions, whose interaction gives rise to the establishment of new neural networks at the base of complex cognitive skills. The third account calls forth a skill learning process: the acquisition of sensory information in the early postnatal period is mediated by specific neural sites whose importance decreases in later life in favor of different brain regions, once the critical period is over (see Figure 2.1).

Further assessment of the three perspectives on human functional brain development will require improved methods for non-invasive functional imaging, such as frequency-domain near-infrared spectroscopy (FD-NIRS).[2] Adopting this technique, Franceschini et al. (2007) were able to monitor the regional difference in the timing of cerebral blood volume (CBV) increase. The first region to show a large increase in CBV is the occipital area, which almost doubles in infants from 0–2.5 to 2.5–5 months. At the same time, there is an increase in CBV in the parietal and temporal regions. In contrast, CBV in the frontal region increases more linearly, until it reaches a plateau between 8 and 9.5 months.

a Maturational

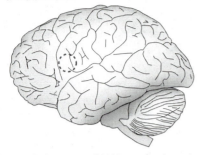
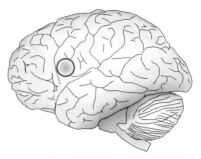

Before successful object retrieval

Successful object retrieval

b Interactive specialization

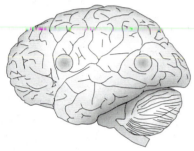
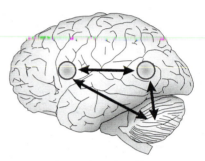

Before successful performance:
poor or disorganized inter-regional interaction

Successful performance:
appropriate interactions established

c Skill learning

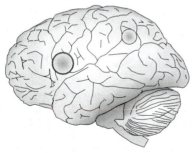
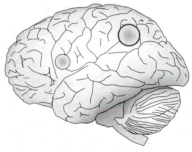

During skill acquistion:
greater activation of frontal regions

After skill acquistion:
greater activation of posterior regions

Nature reviews | Neuroscience

FIGURE 2.1 Three accounts of the neural basis of an advance in behavioral abilities in infants. Reprinted by permission from Macmillan Publishers Ltd: Mark H. Johnson. Functional brain development in humans. *Nature Reviews Neuroscience 2*, 475–483 (July 2001).

The development of the cerebral cortex

Until a few years ago, two general hypotheses about the weight of genetic endowment and experience on cortical development predominated: the protomap and the protocortex. The former postulated that the cortical progenitor zone contains the information that generates specific cortical areas, whereas the latter postulated that thalamic afferent axons, through activity-dependent mechanisms, impose cortical areas' identity on an otherwise homogeneous cortex. Experimental evidence has, however, modified these extreme versions, showing that the development of cortical areas involves a rich array of signals, with considerable interplay between intrinsic cortical mechanisms and mechanisms that are extrinsic to the cortex (Sur and Rubenstein, 2005). It is therefore possible to assume that large-scale cortical regions are formed by graded patterns of gene expression suited for certain computations (protomaps). Inside these spaces, smaller activity-dependent regions develop, associated with the protocortex view (for a review, see Johnson, 2011)

The human brain cortex, phylogenetically the most recent structure, is three times larger than the chimpanzee cortex: present-day chimpanzees of about the same body size as humans and gorillas of considerably larger sizes than humans have brains weighing 300–400 grams, about the size of the brain of early hominids of the genus Australopithecus living some three million years ago. Over the last two million years, the brain of our ancestors increased rapidly to its current weight of 1300–1500 grams. Looking more closely, other important interspecies differences appear: the human cortex has only 1.25 times more neurons than the chimpanzees, the remaining space being filled by axons, dendrites and synapses (Herculano-Houzel, 2012). This space, the neuropil, consists of a dense tangle of axon terminals, dendrites and glial cell processes. It is the locus where synaptic connections are formed between branches of axons and dendrites. Its wide extension in the human brain suggests that the high number and complexity of neural circuitry provide the biological substrate for cognitive postnatal development. It is through this network that an efficient communication among cortical sites, subcortical nuclei, the spinal cord and the cerebellum can be established.

The postnatal synaptogenesis increase is not, however, uniform across the cortex, being more rapid in the visual and primary auditory areas (Huttenlocher and Dabholkar, 1997) and slower in the prefrontal cortex. Changeux and Danchin (1976) analyzed synaptic spine density on the dendrites in a large sample of human prefrontal cortices in subjects ranging in age from newborn to 91 years: the dendritic spine density in childhood exceeds adult values by two- to threefold and begins to decrease during puberty. The long and delayed process of synapse formation to over five years in humans, compared to a few months in other primates, could therefore be considered a potential mechanism contributing to the emergence of postnatal, culturally driven behavior.

At a different level, other features characterize the human brain cortex: a larger development of the left hemisphere planum temporale (Geschwind and Levitsky 1968), a region involved in language and sometimes identified with Wernicke's area, which is a critical component of the language neural network, and a high degree of functional asymmetry between the two hemispheres (for a review, see Denes and Pizzamiglio, 1999).[3]

Cortex development is characterized by regressive and productive events, shaping the neural circuitry and the selection of axons across a variety of phenotypes (Bourgeois and Rakic, 1993). Data obtained from post-mortem or *in vivo* neuroimaging studies converge in showing that, at birth, the majority of neurons have reached their final location in most regions of the brain, a datum consequent with the notions that complex brains require stable conditions and that adult neurogenesis might be an archaic tract, present, in the human brain, only at the level of two restricted cerebral regions outside the neocortex, the sub ventricular zone of the lateral ventricles and the hippocampal dentate gyrus (Eriksson et al., 1998; also see section 2.3.6 of this chapter).

On the contrary, the establishment of the pattern of synaptic connections is a prolonged process that involves overproduction of cells, axons and synapses and a later 'pruning' in response to environmental influences. Developmental exuberance of neural connections is one of the mechanisms at the basis of neural networks: initially related to the formation of transient callosal projections between visual areas of the cat brain during development, it has been later shown that this process is widespread, involving thalamo-cortical, cortico-cortical and cortico-subcortical projections. Two types of exuberance have been described: macroscopic and microscopic. The former involves the temporary formation of afferent and efferent projections to one or more cortical areas, subcortical nuclei, spinal cord and cerebellum. Microscopic exuberance refers to the formation of transient structures, formed by axonal or dendritic branches, synapses and or dendritic spines (small protrusions of the neuron that receive input from synapses, establishing excitatory synapses) in restricted cortical territories that will not be found in the adult brain (Innocenti and Price, 2005).

Most of the thalamo-cortical, cortico-cortical and callosal connections rapidly disappear in the early postnatal period in most mammal species. In humans it has been demonstrated that the corpus callosum, the major bundle of fibers connecting the two hemispheres, is grossly reduced during the end of gestation and in the first postnatal months. The largest number of supranumerary synapses has been recorded in the cerebral cortex of human and nonhuman primates. It is generally accepted that synaptic pruning in the cerebral cortex, including prefrontal areas, occurs at puberty and is completed during early adolescence (Huttenlocher and Dabholkar, 1997). More recent data show, however, that overproduction and developmental remodeling, including substantial elimination of synaptic spines, is a lifelong process, continuing beyond adolescence and throughout the third decade of life before stabilizing at the adult level (Petanjek et al., 2011), followed by a decay in normal and pathological aging. The process of selection and elimination of synapses could provide a high degree of flexibility in the formation of neural circuits and the emergence of new cortical areas (for example, the establishment of the visual word form area; see chapter 4). These areas, in turn, can represent the neural and functional substrate for the development of some uniquely human cognitive capacities following environmental impact – as well as, perhaps, the late onset of specific neuropsychiatric disorders (Rakic et al., 1994).

In addition to the development and selection of dendrites and synapses, the third anatomical factor in the process of brain development is the progressive myelination of cortical axons. Myelin is a sort of insulating shield formed by fatty lipids and proteins, wrapped around the neural axons (the white matter, as opposed to the grey matter, mostly formed by neural cell bodies) essential for an efficient neural transmission. Myelination is not a uniform process: the axon diameters and myelin sheets undergo conspicuous growth during the first two years of life, but reach complete maturation only in adolescence and adulthood. The spinal cord and the brain stem are myelinated first, while prefrontal and temporal myelinate last (Yakovlev and Lecours, 1967). Many studies converge in linking the process of motor, sensory and cognitive development to the timing of myelination, reflecting the increase in the efficiency and speed of communication across brain regions.

> The processes that translate the product of neural activity into human cognition can be considered as the final product of two interwoven mechanisms, the presence and development of species-specific neurological structures and the impact that the postnatal experience has in the process of shaping and refining the anatomy and structure of the brain. Human postnatal development is much longer than other species'; humans take years to fully mature. In addition, postnatal changes are selective, mostly restricted to some regions of the cerebral cortex. These minimally involve neurogenesis (formation of new neurons) but also the formation of dendrites and synapses. These structures allow direct communication between neurons, contributing to the strengthening of genetically programmed neural modules or to the formation of new, experience-dependent functional cerebral mechanisms.

The making of the mind

The issue of pre-existing knowledge versus on-line experience-dependent learning is a fundamental one for the study of cognitive development. Two competing theories are at the forefront: constructivism and nativism.

Developed by the Swiss psychologist Piaget (1957), constructivism had for many years the most profound impact on the field of human perceptual and cognitive development. The kernel of this theory lies in the interaction between genes and the environment: infants construct their own knowledge in response to their experience and interaction with the world around them. The process is stage-like, discontinuous and encouraged by the child's active learning. Piaget was not, however, interested in trying to link the process of cognitive development with anatomical and functional changes, nor did he specify the exact nature of the stage-like cognitive development.

Piaget's empiricist or interactionist position did not go unchallenged. In a series of influential studies, Baillargeon et al. (1985) suggested that the fundamental rules of our knowledge of the physical world, including the properties of objects (e.g. solidity, continuity of motion) are present at birth, but at a primitive stage, evolving in a more sophisticated form as the child develops and its interaction with the external world increases. The novel idea in Baillargeon et al.'s theory (in comparison to Piaget's) was that infants are born with some understanding of the world – a theory that, in recent years, has been actively pursued by linguists and psychologists.

The nativist position assumes that the functional and neural substrates that characterize the process of development and maturation of cognitive skills are innate and represent different phenotypes[4] of certain genotypes that all species have in common. Only the faculty of language, at least in its narrow sense (the recursive faculty[5]), is specifically human, emerging through a process of pre-adaptation or exaptation (a shift of function without changes in anatomical structure, Gould and Vrba, 1982). These skills are organized in modular fashion and conform to the same principles, such as domain specificity (they only operate on certain kinds of inputs), informational encapsulation (no need to refer to other psychological systems in order to operate), obligatory firing (modules process in a mandatory manner), fast speed, shallow outputs (their output is very simple) and having a fixed neural architecture (Fodor, 1983). According to Fodor's original concept, only peripheral systems, such as object perception, auditory and phonological analysis, are modular, while central processes such as memory, reasoning or problem solving are not organized in a modular fashion. More recently, the notion of modularity has been extended to all cognitive processes (the massive modularity thesis, Carruthers, 2006), including reasoning, planning and problem-solving.

At variance with the massive modularity position, a different view advocates that the foundation of cognition is based on the presence of five modules that comprise core knowledge: object, action, number, geometry and social partner representation (Spelke and Kinzler, 2007). These modules, however, do not persist unchanged across the lifespan; in humans, it is the presence of language that modifies infant cognition from an innate modular organization and shapes it into the integrated cognition typical of adulthood (Vallortigara, 2012; Twyman and Newcombe, 2010). A compromise between constructivism and nativism can be made, however, in the light of Darwin's principles of selection: 'inborn' knowledge developed by experience is shared not by single individuals but by the entire human species.

Trying to reconcile the modular view with Piagetian theory, Karmiloff-Smith (1992) supports the view that development proceeds from implicit representations of basic behavioral procedures to successively more complex modules, shaped by experience and learning, with domain-specific outcomes. According to this view, all modules have an evolutionary origin and new skills might recruit evolved modular components.

Cultural recycling of cortical maps

Moscovitch and Umiltà (1990) suggested the existence of complex and in part culturally transmitted modules. These devices have been produced during the processes of evolution and cultural development and are made up of groups of simple modules. Their task is to handle complex information – for example, facial recognition or the processing of written language.

Along the same line, the model proposed by Dehaene and Cohen (2007) is reminiscent of Darwin's preadaptation or exaptation mechanisms at the base of language development in the human species (Hauser et al., 2002). In their model, some biological structures, originally dedicated to different tasks, can readapt or 'recycle' through a process of specific individual learning, supported by brain plasticity, to develop new skills such as written language without significant structural changes.

Their hypothesis predicts the following: each cultural skill should be associated with specific cortical areas consistent across individuals and cultures. In order to develop, they invade evolutionarily older structures, finding a 'neuronal niche' in the brain, whose circuit is set up to perform a similar function

20 Introducing plasticity

and is sufficiently plastic to reorient itself enough to accommodate this novel use. Cultural variability regarding the acquired cognitive processes should be limited due to neural constraints.

The speed and ease of cultural acquisitions should be predictable based on the amount and complexity of the recycling required. Although the acquisition of new skills often leads to significant cognitive gain (literacy improves verbal memory and phonemic awareness,[6] Morais and Kolinsky, 2005), it might be possible to identify small losses in perceptual and cognitive abilities due to competition of the new cultural ability with the evolutionarily older function in relevant cortical regions.

Finally, the connectionist models, that, according to their proponents, are much closer to the way the brain works (Crick, 1989), can be reasonably applied to the processes of cognitive development and plasticity. These models are formed by large sets of neuron-like units (neural networks) interacting locally through connections resembling synapses between neurons. Three main units can be distinguished: input units, which receive signals from outer sources (sensory stimuli, other neural networks); output units, which send signals to outer efferents or to other networks; and hidden units, with efferent and afferent projections internal to the system (see Figure 2.2). The procedures by means of which a neural net can learn to perform a new task are performed by sending appropriate signals to the input units and by computing the discrepancy between output and the target. On a trial and error basis,

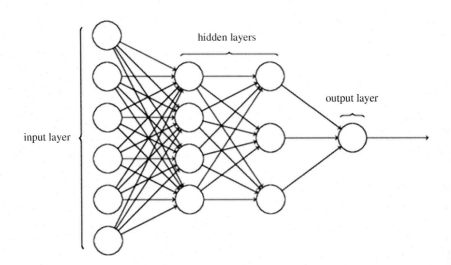

FIGURE 2.2 A simple neural network.

the weights of the connections are modified, with the procedure repeated until the network is able to perform the task (a procedure similar to the Hebbian method, see later in this chapter).

Although, *prima facie*, different from the modular concept of the neural architecture of the mind sketched above, this approach does not deny the existence of a specific neural specialization of some units: connectionist modules could be anatomically and functionally specialized parts of a neural network and they may be the result of a process of evolution in a population of neural networks (for further details, see Rumelhart, 1989; Houghton and Zorzi, 2003).

The mental thesaurus that characterizes humankind has been considered either the product of innate devices (modules or faculties) that activate in the postnatal period or the result of the brain's response to experience and interaction with the outside world. An intermediate position posits that cognitive development starts from innately specified points, becoming, however, domain-specific with the process of development and specific environmental interactions.

Finally, the cultural acquisition of complex domain-specific skills, such as processing written language, could shape the emergence of dedicated modules by recycling brain structures or by combining the work of simple innate modules.

Defining neuroplasticity

Leaving aside the debate between empiricism and nativism, the property of man as a cultural animal (Baumeister, 2005), together and interwoven with the faculty of language, represents the essence of human nature.

Although we share with other species a genetically driven behavior that does not require specific training, our cognitive ability is the final product of a lifelong process of learning by interacting with the environment. This mechanism is based on the human brain's flexibility in response to a variety of stimuli and factors, including instances of functional and anatomical damage, which it achieves by modulating its output as a result of experience and practice and according to different targets or demands. Learning is, therefore, the result of the interaction between intrinsic, robust, innate abilities and those induced by the changes of the functional and anatomical cerebral mechanisms according to environmental needs. This process represents the core of neural plasticity, also referred as brain plasticity, cortical plasticity or brain remapping.

A third factor was added, as outlined in the previous chapter, to the two forms that govern our biological system, including behavior: stochasticism. Stochasticism refers to the inherent variability of the physical properties of the matter, including biological systems. Of particular relevance to the present context is the comparative examination of neural connections: according to Macagno et al. (1973), the formation of neural connections reflects a degree of stochasticism, with no two individuals, even those that are genetically identical and have the same environmental variables, displaying the same neuronal network.

Neural plasticity is defined by Berlucchi and Buchtel (2009: 307) as "the changes in neural organization which may account for various forms of behavioural modifiability, either short-lasting or enduring, including maturation, adaptation to a mutable environment, specific and unspecific kinds of learning, and compensatory adjustments in response to functional losses from ageing or brain damage".

This property not only makes it possible for all members of the human species to learn and share culturally developed skills, not endowed in the genome, but it can also characterize, through the weight of specific experience and environmental variables, the unique traits of single individuals, such as developing talents, confronting the effects of sensory loss, or responding to different forms of brain damage.

The emergence and shaping of the notion of neural plasticity: some historical remarks

Credit must be given to William James who, in his *Principles of Psychology* (1890), first advanced a theory of learning based on a property of the nervous system, plasticity, that allowed for mental changes through a process of habituation of specific brain paths. In James's words (1890, Vol. 1: 105):

> the entire nervous system is nothing but a system of paths between sensory terminus a quo and a muscular, glandular or other terminus ad quem. . . . When a sensory stimulus reaches the cerebral cortex it connects with an effector and on its way out it leaves traces. When the stimulus is repeated, it reinforces old paths or makes new ones. Plasticity, then, in the wide sense of the word, means the possession of a

structure weak enough to yield to an influence, but strong enough not to yield all at once. Each relatively stable phase of equilibrium in such a structure is marked by what we may call a new set of habits. Organic matter, especially nervous tissue, seems endowed with a very extraordinary degree of plasticity of this sort; so that we may without hesitation lay down as our first proposition the following that the phenomena of habit in living beings are due to the plasticity of the organic materials of which their bodies are composed.

In addition, plasticity, James (1890, Vol. 1: 566) added, is crucial not only to reinforce pre-existing paths, but to form new association paths through merging neural components "active together or in immediate succession".

At the same time of the emergence of James's hypothesis, a neurologically oriented theory of the function and nature of neural plasticity and its role in learning started to take hold.

The Italian physiologist Angelo Mosso (1882: 534) first applied an experimental approach to the study of structural brain changes following cognitive activities. He described a "delicately balanced table" that could measure changes in cerebral blood flow associated with mental effort and emotional responses.[7] Although his experiment could at present be considered the forerunner of noninvasive neuroimaging techniques, Mosso's data were somehow neglected. The center stage in the study of neural plasticity was firmly taken by the Spanish anatomist Santiago Ramón y Cajal.

In contrast with the reticular theory proposed by Gerlach and defended by Golgi (for an historical review, see López-Muñoz et al., 2006), according to which the dendrites' only function was nutrition of the neuron, while communication of impulses traveled in the axonal components of a diffuse nerve network, Ramón y Cajal (1895) showed that the relationship between cells was contiguous, rather than continuous: dendrites receive information, while axons send out information centripetally. Although aware of the discoveries of synapses by Sherrington (1906), Ramón y Cajal did not mention the role of synapses in supporting the process of plasticity. Most importantly in the present context, Ramón y Cajal strongly opposed the theory, prevalent in those days, that cortical architecture was rigid and stable: on the contrary, he pursued the concept that the brain had the potential to adapt to the changing conditions of the environment through dynamic histological changes related to the work of mental processes. In his review on the organization of the nervous system (Ramón y Cajal, 1892, quoted by DeFelipe, 2006: 811), he proposed that learning was a product of a sort of "mental gymnastics", a mechanism by which connections between adjacent neurons could be reinforced or formed *de novo* by repeated exercise, thereby improving the abilities of the brain. In Ramón y Cajal's words: "the reinforcement of pre-established organic pathways, the formation of new pathways through ramification and progressive growth of the dendritic arborisation and the nervous terminals represent the neural process for the acquisition of new skills (296)". As a consequence, according to Ramón y Cajal, the different amount of prolonged exercise could therefore explain the inter-individual differences in developing new cognitive skills.

Among the first to fully embrace or even predate (see Berlucchi and Buchtel, 2009) Ramón y Cajal's theories were two Italian neuropsychiatrists, Eugenio Tanzi (1893) and his pupil Ernesto Lugaro (1909). Tanzi approached the question of the facilitating effect of habituation in learning: unaware of the existence of synapses, he postulated that the repetition of activities could cause an hypertrophy of associated neurons, similar to the muscle hypertrophy following physical exercise, by decreasing the distance between adjoining and contiguous neurons, making the inter-neural communication easier. Following Tanzi's theory and strongly influenced by Darwinism, Lugaro proposed that the lifelong processing of learning was possible through a continuous reshaping of the functional organization of the nervous system through the process of plasticity: "The plasticity of the nervous elements, which allows the internal relations to be molded according to the external stimuli, decreases as the years go by: this property, which represents a continuum in the adult of the formative drive of the embryo, declines progressively and reaches an almost complete annulment in a variable time from an individual to other" (written in 1898, English translation by Berlucchi and Buchtel, 2009: 311).

The interest in neural plasticity, as proposed by James and Ramón y Cajal and based on reinforcement of specific pre-existing or formation of neural circuits, was neglected in the following years, mostly following the influence and diffusion of the Mass Theory and Equipotentiality theory proposed by Lashley, an eminent Harvard psychologist. Mass action postulates that certain types of learning are mediated by the cerebral cortex as a whole, contrary to the view that every psychological function is localized at a specific place on the cortex. Equipotentiality, associated chiefly with sensory systems such as vision, relates to the finding that some parts of a system take over the functions of other parts that have been damaged. According to Lashley (1924), cerebral functions involve the combination of localization and decentralization theories, from limited point-to-point correspondence of cells to a condition of absolute nonspecificity.

In addition, the diffusion of psychodynamic theories that emphasize the role of psychological factors in shaping behavior, neglecting the role of physiological mechanisms, shifted the interest of psychologists far from the study of neural plasticity.

It was only in 1948, after the end of the second World War, that J. Konorski, a Polish neuroscientist and, a year later, Donald Hebb (1949), a Canadian neuropsychologist, proposed a theory of learning based on the changes that occur in the brain organization following experience. Repetition of the same stimulus (habituation) shapes the neural base of learning: pre-existing or newly formed neural pathways are reinforced by strengthening specific synapses. In Hebb's words (1949: 62):

> When an axon of cell A is near enough to excite a cell B and repeatedly or persistently takes part in firing it, some growth process or metabolic change takes place in one or both cells such that A's efficiency, as one of the cells firing B, is increased: the frequent co-activation makes the link stable (consolidated), while links that are seldom co-active get weaker and disappear.

The end product of this process is the formation of dynamically shaped neural networks of different size and complexity, modulating the neural and cognitive architectures of the brain. Almost 60 years later, in a series of elegant experiments using Transcranial Magnetic Stimulation (TMS), Pascual-Leone and colleagues (2005) were able to experimentally confirm Ramón y Cajal's intuitions. They mapped the cortical motor areas, targeting the contralateral long finger flexor and extensor muscles in subjects learning a one-handed, five-finger exercise on a keyboard. The process of acquisition of the necessary motor skill involved two different mechanisms, with the first process consisting of a rapid but reversible modulation of the existing pattern. As the task became over-learned over the course of five weeks, the pattern of cortical activation changed as other neural structures were involved, leading to long-term structural changes (see section 2.9.3).

Interest in neural plasticity has become widespread in recent years, becoming one of the most important fields of interest both for psychologists and neurologists. Several factors contributed to this change:

- the recognition that specific factors can influence or limit the process of neural plasticity.
- the advent of advanced neuroimaging studies such as Magnetic Resonance Imaging (MRI) and functional MRI (fMRI), leading to the recognition that, in animal as well as human brains, structural and functional changes can occur and can be mapped *in vivo* following behavioral modifications induced by experience and other factors.
- the experimental demonstration that specific rehabilitation methods can enhance cerebral plasticity by actively modifying the pre-existing damaged pathways.

In the following paragraphs, some of the factors critical for the understanding of neural plasticity will be outlined.

> The functions and, up to a certain degree, the anatomical structures of the brain show a remarkable degree of reactivity to environmental changes and various forms of learning. This process, neural plasticity (NP), is, in addition, crucial in the process of adjustment to functional losses, ranging from sensory deprivation to aging to acquired brain damage.
>
> According to Hebb, repetition of the same stimulus is at the base of learning. This process shapes the neural base of acquiring new information and modifies the behavior by reinforcing or forming new neural pathways by strengthening specific synapses' networks.
>
> NP-induced changes can affect brain organization at temporal and spatial levels. Changes can extend from microseconds to the entire lifespan. Similarly, spatial changes can induce large-scale modifications or modifications restricted to local neural circuits.

Structural and functional plasticity

Life changes determined by age, experience, and pathological processes affect different levels of cerebral organization. Two forms of brain plasticity can be roughly distinguished: structural and functional. The first refers to the morphological changes following acquisition of new knowledge or decreased processing efficiency. Functional plasticity, on the other side, refers to the reorganization of the neural activity, supported by a process of the modifiability of synaptic transmission between neurons.[8]

The changes in brain organization can be examined at different spatial and temporal levels and at various levels of complexity. In time, plasticity extends from microseconds, with instantaneous spiking of synapses, to life-long stable modifications.

The spatial scale at which plastic changes occur varies and can be distinguished into macromaps, mesomaps and micromaps. Macromaps describe how the different brain areas are spatially organized in relation to contiguous regions, with a scale up to several centimeters; mesomaps characterize the global spatial structure within a given brain area; micromaps refer to the fine-grained structure by which small regional parts of a specific area process information (for a review, see Dehaene and Cohen, 2007). At macroscale level, neural plasticity acts by changing the spatial pattern of activation of different brain regions and their corresponding inter-regional connections (Sporns, 2012): for example, Seitz et al. (1995), in a positron emitting tomography (PET) study, showed that slowly developing neoplastic lesions in the motor region of one cerebral human hemisphere can induce large-scale reorganization that is not confined to changes within the somatotopic body representation. Along the same line, in a magnetoencephalography (MEG) study, Rossini et al. (1998) found that, in unilaterally brain damaged stroke subjects, the cortical 'hand area' representation was significantly larger in the damaged hemisphere in comparison to the unaffected hemisphere, suggesting that brain areas outside the normal boundaries may act, following spontaneous or therapy-induced improvement, as supplementary somatosensory hand centers. At mesoscale level, plasticity leads to a modification of the long-range or local cortical and subcortical circuits, as shown by the effect of monocular deprivation (see section 7.2.3) described by Hubel and Wiesel (1998). At microscale level, following the intuitions of Ramón y Cajal and Hebb, physiologists have convincingly demonstrated modifications of cellular and molecular mechanisms underlying synaptic plasticity (Ganguly and Poo, 2013).

Structural plasticity

Morphological brain changes in non-human species have been repeatedly demonstrated, although in different measure, ranging from axonal sprouting, to input specific, activity-dependent synaptic modifications, in response to normal and pathological stimuli and conditions (Hebb's basic process of learning and memory). In addition, the influence of neurotrophic factors on neurogenesis has been experimentally observed in many studies. The last and perhaps the most important factor shaping structural plasticity is, however, represented by the white matter changes.

In humans, the increasing development and use of neuroimaging techniques has evidenced grey and white matter changes linked to the process of neuronal plasticity following a number of factors, such as experience or brain injury.

The dynamics of dendritic spines

Following the theories of Ramón y Cajal and Hebb about the role of inter-neural connectivity as the main factor of neural plasticity, the research on the structural basis of neural plasticity focused on modification of dendritic spines and axons. The notion took hold that the major factor shaping structural neural plasticity derived from the combined actions of the outgrowth of new axonal branches or 'sprouts' (collateral *sprouting*) and the property that a subset of dendritic spines manifests following contact with specific excitatory synaptic structures: while some dendritic spines are life-long structures, other spines grow and retract, linking pre-existing neurons to new neural networks. The dynamics of this turnover are regulated by sensory experience, brain damage, and sensory deprivation (for a review, see Holtmaat and Svoboda, 2009).

At the experimental level, the best-known example of activity-dependent synaptic plasticity is the phenomenon of long term potentiation (LTP) of spine synapses in the hippocampus of rats. LTP is expressed as a persistent increase in the size of the synaptic component of the evoked response, induced by repetitive stimulation and recorded from individual cells or a group of neurons. LTP has been found in all excitatory pathways of the hippocampus, as well as in other brain regions (Bliss and Collingridge, 1993). The opposite phenomenon, long term depression (LTD), another form of activity-dependent plasticity, follows persistent weak synaptic stimulation and it is associated with spine shrinkage and pruning and reduced spine motility (for a review, see Kasai et al., 2010). This active spine dynamic, together with axonal sprouting, the most important means of shaping the process of structural plasticity.

Therefore, it is tempting to speculate that the plastic changes in spine morphology reflect the dynamic state of its associated synapses, which can be considered responsible to some extent for neuronal circuitry remodeling. For example, Hihara et al. (2006) showed, in monkeys trained in tool using, the emergence of novel projections from the higher visual centers to the intra-parietal area, in the vicinity of the temporo-parietal junction and the ventro-lateral prefrontal areas.

It must, however, be remembered that the rate of synaptic changes is influenced not only by activity, but is age dependent. As described in 2.1.5, during the developmental period the infant's cerebral cortex is subjected to a large amount of fiber and synaptic pruning as part of normal development. This process is entirely positive and adaptive, similar to a 'sculpting' (Craik, 2008) of learned behaviors. On the contrary, synaptic loss in aging is more akin to erosion. The same biological process can apparently have different functions and consequences at different life stages.

Neurotrophins

Neurotrophins are a group of proteins that include nerve growth factor (for a review, see Levi-Montalcini and Angeletti, 1988); they represent, together with their receptors, a key factor in the process of regulation of neural development and survival of the axonal and dendritic networks, enhancing synaptic plasticity through modulation of synaptic strength. The brain-derived neurotrophic factor (BDNF) gene, coding for the BDNF protein, is located on chromosome 11 and has been investigated in a wide range of neuroplasticity-related areas, including differences in gross brain morphology, learning, and memory, interactions with plasticity-inducing brain stimulation protocols, and recovery after brain insult; it has been linked to a wide diversity of neurological disorders (for a review, see Chaieb et al., 2014). Various *in vivo* models converge in postulating that BDNF could offer a therapeutic tool for the treatment of a number of neurological diseases (for a review, see Longo and Massa, 2013).

Neurogenesis

A further component was recently added to the mechanisms of structural plasticity: the ability to generate new nerve cells (neurogenesis) in adult life. Although in non-mammal species adult neurogenesis is widespread, until a few years ago many neurobiologists thought that the process of neurogenesis was absent in mammals. According to Ramón y Cajal (1913–14), "Once development was ended, the fonts of growth and regeneration of the axons and dendrites dried up irrevocably. In adult centers, the nerve paths are something fixed and immutable: everything may die, nothing can be regenerated" (375–392). On the contrary, since the pioneering observations of Altman (1962), it is now widely accepted that new neurons continue to be generated beyond development and in adulthood. The process is limited to particular brain regions (the subventricular zone [SVZ] of the lateral ventricles and the dentate gyrus [DG] of the hippocampus) and mostly occurs in the first postnatal period.

The search of newly formed neurons' functional role is more complex: adult neurogenesis has been often considered an archaic trait that has undergone a 'phylogenetic reduction' from amphibian ancestors to the lateral ventricles of humans, whose higher level of cognition needs stable neural circuits in the adult brain (Kempermann, 2012).

Sawada and Sawamoto (2013) have summarized their and other findings on the regulatory mechanisms of SVZ neurogenesis across numerous species. Both SVZ and DG neural stem cells[9] generate new neurons that form cell aggregates that integrate with the already present neural network, allowing the process of postnatal neurogenesis to play an active role both in the recovery from brain injuries and in learning and adaptation. At variance with the above hypothesis, Akers et al. (2014) showed that in mice high levels of neurogenesis lead, mostly during the developmental period, to degradation or forgetting of established memories. According to Akers et al., the process of neurogenesis reconfigures hippocampal circuits, destabilizing pre-existing synaptic connections, labilizing previously encoded memories or impairing the ability of a given set of cues to reactivate the same pattern of activity. During infancy, when neurogenesis levels are elevated, high rates of decay render hippocampus-dependent memories inaccessible at later time points. During adulthood, when neurogenesis levels are lower, memories are more resistant to decay.

Tornero et al. (2013) induced human pluripotent stem cells toward a functional cortical phenotype, providing a potentially useful tool for a stem-cell based therapeutics for stroke. Andres et al. (2011) showed that, in ischemic rat brains, human neural progenitor cell grafting can increase dendritic plasticity in both experimentally damaged and normal contralateral cortex, as well as enhancing axonal transport and sprouting inhibited by the vascular damage. Although very preliminary and, at least up to now, without any evidence of *in vivo* functional effect, these data must be taken into proper consideration in the light of a possible cell therapy following acquired brain damage.

Grey and white matter changes: neuroimaging studies

The third factor involved in the process of structural plasticity is white matter. We already mentioned its changes in the developmental process, as demonstrated by a variety of anatomical studies showing an age-related increase of the thickness of the myelin sheaths and axonal diameters that, in some cortical regions, extends well beyond adolescence. In the following paragraphs, the contribution of neuroimaging studies to understanding the role of white matter in the process of neural plasticity will be described in some detail.

Neuroimaging and neural plasticity

Morphological (magnetic resonance, MRI) and functional neuroimaging studies (functional magnetic resonance, fMRI) have been applied with increased frequency to the study of structural and functional changes in both normal and injured brains. The *in vivo* measures of the morphometric changes in the normal and damaged brain represent, although with some limitations (see chapter 8) the best tool to correlate, in humans, the behavioral changes induced by experience and other factors to the corresponding neural changes. The bulk of studies involve the white matter, the most malleable part of the nervous system, capable of reacting to the influence of development, experience and brain damage.

Two contrasting approaches have been used to apply neuroimaging research to the study of neuroplasticity: cross-sectional and longitudinal studies.

Cross-sectional studies (also known as cross-sectional analyses, transversal studies, or prevalence studies) form a class of research methods that involve observation of a particular function and its anatomical or functional neural substrate in different groups of people at a given period of time. Although largely applied in the study of animal and human brain plasticity involving different skills, this research method is not faultless, since these studies do not distinguish between the possibilities that brain structure varies in response to behavioral variability and vice versa. It is possible, for example, to interpret the group differences as the consequence of possible pre-existing (genetic?) factors, making some subjects more prone to engage in practicing a specific skill, but it is also possible to interpret the anatomical or functional differences as the consequence of the treatment (training, therapy, etc.).

Longitudinal studies or interventional studies are required to help parse causality between brain structure and behavior. Typically, they involve repeated (two or more) measures over time (minutes, hours, days or years) on the same subject(s) of the changes in a skill and/or its anatomical substrate, and they follow a known variable, such as age or specific training. The advantage of this often time-consuming method is to unveil dynamic properties of treatment-related plastic changes. Before describing in more detail the application of these two methods to different subsets of neural plasticity in the following chapters, two examples of the above studies will be provided. One involves grey matter; the second, white matter.

Grey matter changes

By far, the best-known example of structural grey matter plasticity derives from MRI volumetric changes in the hippocampus that were observed in London taxi drivers.

In comparison to sedentary species, small mammals and birds engaged in spatial memory tasks such as food storing show an increased hippocampal volume relative to body size, suggesting a specific role for such a structure in storing spatial representation (see chapter 5). A limit of these studies is, as outlined above, the difficulty to understand whether the differences in brain anatomy are predetermined or are the consequence of the specific navigation training. Maguire et al. (2000) tried to disentangle the above problem by examining morphological hippocampal changes in healthy humans with extensive experience of spatial navigation – specifically, London taxi drivers (LTD). In order to obtain a valid license, LTD must undergo an extensive training (about 2 years), allowing them to successfully navigate across the wide street web of the city. In an MRI study involving LTD, Maguire et al. (2000)

reported an increase of grey matter volume in the hippocampus relative to controls, with a positive correlation of hippocampus volume to the time spent driving. While these grey matter differences could result from using and updating spatial representations, they might instead be influenced by factors such as self-motion, driving experience, and stress. In a further study, Maguire et al. (2006) examined the contribution of these factors by comparing LTD with London bus drivers (LBD), who were matched for driving experience and levels of stress, but differed in navigation learning because they follow a constrained set of routes. Compared with LBD, LTD had greater grey matter volume in mid-posterior hippocampi and less volume in anterior hippocampi. Furthermore, years of navigation experience correlated with hippocampal grey matter volume only in LTD. This last finding suggests that spatial knowledge, and not stress, driving, or self-motion, is associated with the pattern of hippocampal grey matter volume in taxi drivers.

More recently, Gaser and Schlaug (2003), using a voxel-by-voxel morphometric technique, found grey matter volume differences in motor, auditory, and visual–spatial brain regions when comparing professional musicians (keyboard players) with a matched group of amateur musicians and non-musicians. Although some of these multiregional differences could be attributable to innate predisposition, they may represent structural adaptations in response to long-term skill acquisition and the repetitive rehearsal of those skills. The strong associations among structural differences, musician status, and practice intensity support this hypothesis.

Caution, however, must be used in interpreting the grey matter changes shown in MRI studies in humans. First and utmost, it is important to mention that grey matter is not composed only of neurons, but of initial axon segments, dendritic processes and arborizations, glial cells, capillaries and vascular support. Second, as outlined in the previous pages, the process of neurogenesis in the postnatal and adult brain is absent, or at least limited to the early postnatal period; in mice and rats, which show neurogenesis following training, the process is slow and it is maintained over time. On the contrary, the grey matter changes shown in MRI in longitudinal and cross-sectional studies in humans are fast and unstable, returning to the baseline when subjects stop training (for a review, see Driemeyer et al., 2008). This time-course favors quickly adjusting neuronal systems, such as spine and synapse turnover or even changes in blood flow or interstitial fluids, as the underlying factors for grey matter increase, rather than slowly evolving mechanisms such as neuronal or glial cell genesis.

At present it seems much more reasonable to attribute the grey matter changes, observed with neuroimaging techniques, to axonal sprouting and new dendritic spine formation inside the grey matter rather than to a process of neurogenesis.

White matter changes

The white matter plays an essential role in shaping brain plasticity in normal development, as well as in adulthood, as substantiated by a series of anatomical and neuroimaging data.

The massive brain postnatal myelination process, involving an increase in thickness of myelin sheaths and axonal diameters, very active in the early infancy (see previous sections), extends into late childhood and adolescence for motor and sensory cortical areas and into late adulthood for higher order, cortical, associative areas (Giedd et al., 1999).

In adults, Schlaug (for a summary, see Schlaug et al., 2009) found that intensive musical training influences an increased development of the midsagittal motor-related parts of the corpus callosum (the biggest inter-hemispheric bundle of myelinated fibers connecting the two hemispheres), suggesting a development of stronger anatomical inter-hemispheric connection between motor cortical areas. This development was more evident in musicians who started their musical training at the age of 7, as compared with those who started later in life. Working in the same field, Amunts et al. (1997) measured through MRI the length of the posterior wall of the precentral gyrus bordering the central sulcus (intrasulcal length of the precentral gyrus, ILPG) in horizontal sections through both hemispheres of right-handed keyboard players and of an age- and handedness-matched control group. ILPG is assumed to be a measure of the size of the primary motor cortex. Whereas controls exhibited a pronounced left-larger-than-right asymmetry, keyboard players had more symmetrical ILPG. The most pronounced differences in ILPG between keyboard players and controls were seen in the most dorsal part of the presumed cortical hand representation of both hemispheres. This was especially true in the nondominant right hemispheres of violinists, which control the left hands they use intensively to manipulate the instrument.

As a further example, Draganski et al. (2004) have associated selective and transient changes in activity-dependent white matter, as well as grey matter, with the processing and storage of complex visual motion tasks (three-ball cascade juggle learning) in the region corresponding to the interparietal sulcus, possibly reflecting a exercise-dependent effect on myelin formation and axonal diameter (Scholz et al., 2009).

Summing up the data obtained by the application of MRI techniques to the study of neural plasticity (both in laboratory animals as well as in humans) published so far, we can conclude that structural changes, mostly following extensive training, can follow; these changes, however, are not widespread but related to the type of practiced task. The structural changes do not involve neurogenesis, but reflect an increase of dendritic spine and axonal sprouting. Particularly important from a functional point of view are the visible changes in white matter – the thickness of the myelin sheet coupled with an increase of the axonal diameter following intensive visuomotor training (Scholz et al., 2009) – possibly reflecting the need to transmit signals at a high rate and in the correct order according to the specific rules of the trained skill.

> Two forms of neural plasticity have been described: structural and functional. Structural plasticity involves morphological changes of grey and white matter. Neurogenesis, the process of generation of new neurons in response to learning or to brain damage, is, in man, at best limited, and its role is far from being defined. On the other hand, the process of structural white matter plasticity is much more active, its development persisting up to adulthood and showing consistent modifications following training. Functional plasticity refers to the reorganization of the neural activity following experience, training or brain damage, without anatomical modifications.
>
> The introduction in clinical and research practice of morphological (MRI) and functional (fMRI) neuroimaging methods has considerably increased the chance to correlate, *in vivo*, the behavioral modifications following learning and other factors of brain-induced modification. Longitudinal (repeated observations on the same subject or group of subjects of the anatomical changes coupled to behavioral modifications following a specific variable) and cross-sectional (observations of functional and anatomical differences in two different groups) studies have been used.
>
> Grey matter and white matter plastic changes, following training or experience, have been recorded. Grey matter neuroimaging visible changes are attributable to axonal sprouting rather than neurogenesis. These modifications are, however, unstable, returning to baseline once training is over. Increase of white matter following prolonged exercise probably reflects the process of fast transmitting signals according to the needs of the trained skill.

Functional plasticity

The ability of the brain, mostly in the developmental phase, but with increasing evidence even in adulthood and aging, to functionally modify its architecture following experience, sensory deprivation and acquired brain lesion, is at the base of functional plasticity.

Functional changes can be observed at synaptic level, or they can involve a remapping of specific cortical areas or neural circuits. The young and adult primate brains are, in fact, capable of modifying rapidly the size of cortical receptive fields or motor output modules in response to experience, training or altered synaptic input, as will be demonstrated by the following examples.

Synaptic functional plasticity

The core of functional plasticity is considered to lie on a mechanism that changes the strength of a single synapse by modifying its amplification within a hard-wired network structure (Butz et al., 2009.) Long term depression (LTD) and long term potentiation (LTP) are the main factors of this process. They are widely considered the basis for the cellular and molecular mechanisms that underlie synaptic changes during the process of learning (Massey and Bashir, 2007; Malenka and Bear, 2004). Additional mechanisms flanking synaptic plasticity in the process of learning have been recently proposed: information storage may involve activity-dependent changes in the intrinsic excitability of neurons. This type of plasticity could further extend to a large number of synapses, thereby creating a more global change in signal integration (for a review, see Hansel et al., 2001).

The remapping of cortical space

Space in the brain is represented in numerous spatial maps: specific cortical neurons respond, for example, to multisensory (visuo-tactile) stimuli presented in the space immediately adjacent to the face and peripersonal space (Rizzolatti et al., 1997). In a seminal paper, Iriki et al. (1996) found that soon after the monkeys retrieved distant pieces of food pellets with a hand-held rake, the receptive fields corresponding to the peripersonal space located in the caudal part of the post central gyrus were enlarged, as the image of the tool was incorporated into that of the hand. The re-sizing of the personal space is, however, dynamic, since it shrinks backwards following the discontinuation of the active use of the tool (for a review, see Farné et al., 2007).

The effect of training

Adult motor cortex functional plasticity during motor skill learning has been extensively reported. In a Positron Emission Tomography (PET) study, Jenkins et al. (1994) reported a positive correlation between behaviorally controlled hand use and the corresponding cortical somato-sensory area; the map of the hand representation was enlarged about five times compared to the pretreatment finding. Similar changes have been found by Pascual-Leone et al., (1995) in a Transcranial Magnetic Study (TMS) in normal subjects acquiring new fine motor skills (see following section).

Large scale remapping following brain injury

As it will be detailed in the chapter specifically devoted to the role of neural plasticity in the process of recovery, much of the improvement following an acquired brain injury is the consequence of the capacity of the undamaged portions of the brain to take over the functions previously performed by the damaged regions. Seitz et al. (1995) used PET to map the regional cerebral blood flow changes related to voluntary finger movements in patients with low-grade cerebral tumors occupying the hand area of motor cortex. All patients showed activations solely outside the tumor. Compared with the unaffected side, the activations were shifted by 9–43 mm either along the mediolateral body representation of motor cortex or into the premotor or parietal somatosensory cortex. These results provide evidence that slowly developing lesions can induce large-scale reorganization that is not confined to changes within the somatotopic body representation in motor cortex.

By far the most evident example of large scale remapping comes from the report of language development after removal of the left hemisphere. Vargha-Khadem et al. (1997) reported impressive language development, well after the critical period, in a Sturge-Weber[10] subject, affecting the left hemisphere. The boy failed to develop speech and his comprehension was age equivalent to 3–4 years. At the age of 8, after having been operated upon, he began to acquire speech, up to a level of 8–10 years. More recently, Danelli et al. (2013) reported the case of a right-handed boy who underwent a left hemispherectomy at the age of 2.5 years for removal of a large congenital malformation. After initial aphasia, his language skills recovered almost at normal level; his only remaining deficit was in lexical competence. fMRI patterns in the right hemisphere when engaged in linguistic skills were similar to those observed in the left hemisphere in typically developed age-matched subjects, with the addition of a more widespread frontal recruitment, suggesting a more functionally demanding neural activity for linguistic tasks.

It must be furthermore noted that the extent of functional plasticity is not constant: Ward et al. (2003), in a longitudinal study, investigated the changes of spatial distribution of task-related motor activation in a group of unilateral motor-impaired stroke patients. Using fMRI, they found a consistent pattern of decreased brain activation in a number of primary and non-primary motor regions as the process of motor recovery increased. This pattern reflected, according to Ward et al., a massive recruitment of areas in the motor system in the early stages of recovery. Thereafter, the surviving elements of the motor system are again employed, to facilitate the transition from a highly attention-dependent movement to an automated motor performance. This is accompanied by a recovery-dependent decrease of cerebral activation. Such pattern is reminiscent of that observed in the normal brain during motor skill learning (see following section).

Structural and functional plasticity: two distinct processes?

Behaviorally relevant experience, such as training or alterations in the central and peripheral inputs, may reshape brain networks at both functional and structural levels, as described in the previous sections of this chapter. Similarly, chronic or acute brain damage may bring about a functional and structural reorganization of the cortico-subcortical networks that can be associated with the process of recovery of the functions supported by the damaged areas.

A consistent number of animal studies have shown a co-localization of structural and functional plasticity after prolonged exercise. For example, Swain et al. (2003) reported chronic functional and structural changes in the primary motor cortex of rats submitted to prolonged motor training.

The problem of the co-occurrence in the human brain of functional and structural adaptive plasticity, defined by Paillard (1976) as the capacity of the neural system to change its own structure and expand its behavioral repertoire, has started to be experimentally explored only recently following the development of high resolution morphological (MRI) and functional (fMRI) neuroimaging techniques, coupled with the use of neuropsychological techniques. Schaechter et al. (2006) submitted a group of chronic hemiparetic stroke patients to structural MRI and fMRI during unilateral tactile stimulation of the affected side. In comparison with controls, patients showed an enhanced activation of the ventral post-central gyrus (a part of the sensory area). The same area showed, at the morphological level, a significant increase in cortical thickness, absent in the control cortical areas. Summing up the above results, it seems at present possible to have a clearer picture of the links between structural and functional plasticity and the temporal relations in the process of recovery.

> Following specific training, cortical maps can be extensively modified – as, for example, in the cerebral areas of professional musicians. In a similar way, the process of recovery following brain damage, both in developmental and adult life, is a consequence of intact regions taking over the functions of the damaged region, and it can involve areas of the same or contralateral hemisphere. Critical factors are age and the way the damage develops, with slow-growing lesions allowing a better adjustment.

Spatial and temporal characteristics of neural plasticity

The advances in neuroimaging and non-invasive brain stimulation techniques have provided a sound experimental data set about the time course and spatial distribution of the neurological processes subserving neural plasticity. The study of the mechanisms involved in motor skill learning, their evolution over time and the involvement of different interconnected brain regions has been particularly fruitful. In particular, the analysis of the processes that require learning of sequential simple or complex motor sequence movements, their time course and their consolidation has provided a new and further insight into the anatomo-functional processes subserving neural plasticity (for a review, see Dayan and Cohen, 2011).

In some cases, motor skill learning is simple and fast, requiring few or even a single training session to reach an asymptotic level, whereas acquisition of motor musical skills, like those involved in piano or violin playing, often requires long and often painful training sessions, with considerable inter-individual variations.

Motor skill acquisition development can be divided into two phases: a first rapid phase, measured over the course of a single training session, followed by a later, slower phase, characterized by incremental gains over multiple sessions of practice. The duration of fast and long learning is obviously task dependent: learning a four-component key press sequence could be accomplished in few minutes, whereas the fast stage of learning a full piano or violin musical piece could last months.

Fast motor skill learning

The results of the functional neuroimaging studies (PET, fMRI) in human fast learning of sequential motor tasks show an increased activation in the dorsolateral prefrontal cortex, primary motor areas and pre supplementary motor area (Floyer-Lea and Matthews, 2005). As learning progresses, these areas show decreased activation: increased activation is considered to reflect recruitment of additional nervous structures, whereas later deactivation suggests the task can be carried out using fewer neuronal resources, as the process of learning proceeds (Poldrack, 2000).

Slow motor skill learning

As in fast learning, the time course and degree of neural changes associated with slow learning are task dependent (Ungerleider et al., 2002). As a rule, performance gains develop at a slower pace than fast learning, but can continue over many years, as, for example, in playing musical pieces, whose execution can become, under certain situations, automatic and less susceptible to interference (Doyon and Benali, 2005).

The neurological mechanisms active in the slow learning process tend to shift from the more anterior cortical region involved in fast learning to the more posterior region of the brain. While short-term motor skill learning seems associated primarily with activation in a cortical network specific for the learned movements, long-term learning involves increased activation of a bihemispheric cortical-subcortical network, including the striatum. According to Floyer-Lea and Matthews (2005), such a pattern suggests a "plastic" development of new representations for both motor output and somatosensory afferent information, pointing to a lesser involvement of attentional and executive resources (Kelly and Garavan, 2005).

Once acquired, motor learning skills can be retained over long periods of time or forgotten. As well known to professional musicians, daily practice plays a crucial role. (There's a funny story about Paderewski, who said, *If I don't practice for one day, I know it; if I don't practice for two days, my friends know it. If I don't practice for three days, EVERYBODY knows it.*) Other factors have been found to positively affect the process of consolidation, ranging from reward to sleep. Reward involves activating the striatum, ventral tegmental area and hippocampus, as shown by Wittmann et al. (2011) in an fMRI study.

Consolidation of explicit motor sequence learning has been correlated with the amount of stage II non-rapid eye movement sleep by Walker et al. (2002; but see Rickard, 2008).

Structural plasticity associated with slow learning

As described in the previous sections, the process of plasticity can induce grey and white matter changes.

Given their long period of learning and practice, expert musicians have served as a model group for studying neural plasticity involving long-term motor learning and consolidation. A tremendous amount of practice is, in fact, required to achieve the kind of movement speed for playing musical instruments at professional levels: professional pianists and violinists practice for 7500 hours before reaching the age of 18 years (Ericsson et al., 1993; Ericsson and Lehmann, 1996). In a series of cross-sectional studies, musicians show, in comparison to non-musicians, a higher grey matter volume in sensorimotor and premotor areas, as well as in the cerebellum (Han et al., 2009). Significant changes in the size of corpus callosum have been found in musicians, more evident in those subjects who began musical training before the age of 7 (for a review, see Jäncke, 2009). Similarly, diffusion MRI-based studies such as fractional anisotropy (FA)[11] have shown a relationship between FA values on the cortico-spinal fibers (CSF) from the primary sensorimotor and premotor cortices and the number of practice hours during childhood in skilled musicians (Imfeld et al., 2009), suggesting plastic changes in the CSF in professional musicians. These changes are not, however, stable (Jäncke, 2009) and tend to return to the baseline when the subjects stop practicing (the rule *use it or lose it* is, in many fields, valid!).

The time to acquire a new skill is dependent on its difficulty, and different neural mechanisms are at work for fast and slow (more stable) learning. Fast learning is associated with activation of prefrontal cortex, while slow learning requires activation of a cortico-subcortical network, including the striatum.

Unimodal and cross-modal brain plasticity

A key question with regard to neuroplasticity is the search for the anatomical and functional loci subserving the ability of the normal brain to be shaped by environmental inputs. Of equal weight is the study of the neurological and functional bases subserving the process of recovery following brain damage or sensory deprivation (see chapters 7 and 8). The above questions are strictly interlinked with the time of information acquisition or loss, whether the latter occurs in the developmental period or in adulthood. A further factor is represented by the specificity (innate and irreversible, or acquired during postnatal development, Bates and Roe, 2001) or flexibility of the brain areas dedicated to processing single domains such as language or face processing or sensory inputs (e.g. vision).

According to a first hypothesis, brain plasticity is unimodal. Dedicated brain areas are domain specific, perhaps through a gradual specialization of an initially more general-purpose system (De Haan, 2001). As a consequence, the process of plasticity, either in the normal development or following damage, is domain specific.

Conversely, a wealth of experimental animal studies and neuroimaging human observations has documented the remarkable ability of the brain to reshape its organization through a process of cross-modal plasticity, which is thought to refine the processing of the spared modalities and/or sensory systems.

Examples of unimodal neural plasticity can be found at different levels. Rapid activity-dependent changes that occur locally have been recorded at specific synapses, such as long term potentiation or depression (Malenka and Bear, 2004). For instance, depriving rodents of vision by dark exposure enhances AMPA receptors in some layers of the primary visual cortex, while at the same time reducing them at the level of primary somatosensory and auditory cortices (Goel and Lee, 2007).

More broadly, the process of unimodal plasticity involves the recruitment of specific sensory and motor areas to improve a specific skill through learning. For example, as seen in the previous sections, in professional musicians submitted to a long training, the cerebral motor area is enlarged, both compared to that of non-musicians and to its own previous size. Also, a number of neuroimaging studies associate the process of recovery of language impairment (aphasia following left-hemisphere acquired damage) with neuroplastic changes in the perilesional language areas of the same hemisphere (see section 8.3.2).

In addition, unimodal plasticity is thought to enhance tactile and auditory perception in unimodal visually deprived subjects by recruiting the deprived cortex for processing the remaining sense (He et al., 2012). In comparison with sighted animals, rats deprived of vision at birth show a better maze performance, mediated by somatosensory perception through the use of their whiskers (Toldi et al., 1994). Similar changes have been reported in unimodal sensory deprived persons (see chapter 7). The visual cortex of congenitally blind subjects is 'invaded' by the somatosensory and auditory systems and found to be active in auditory and tactile skills, such as Braille reading (Sadato et al., 1996; Weeks et al., 2000). In an fMRI study, Merabet et al. (2008) found that after five days of complete visual deprivation, normally sighted subjects showed an increase in Blood-oxigen-level (BOLD) signal within the occipital cortex in response to tactile stimulation. This increase in signal was, however, no longer present 24 hours after blindfold removal. Similarly, congenitally blind persons have enhanced tactile, auditory pitch and sound localization skills (for a review, see Gori et al., 2014). These functional changes could reflect anatomical reshaping; in cats subjected to visual and somatic deafferentation, a hypertrophy of the auditory cortex has been found (for a review, see Bavelier and Neville, 2002).

On the other hand, a wealth of experimental animal studies and neuroimaging human observations has documented the remarkable capacity of the brain to reshape the organization of cortical functions through a process of cross-modal plasticity following acquired brain lesions and in unimodal sensory deprived subjects. Two mechanisms have been hypothesized to support cross-modal plasticity: changes in local connectivity and changes in subcortical connectivity (Bavelier and Neville, 2002).

Changes in local connectivity: the best-studied examples of this type of plasticity have been observed in the sensory maps of animals after sensory stimulation or deafferentation. Qi et al. (2010) have recently described a reorganization of the sensory cortex to over-represent the surviving input in monkeys reared from infancy with a sensory loss experimentally produced by a lesion of somatosensory afferents in the dorsal columns of spinal cords. In addition, they have found that inputs from the reorganized cortex provide sensory information to the motor cortex. This new acquired information could affect the shape and function of the motor map in the primary motor cortex.

Examples of disrupted cross-modal connectivity in humans have been convincingly demonstrated in a number of neuroimaging studies. Stroke-induced lesions not only affect the connections between motor cortex and spinal cord, but may also negatively impact the interaction between the affected areas and those distant from the lesion. The malfunction may affect the damaged hemisphere network or spread to the opposite hemisphere (Grefkes and Fink, 2011). Agosta et al. (2013) found that global and local functional networks are altered in the behavioral variant of frontotemporal dementia (FTD). FTD patients showed the greatest decrease in inter-regional connectivity among the frontal and occipital regions; the insular cortices; and occipital, temporal, subcortical, frontal regions. These altered global network properties correlated with executive dysfunction, suggesting a loss of efficiency in information exchange between both distant and close brain areas.

Finally, it must be remembered that cross-modal plasticity has its limits, and it cannot fully compensate for the damage from the loss of a sensory modality with a greater enhancement of other senses. Gori et al. (2014) showed that congenitally blind subjects are severely impaired in auditory spatial localization tasks; the deficit was specific for the spatial bisection task, which requires encoding and remembering the position of the perceived sound sequence. These findings suggest that some perceptual functions, such as the development of the auditory sense of space, need a cross-sensory calibration between visual and auditory modalities (Gori et al., 2011).

> The ability of the nervous system to modify and adapt behavior according to the weight of experience and to react to the impact of sensory deprivation or to brain damage can be viewed as the result of two different mechanisms: unimodal and cross-modal plasticity. According to a first view, the process of recovery of modality-specific (e.g. auditory, visual) sensory loss derives from the activity of domain-specific dedicated brain areas. A second view posits that the brain reshapes its organization following unimodal sensory deprivation through a process of cross-modal plasticity, involving additional sensory areas.

Maladaptive plasticity

Focal Dystonias: Writer's Cramp and Musical Dystonia

Dystonia is a neurological movement disorder, in which sustained muscle contractions of agonist and antagonist muscles of the body cause twisting and repetitive movements or abnormal postures. It most often affects the large axial muscles of the trunk and limb gir-dle ... The disorder may be hereditary or caused by other factors such as birth-related trauma, infection, poisoning or reaction to pharmaceutical drugs, particularly neuroleptics. In some cases dystonia is focal, affecting a muscle or group of muscles in a specific part of the body causing involuntary muscular contractions and abnormal postures. For example, in focal hand dystonia, the fingers either curl into the palm or extend outward without control. A series of recent data suggest a pattern of abnormal plasticity within sensorimotor circuits, including basal ganglia circuits active in primary dystonia (for a review, see Quartarone and Hallet, 2013).

Of particular interest in the present context are two types of focal dystonia, affecting the manual skills on non-brain damaged persons performing tasks demanding high levels of sensorimotor integration, such as writing (Writer Cramp or Writing Dystonia, Sheeny and Mardsen, 1982) or playing musical instruments at professional level (Musician Dystonia). Although the exact pathogenesis of these form of dystonia is not completely clear, the hypothesis of abnormal regulation of neural plasticity within sensorimotor circuits, prompted by prolonged exercise, is very attractive Dystonia could be the result of an ex-cessively responsive neuronal machinery with an increased tendency to form sensorimotor associations. The resulting excessive neuronal plastic changes and 'noise' could degrade motor control and lead to the clinical symptoms.

Writer's cramp

Writer's cramp has been recognized for over a century, and originally was considered as a motor disorder, whose origin was considered functional, without any discernible organic cause (occupational neurosis, Gowers, 1881), The unfortunate use of the term neurosis was, for many years, an obstacle to consider the writer's cramp was is a real focal motor disorder. Electro-myographic studies (EMG) reveal a characteristic pattern of cocontraction of the agonist and antagonist muscles, with abnormally prolonged bursts in the active muscles, In addition, there is a difficulty in selecting the appropriate muscle to carry out the task. (for a review, see Marsden and Sheehy, 1990). some cases, it can play a maladaptive role, both in non-brain damaged subjects and in patients affected by acquired brain lesions or sensory deprivation.

Whereas the role of maladaptive plasticity (MP) in impairing the process of motor or sensory recovery following acquired brain damage or sensory deafferentation (phantom limb) will be treated in chapter 6, this chapter will focus on some examples of maladaptive plasticity in non-brain damaged adults affecting the motor and sensory systems. The best-known examples of MP in people without damage to the brain or limbs are focal dystonia (writer's cramp and musician's dystonia) and chronic pain syndrome.

Musician's dystonia

Musician's dystonia (MD) or musicians' cramp is characterized by incoordi-nation or loss of voluntary movement control of extensively trained move-ments (Altenmüller et al., 2012). The affected persons ($\approx$ 1% of musicians, the first recorded case being Robert Schumann) experience abnormal activation, sometimes painful, of agonist and antagonist muscles. MD is task specific, affecting the coordination of the muscles activated in instrument playing and triggered by task performance.

MD has been classified according to the task or instrument specifically involved. Embouchure dystonia, affecting brass and wind players, impairs coordi-nation of lips, tongue, facial muscles and breathing. The most frequently described violin and piano MD affects the control of finger and isolated arm movements.

MD is not equally distributed. For example, MD seems to be more frequent in high strings (violin) than in low strings (cello) players. Among players of instruments with different workloads, MD appears in the most heavily used hand: keyboard instruments (piano, organ, harpsichord) players are mainly affected in the right hand, the one that carries the higher workload; string players are predominantly affected in the left hand, which carries a higher and more rapid complexity of movements (Conti et al., 2008).

Several studies have suggested that MD can represent a syndrome of maladaptive or excessive neural plasticity (Münte et al., 2002). Following intensive practice, professional musicians develop an enlarged sensory motor area of the single digits and both motor excitability and long term potentiation/long term depression–like plasticity are enhanced (Rosenkranz et al., 2008). In MD, the spatial differentiation of single digits disappears and the receptive fields are topographically disorganized.

The fact that, as said before, MD develops only in a tiny minority of professional musicians has enhanced a number of hypotheses about its causative role. Based on a series of neurophysiological, genetic and epidemiological data, Altenmüller et al. (2012) proposed a model, based on genetic predisposition, by which MD patients are affected by a deficit in inhibitory mechanisms in sensory motor networks on several levels of the central nervous system. This translates into a pattern of temporal and spatial overshoot in motor activation. Similarly, in monkeys required to perform repetitive fine motor tasks, cortical receptive fields are abnormally increased with breakdown of normal topographic boundaries (Byl et al., 1996).

Chronic pain

Acute pain, usually associated with actual and potential tissue damage, has a clear functional and prospective role, and it usually disappears when the underlying cause of pain has been treated or has healed. In a consistent minority of patients, however, there is a transition to a chronic pain status, loosely defined by a pain that persists beyond the normal time of healing (IASP, Merskey, 1986). The pain is described in vague terms of an "electric" nature and, in many cases, is hardly sensible to analgesic medications (Dworkin et al., 2011). In contrast with acute pain that can be considered mainly a physiological response, chronic pain involves psychological and behavioral mechanisms in addition to physiological ones (for a review, see Verhaak et al., 1998), and it is correlated to cognitive and mood disorders (McWilliams et al., 2003).

According to a number of recent neuroimaging studies (for a review, see Saab, 2013), the transition from acute to chronic pain may be explained by excessive plasticity, leading to a structural remapping and functional reorganization of the cortico-subcortical connectivity involving thalamo-cortical circuits. As a consequence of this reorganization, ectopic firing in the sensory neurons of the thalamus can spontaneously occur or show reduction of firing thresholds.

Recent studies (for a review, see Loggia et al., 2015) have, however, focused on the role of microglia and astrocytes in the central nervous system (CNS), as well as neuro-glial interactions, in the establishment and maintenance of persistent pain. Both microglia and astrocytes respond to acute injures of CNS by undergoing a series of cellular responses collectively known as 'glial activation'. This response includes proliferation, morphological changes and production of cytokines and other inflammatory mediators. Glial activation is an adaptive defensive mechanism that can contribute to handling acute stress, limiting tissue damage, and restoring homeostasis. However, when malfunctioning (and, in particular, when it does not get resolved during the post-acute stage after an injury event) glial activation can have deleterious effects and turn into the primary pathogenic element (Pekny and Pekna, 2014). Several animal studies have now established that glial activation is a key contributing factor in chronic pain.

Related to chronic pain syndrome is Hyperalgesia, a state of increased intensity of pain sensation induced by either noxious or ordinarily non-noxious stimulation of peripheral tissue (Hardy et al., 1950), and Allodynia, a pain sensation following a test stimulus that is not capable of activating nociceptors (Sandkühler, 2009). These phenomena are not per se pathological or a sign of an inadequate response, but may rather be an appropriate shift in pain threshold to prevent further tissue damage. According to Melzack et al. (2001), the appearance of these symptoms could be due to the influence of prior similar inputs that have modified specific neural systems; as a consequence, the behavioral output is significantly influenced by the "memory" of these prior events.

In some cases, the process of plasticity is not beneficial, leading to deleterious consequences and impaired functionality (maladaptive plasticity) both in non-brain-damaged subjects and in sensory deprived or brain-damaged people (e.g. auditory, visual, etc.). The most cited examples of this dysfunction are musician's dystonia and chronic pain. Both are interpreted as the effects of an impaired functional brain remapping that follows extensive training or noxious stimuli whose effect continues after the decrease of intensive practice or, in the second case, after the disappearance of the source of pain.

SUMMARY

Experience is, at the behavioral level, the critical factor of the postnatal, culturally acquired learning process. It represents, at the neural level, the most important factor of brain plasticity, the process by which the brain can change structure and function to cope with new experiences and react to the effect of acquired damage or sensory deprivation. This process produces changes in the brain, both at anatomical and functional levels. At the morphological level, the modifications are at the synaptic level rather than stimulating the process of neurogenesis. At the functional level, neural plasticity refers to the reorganization of the neural activity following experience, training or brain damage, without anatomical modifications.

Specific factors, from age to brain damage, can enhance or limit the process of neural plasticity. Similarly, plasticity is not a widespread process across the brain; some brain regions can adapt more easily than others to the changing environment.

While in the past the morphological aspects of neural plasticity could be experimentally studied only in non-human species, the advent of neuroimaging studies such as magnetic resonance imaging (MRI) and functional MRI (fMRI) allow the recognition that, in animal as well as human brains, structural and functional changes can occur and can be mapped *in vivo*, following behavioral modifications induced by experience and other factors.

The process of plasticity can involve modality-specific brain areas or can extend through a process of cortical and subcortical connectivity to additional cerebral areas.

Finally, it must be noted that the process of cerebral plasticity is, at least in some cases, maladaptive, as in musician's dystonia or chronic pain.

Notes

1 A term introduced by Francis Galton, cousin of Charles Darwin.
2 Near-infrared spectroscopy (NIRS), a noninvasive optical technique, measures changes in the hemoglobin oxygenation state in the human brain (for a review, see Hoshi, 2003; Hebden, 2003). Unlike PET and fMRI, NIRS does not require strict motion restriction nor use of radioactive substances (PET). It therefore represents a useful tool for studying the brain mechanisms of the youngest developmental populations from birth to the toddler years. Apart from its clinical use (monitoring cerebral oxygenation and hemodynamics in preterm infants affected by cerebral hypoxic-ischemia and admitted to an intensive care unit), it represents a potential tool for functional mapping studies. NIRS has proven

to be an excellent research tool for studies of functional activation (functional near-infrared spectroscopy, fNIRS); it has, for example, clarified the origins of the left lateralization of language processing in the brain, revealing lateralization to the native language at birth (Gervain et al., 2008).
3 Apes, however, seem to possess some hemispheric asymmetries, including the *planum temporale* (for a review, see Hopkins and Vauclair, 2012).
4 The observable physical or biochemical characteristics of an organism, as determined by both genetic makeup and environmental influences.
5 The capacity of producing an infinite number of correctly grammatical sentences, based on a finite number of elements, by combining them in appropriate ways (for a review, see Hauser, Chomsky and Fitch, 2002).
6 Phonemic awareness (PA) consists of the ability to hear, identify, and manipulate phonemes, such as separating a spoken word into distinct phonemes. Development of PA predicts reading acquisition – or, on the contrary, could be a consequence of the process of learning to read.
7 A contemporary replication of Mosso's (1882) historical experiments was recently published in *Brain* (Field and Inman, 2014).
8 This distinction is not, however, unanimously accepted. Paillard (1976) claims that the term *plasticity* should denote a "process of acquisition of new knowledge associated with structural brain changes that have functional consequences. Conversely, a change in neural activity in existing pathways could be defined more precisely by the term *flexibility*" (Will et al., 2008: 2–11).
9 Stem cells are undifferentiated cells that have the potential to develop into many different cell types that carry out different functions. Pluripotent stem cells, found in embryos, can give rise to all the cells found in the human body – cells as diverse as those found in the brain, bone, heart and skin. In adults, neural stem cells can generate only specific types of cells.
10 Sturge–Weber syndrome is an embryonal developmental anomaly characterized by neurological and skin disorder. It is often associated with port-wine stains of the face, glaucoma, seizures, mental retardation, and ipsilateral leptomeningeal angioma. Normally, only one side of the brain is affected.
11 Fractional anisotropy (FA) is a useful MRI measure of connectivity to evaluate white matter fiber tracts, derived from the diffusion tensor imaging (DTI) dataset.

Bibliography

Agosta F., Sala S., Valsasina P., Meani A., Canu E., Magnani G., Cappa S.F., Scola E., Quatto P., Horsfield M.A., Falini A., Comi G., Filippi M. (2013), Brain network connectivity assessed using graph theory in frontotemporal dementia. *Neurology, 81*(2): 134–143.

Akers K.G., Martinez-Canabal A., Restivo L., Yiu A.P., De Cristofaro A., Hsiang H.L., Wheeler A.L., Guskjolen A., Niibori Y., Shoji H., Ohira K., Richards B.A., Miyakawa T., Josselyn S.A., Frankland P.W. (2014), Hippocampal neurogenesis regulates forgetting during adulthood and infancy. *Science, 344*(6184), 598–602.

Alivisatos A.P., Chun M., Church G.M., Deisseroth K., Donoghue J.P., Greenspan R.J., Mceuen P.L., Roukes M.L., Sejnowski T.J., Weiss P.S., Yuste R. (2013), Neuroscience. The brain activity map. *Science, 339*(6125): 1284–1285.

Altenmüller E., Baur V., Hofmann A., Lim V.K., Jabusch H.C. (2012), Musician's cramp as manifestation of maladaptive brain plasticity: arguments from instrumental differences. *Annals of New York Academy of Sciences, 1252*: 259–265.

Altman J. (1962), Are new neurons formed in the brains of adult mammals? *Science, 135*(3509): 1127–1128.

Amunts K., Schlaug G., Jäncke L., Steimetz H., Schleicher A., Dabringhaus A., Zilles K. (1997), Motor cortex and hand motor skills: structural compliance in the human brain. *Human Brain Mapping, 5*(3): 206–215.

Andres R.H., Horie N., Slikker W., Keren-Gill H., Zhan K., Sun G., Manley N.C., Pereira M.P., Sheikh L.A., McMillan E.L. Schaar B.T., Svendsen C. N, Bliss T.M., Steinberg G.K. (2011), Human neural stem cells enhance structural plasticity and axonal transport in the ischaemic brain. *Brain, 134*(6): 1777–1789.

Baillargeon R., Spelke E.S., Wasserman S. (1985), Object permanence in five-month-old infants. *Cognition, 20*: 191–208.

Bates E. And Roe K. (2001), Language development in children with unilateral brain injury. In: Nelson C.A. and Luciana M. (eds), *Handbook of developmental cognitive neuroscience*, Cambridge (MA), MIT Press, 281–307.

Bateson P. and Gluckman P. (2011), *Plasticity, Robustness, Development and Evolution*, Cambridge (MA), Cambridge University Press.

Baumeister R.F. (2005), *The Cultural Animal: Human Nature, Meaning, and Social Life*. New York, Oxford University Press.

Bavelier D. and Neville H.J. (2002), Cross-modal plasticity: where and how? *Nature Reviews Neuroscience, 3*(6): 443–452.

Berlucchi G. and Aglioti S.M. (2001), The body in the brain revisited. *Experimental Brain Research, 200*(1): 25–35.

Berlucchi G. and Buchtel H.A. (2009), Neuronal plasticity: historical roots and evolution of meaning. *Experimental Brain Research, 192*(3): 307–319.

Bisiach E. (1999), Unilateral neglect and related disorderes, In: Denes G. and Pizzamiglio L. (eds), *Handbook of clinical and experimental neuropsychology*, Hove (UK), Psychology Press, 479–496.

Bliss T.V. and Collingridge G.L. (1993), A synaptic model of memory: long-term potentiation in the hippocampus. *Nature, 361*(6407): 31–39.

Bourgeois J.P. and Rakic P. (1993), Changes of synaptic density in the primary visual cortex of the macaque monkey from fetal to adult stage. *Journal of Neuroscience, 13*(7): 2801–2820.

Butz M., Wörgötter F., Van Ooyen A. (2009), Activity-dependent structural plasticity. *Brain Research Reviews, 60*(2): 287–305.

Byl N.N., Merzenich M.M., Jenkins W.M. (1996), A primate genesis model of focal dystonia and repetitive strain injury: I. Learning-induced dedifferentiation of the representation of the hand in the primary somatosensory cortex in adult monkeys. *Neurology, 47*(2): 508–520.

Carruthers P. (2006), *The Architecture of the Mind: Massive Modularity and the Flexibility of Thought*, Oxford, University Press.

Cashmore A.R. (2010), The Lucretian swerve: The biological basis of human behavior and the criminal justice system. *Proceedings of the National Academy of Sciences USA, 107*: 4499–4504.

Chaieb L., Antal A., Ambrus G.G., Paulus W. (2014), Brain-derived neurotrophic factor: its impact upon neuroplasticity and neuroplasticity inducing transcranial brain stimulation protocols. *Neurogenetics, 15*(1): 1–11.

Changeux J.P. and Danchin A. (1976), Selective stabilisation of developing synapses as a mechanism for the specification of neuronal networks. *Nature, 264*: 705–712.

Charrier C., Joshi K., Coutinho-Budd J., Kim J.E., Lambert N., De Marchena J., Jin W.L., Vanderhaeghen P., Ghosh A., Sassa T., Polleux F. (2012), Inhibition of SRGAP2 function by its human-specific paralogs induces neoteny during spine maturation. *Cell, 149*(4): 923–935.

Chen F.C. and Li W.H. (2001), Genomic divergences between humans and other hominoids and the effective population size of the common ancestor of humans and chimpanzees. *American Journal of Human Genetics, 68*: 444–456.

Conti A.M., Pullman S., Frucht S.J. (2008), The hand that has forgotten its cunning – lessons from musicians' hand dystonia. *Movement Disorders, 23*(10): 1398–1406.

Craik F.I. (2008), Memory changes in normal and pathological aging. *Canadian Journal of Psychiatry, 53*(6): 343–345.

Crick F. (1989), The recent excitement about neural networks. *Nature, 337*(6203): 129–132.

Danelli L., Cossu G., Berlingeri M., Bottini G., Sberna M., Paulesu E. (2013), Is a lone right hemisphere enough? Neurolinguistic architecture in a case with a very early left hemispherectomy. *Neurocase, 19*(3): 209–231.

Dayan E. and Cohen L.G. (2011), Neuroplasticity subserving motor skill learning. *Neuron, 72*(3): 443–454.

DeFelipe J. (2006), Brain plasticity and mental processes: Cajal again. *Nature Reviews Neuroscience, 7*: 811–817.

De Haan M. (2001), The neuropsychology of face processing during infancy and childhood, In: Nelson C.A. and Luciana M. (eds), *Handbook of developmental cognitive neuroscience*, Cambridge (MA), MIT Press, 381–398.

Dehaene S. and Cohen L. (2007), Cultural recycling of cortical maps. *Neuron, 56*(2): 384–398.

Denes G. (1999), Disorders of body awareness and body knowledge. In: Denes G. and Pizzamiglio L. (eds), *Handbook of clinical and experimental neuropsychology*, Hove (UK), Psychology Press, 497–508.

Denes G. and Pizzamiglio L. (eds) (1999), *Handbook of clinical and experimental neuropsychology*, Hove (UK), Psychology Press.

Doyon J. and Benali H. (2005), Reorganization and plasticity in the adult brain during learning of motor skills. *Current Opinion in Neurobiology, 15*(2): 161–167.

Draganski B., Gaser C., Busch V., Schuierer G., Bogdahn U., May A. (2004), Neuroplasticity: changes in grey matter induced by training. *Nature, 427*(6972): 311–312.

Driemeyer J., Boyke J., Gaser C., Büchel C., May A. (2008), Changes in gray matter induced by learning – revisited. *PLoS ONE, 3*(7): e2669.

Dworkin R.H., Turk D.C., Basch E., Berger A., Cleeland C., Farrar J.T., Haythornthwaite J.A., Jensen M.P., Kerns R.D., Markman J., Porter L., Raja S.N., Ross E.,

Todd K., Wallace M., Woolf C.J. (2011), Considerations for extrapolating evidence of acute and chronic pain analgesic efficacy. *Pain, 152*(8): 1705–1708.

Ericsson K.A., Krampe R.T., Tesch-Romer C. (1993), The role of deliberate practice in the acquisition of expert performance. *Psychological Review, 100*: 363–406.

Ericsson K.A. and Lehmann A.C. (1996), Expert and exceptional performance: evidence of maximal adaptation to task constraints. *Annual Review of Psychology, 47*: 273–305.

Eriksson P.S., Perfilieva E., Björk-Eriksson T., Alborn A., Nordborg C., Peterson D.A., Gage F.H. (1998), Neurogenesis in the adult human hippocampus. *Nature Medicine, 4*: 1313–1317.

Fagiolini M., Jensen C.L., Champagne F.A. (2009), Epigenetic influences on brain development and plasticity. *Current Opinion in Neurobiology, 19*(2): 207–212.

Farnè A., Serino A., Làdavas E. (2007), Dynamic size-change of peri-hand space following tool-use: determinants and spatial characteristics revealed through cross-modal extinction. *Cortex, 43*(3): 436–443.

Field D.T. and Inman L.A. (2014), Weighing brain activity with the balance: a contemporary replication of Angelo Mosso's historical experiment. *Brain, 137*(2): 634–639.

Floyer-Lea A. and Matthews P.M. (2005), Distinguishable brain activation networks for short- and long-term motor skill learning. *Journal of Neurophysiology, 94*(1): 512–518.

Fodor J.A. (1983), *The Modularity of Mind: An Essay on Faculty Psychology*, Cambridge (MA), MIT Press.

Franceschini M.A., Thaker S., Themelis G., Krishnamoorthy K.K., Bortfeld H., Diamond S.G., Boas D.A., Arvin K., Grant P.E. (2007), Assessment of infant brain development with frequency-domain near-infrared spectroscopy. *Pediatric Research, 61*: 546–551.

Ganguly K. and Poo M.M. (2013), Activity-dependent neural plasticity from bench to bedside. *Neuron, 80*(3): 729–774.

Gaser C. and Schlaug G. (2003), Gray matter differences between musicians and non-musicians. *Annals of the New York Academy of Science, 999*: 514–517.

Gervain J., Macagno F., Cogoi S., Peña M., Mehler J. (2008), The neonate brain detects speech structure. *Proceedings of the National Academy of Sciences USA, 105*(37): 14222–14227.

Geschwind D.H. and Konopka G. (2012), Neuroscience: genes and human brain evolution. *Nature, 486*(7404): 481–482.

Geschwind N. and Levitsky W. (1968), Human brain: left-right asymmetries in temporal speech region. *Science, 161*(3837): 186–187.

Giedd J.N., Blumenthal J., Jeffries N.O., Castellanos F.X., Liu H., Zijdenbos A., Paus T., Evans A.C., Rapoport J.L. (1999), Brain development during childhood and adolescence: a longitudinal MRI study. *Nature Neuroscience, 2*(10): 861–863.

Goel A. and Lee H.K. (2007), Persistence of experience-induced homeostatic synaptic plasticity through adulthood in superficial layers of mouse visual cortex. *Journal of Neuroscience, 27*(25): 6692–6700.

Gori M., Mazzilli G., Sandini G., Burr D. (2011), Cross-sensory facilitation reveals neural interactions between visual and tactile motion in humans. *Frontiers in Psychology, 2*: 55.

Gori M., Sandini G., Martinoli C., Burr D.C. (2014), Impairment of auditory spatial localization in congenitally blind human subjects. *Brain, 137*(1): 288–293.

Gould S.J. (1977), *Ontogeny and Phylogeny*, Cambridge (MA), Harvard University Press.

Gould S.J. and Vrba E.S. (1982), Exaptation – a missing term in the science of form. *Paleobiology, 8*(1): 4–15.

Gowers W.R. (1886–1888), *A manual of diseases of the nervous system*. Vol II. 1st ed. London: J and A Churchill.

Greenough W.T. and Chang F.F. (1989), Plasticity of synapse structure and pattern in the cerebral cortex. In: Peters A. and Jones E.G. (eds), *Cerebral cortex*, New York, Plenum Press, 7: 391–440.

Grefkes C. and Fink G.R. (2011), Reorganization of cerebral networks after stroke: new insights from neuroimaging with connectivity approaches. *Brain, 134*(5): 1264–1276.

Han Y., Yang H., Lv Y.T., Zhu C.Z., He Y., Tang H.H., Gong Q.Y., Luo Y.J., Zang Y.F., Dong Q. (2009), Gray matter density and white matter integrity in pianists' brain: a combined structural and diffusion tensor MRI study. *Neuroscience Letters, 459*(1): 3–6.

Hansel C., Linden D.J., D'Angelo E. (2001), Beyond parallel fiber LTD: the diversity of synaptic and non-synaptic plasticity in the cerebellum. *Nature Neuroscience, 4*(5): 467–475.

Hardy J.D., Wolff H.G., Goodell H. (1950), Experimental evidence on the nature of cutaneous hyperalgesia. *Journal of Clinical Investigation, 29*(1): 115–140.

Hauser M.D., Chomsky N., Fitch W.T. (2002), The faculty of language: what is it, who has it, and how did it evolve? *Science, 298*(5598): 1569–1579.

He K., Petrus E., Gammon N., Lee H.K. (2012), Distinct sensory requirements for unimodal and cross-modal homeostatic synaptic plasticity. *Journal of Neuroscience, 32*(25): 8469–8474.

Hebb D.O. (1949), *The Organization Of Behaviour*, New York, John Wiley and Sons.

Hebden J.C. (2003), Advances in optical imaging of the newborn infant brain. *Psychophysiology, 40*(4): 501–510.

Herculano-Houzel S. (2012), The remarkable, yet not extraordinary, human brain as a scaled-up primate brain and its associated cost. *Proceedings of the National Academy of Sciences USA, 109*(1): 10661–10668.

Hihara S., Notoya T., Tanaka M., Ichinose S., Ojima H., Obayashi S., Fujii N., Iriki A. (2006), Extension of corticocortical afferents into the anterior bank of the intraparietal sulcus by tool-use training in adult monkeys. *Neuropsychologia, 44*(13): 2636–2346.

Holtmaat A. and Svoboda K. (2009), Experience-dependent structural synaptic plasticity in the mammalian brain. *Nature Reviews Neuroscience, 10*(9): 647–658.

Hopkins W.D. and Vauclair J. (2012), Evolution of behavioral and brain asymmetries in primates. In: Tallerman M. and Gibson K. (eds), *Handbook of language evolution*, Oxford (UK), Oxford University Press, 184–197.

Hoshi Y. (2003), Functional near-infrared optical imaging: utility and limitations in human brain mapping. *Psychophysiology, 40*(4): 511–520.

Houghton G. and Zorzi M. (2003), Normal and impaired spelling in a connectionist dual-route architecture. *Cognitive Neuropsychology, 20*: 115–162.

Hubel D.H. and Wiesel T.N. (1998), Early exploration of the visual cortex. *Neuron,* 20(3): 401–412.
Huttenlocher P.R. and Dabholkar A.S. (1997), Regional differences in synaptogenesis in human cerebral cortex. *Journal of Comparative Neurology, 387*(2): 167–178.
Imfeld A., Oechslin M.S., Meyer M., Loenneker T., Jäncke L. (2009), White matter plasticity in the corticospinal tract of musicians: a diffusion tensor imaging study. *Neuroimage, 46*(3): 600–607.
Innocenti G.M. (2011), Development and evolution: two determinants of cortical connectivity. *Progress in Brain Research, 189*: 65–75.
Innocenti G.M. and Price D.J. (2005), Exuberance in the development of cortical networks. *Nature Reviews Neuroscience, 6*: 955–965.
International Human Genome Sequencing Consortium. (2004), Finishing the euchromatic sequence of the human genome. *Nature, 431*: 931–945.
Iriki A., Tanaka M., Iwamura Y. (1996), Coding of modified body schema during tool use by macaque postcentral neurones. *Neuroreport, 7*(14): 2325–2330.
James W. (1890), *The Principles of Psychology*, New York, Holt.
Jäncke L. (2009), The plastic human brain. *Restorative Neurology and Neuroscience, 27*(5): 521–538.
Jenkins I.H., Brooks D.J., Nixon P.D., Frackowiak R.S., Passingham R.E. (1994), Motor sequence learning: a study with positron emission tomography. *Journal of Neuroscience, 14*(6): 3775–3790.
Johnson M.H. (2001), Functional brain development in humans. *Nature Reviews Neuroscience, 2*: 475–483.
Johnson M.H. (2011), *Developmental Cognitive Neuroscience*, (3rd edition), New York, John Wiley & Sons.
Karmiloff-Smith A. (1992), *Beyond Modularity: A Developmental Perspective on Cognitive Science*, Cambridge (MA), MIT Press.
Karni A., Meyer G., Rey-Hipolito C., Jezzard P., Adams M.M., Turner R., Ungerleider L.G. (1998), The acquisition of skilled motor performance: fast and slow experience-driven changes in primary motor cortex. *Proceedings of the National Academy of Sciences USA, 95*(3): 861–868.
Kasai H., Fukuda M., Watanabe S., Hayashi-Takagi A., Noguchi J. (2010), Structural dynamics of dendritic spines in memory and cognition. *Trends in Neurosciences, 33*: 121–129.
Kelly A.M. and Garavan H. (2005), Human functional neuroimaging of brain changes associated with practice. *Cerebral Cortex, 15*(8): 1089–1102.
Kempermann G. (2012), New neurons for 'survival of the fittest'. *Nature Reviews Neuroscience, 13*(10): 727–736.
Khaitovich P., Weiss G., Lachmann M., Hellmann I., Enard W., Muetzel B., Wirkner U., Ansorge W., Pääbo S. (2004), A neutral model of transcriptome evolution. *PLoS Biology, 2*(5): e132.
Konopka G., Bomar J.M., Winden K., Coppola G., Jonsson Z.O., Gao F., Peng S., Preuss T.M., Wohlschlegel J.A., Geschwind D.H. (2009), Human-specific transcriptional regulation of Cns development genes by FOXP2. *Nature, 462*(7270): 213–217.
Konorski J. (1948), *Conditioned Reflexes and Neuron Organization*, Cambridge (UK), Cambridge University Press.

Lashley K.S. (1924), Studies of cerebral function in learning. VI. The theory that synaptic resistance is reduced by the passage of the nerve impulse. *Psychological Review*, *31*: 369–375.

Levi-Montalcini R. and Angeletti P.U. (1988), Nerve growth factor. *Physiological Reviews*, *48*(3): 534–569.

Liu X., Somel M., Tang L., Yan Z., Jiang X., Guo S., Yuan Y., He L., Oleksiak A., Zhang Y., Li N., Hu Y., Chen W., Qiu Z., Pääbo S., Khaitovich P. (2012), Extension of cortical synaptic development distinguishes humans from chimpanzees and macaques. *Genome Research*, *22*(4): 611–622.

Loggia M.L., Chonde D.B., Akeju O., Arabasz G., Catana C., Edwards R.R., Hill E., Hsu S., Izquierdo-Garcia D., Ji R.R., Riley M., Wasan A.D., Zürcher N.R., Albrecht D.S., Vangel M.G., Rosen B.R., Napadow V., Hooker J.M. (2015), Evidence for brain glial activation in chronic pain patients. *Brain*, *12*(138): 604–615.

Longo F.M. and Massa S.M. (2013), Small-molecule modulation of neurotrophin receptors: a strategy for the treatment of neurological disease. *Nature Reviews Drug Discovery*, *12*(7): 507–525.

López-Muñoz F., Boya J., Alamo C. (2006), Neuron theory, the cornerstone of neuroscience, on the centenary of the Nobel Prize award to Santiago Ramón y Cajal. *Brain Research Bulletin*, *70*(4–6): 391–405.

Lugaro E. (1909), *Modern Problems in Psychiatry*, Manchester, University Press.

Macagno E.R., Lopresti V., Levinthal C. (1973), Structure and development of neuronal connections in isogenic organisms: Variations and similarities in the optic system of Daphnia magna. *Proceedings of the National Academy of Sciences USA*, *70*: 57–61.

Maguire E.A., Gadian D.G., Johnsrude I.S., Good C.D., Ashburner J., Frackowiak R.S., Frith C.D. (2000), Navigation-related structural change in the hippocampi of taxi drivers. *Proceedings of the National Academy of Sciences USA*, *97*(8): 4398–4403.

Maguire E.A., Nannery R., Spiers H.J. (2006), Navigation around London by a taxi driver with bilateral hippocampal lesions. *Brain*, *129*(11): 2894–2907.

Marsden C.D. and Sheehy M.P. (1990), Writer's cramp.-a focal dystonia. *Trends in Neurosciences*, *13*(4): 148–153.

Malenka R.C. and Bear M.F. (2004), Ltp and LTD: an embarrassment of riches. *Neuron*, *44*(1): 5–21.

Massey P.V. and Bashir Z.I. (2007), Long-term depression: multiple forms and implications for brain function. *Trends in Neurosciences*, *30*(4): 176–184.

Mcwilliams L.A., Cox B.J., Enns M.W. (2003), Mood and anxiety disorders associated with chronic pain: an examination in a nationally representative sample. *Pain*, *106*(1–2): 127–133.

Meltzoff A.N. (1990), Towards a developmental cognitive science. The implications of cross-modal matching and imitation for the development of representation and memory in infancy. *Annals of the New York Academy of Sciences*, *608*: 1–31.

Melzack R. (1990), Phantom limbs and the concept of a neuromatrix. *Trends in Neuroscience*, *13*(3): 88–92.

Melzack R., Coderre T.J., Katz J., Vaccarino A.L. (2001), Central neuroplasticity and pathological pain. *Annals of the New York Academy of Sciences*, *933*: 157–174.

Merabet L.B., Hamilton R., Schlaug G., Swisher J.D., Kiriakopoulos E.T., Pitskel N.B., Kauffman T., Pascual-Leone A. (2008), Rapid and reversible recruitment of early visual cortex for touch. *PLoS One, 3*(8): e3046.

Merskey H. (ed) (1986), Classification of chronic pain. Descriptions of chronic pain syndromes and definitions of pain terms. Prepared by the International Association for the Study of Pain, Subcommittee on Taxonomy. *Pain Supplement, 3*: S1–226.

Morais J. and Kolinsky R. (2005), Literacy and cognitive change. In: Snowling M. and Hulme C. (eds), *The science of reading: A handbook*, Oxford, Blackwell, 188–203.

Moscovitch M. and Umiltà C. (1990), Modularity and neuropsychology. In: Schwartz M. (ed), *Modular processes in Alzheimer Disease*, Cambridge (MA), MIT Press.

Mosso A. (1882), Applicazione della bilancia allo studio della circolazione del sangue nell'uomo. *Reale Accademia delle Scienze di Torino, 17*: 534–5.

Müller G.B. (2007), Evo-Devo: Extending the evolutionary synthesis. *Nature Reviews Genetics*, 8(12): 943–950.

Münte T.F., Altenmüller E., Jäncke L. (2002), The musician's brain as a model of neuroplasticity. *Nature Reviews Neuroscience, 3*(6): 473–478.

Paillard J. (1976), Réflexions sur l'usage du concept de plasticité en Neurobiologie. *Journal de Psychologie Normale et Pathologique, 1*: 33–47.

Pekny M. and Pekna M. (2014), Astrocyte reactivity and reactive astrogliosis: costs and benefits. *Physiological Reviews, 94*: 1077–98.

Pascual-Leone A., Amedi A., Fregni F., Merabet L.B. (2005), The plastic human brain cortex. *Annual Review of Neuroscience, 28*: 377–401.

Pascual-Leone A., Nguyet D., Cohen L.G., Brasil-Neto J.P., Cammarota A., Hallett M. (1995), Modulation of muscle responses evoked by transcranial magnetic stimulation during the acquisition of new fine motor skills. *Journal of Neurophysiology*, 74(3): 1037–1045.

Petanjek Z., Judaš M., Šimic G., Rasin M.R., Uylings H.B., Rakic P., Kostovic I. (2011), Extraordinary neoteny of synaptic spines in the human prefrontal cortex. *Proceedings of the National Academy of Sciences USA, 108*(32): 13281–13286.

Piaget J. (1957), *The Construction of Reality in the Child*, London, Routledge & Kegan Paul.

Poldrack R.A. (2000), Imaging brain plasticity: conceptual and methodological issues – a theoretical review. *Neuroimage, 12*(1): 1–13.

Preuss T.M. (2009), The cognitive neuroscience of human uniqueness. In: Gazzaniga M.S. (ed), *The cognitive neurosciences* (4th edition), Cambridge (MA), MIT Press, 49–64.

Qi H.X., Jain N., Collins C.E., Lyon D.C., Kaas J.H. (2010), Functional organization of motor cortex of adult macaque monkeys is altered by sensory loss in infancy. *Proceedings of the National Academy of Sciences USA, 107*(7): 3192–3197.

Rakic P., Bourgeois J.P., Goldman-Rakic P.S. (1994), Synaptic development of the cerebral cortex: implications for learning, memory, and mental illness. *Progress in Brain Research, 102*: 227–243.

Ramachandran V.S. and Hirstein W. (1998), The perception of phantom limbs. The D.O. Hebb lecture. *Brain, 121*(9): 1603–1630.

Ramachandran V.S. and Rogers-Ramachandran D. (2000), Phantom limbs and neural plasticity. *Archives of Neurology, 57*(3): 317–320.

Ramón Y Cajal S. (1892), El nuevo concepto de la histología de los centros nerviosos. *Revista de Ciencias Médicas, 18*: 361–376, 457–476, 505–520, 529–541.

Ramón Y Cajal S. (1895), Algunas conjeturas sobre el mecanismo anatómico de la ideación, asociación y atención. *Revista de Medicina y Cirugía prácticas, 36*: 497–508.

Ramón Y Cajal S. (1913–1914), *Estudios sobre la Degeneración y Regeneración del Sistema Nervioso*, Madrid, Moya.

Rickard T.C., Cai D.J., Rieth C.A., Jones J., Ard M.C. (2008), Sleep does not enhance motor sequence learning. *Journal of Experimental Psychology Learning Memory and Cognition, 34*(4): 834–842.

Rizzolatti G., Fadiga L., Fogassi L., Gallese V. (1997), The space around us. *Science, 277*(5323): 190–191.

Rosenkranz K., Butler K., Williamon A., Cordivari C., Lees A.J., Rothwell J.C. (2008), Sensorimotor reorganization by proprioceptive training in musician's dystonia and writer's cramp. *Neurology, 70*(4): 304–315.

Rossini P.M., Caltagirone C., Castriota-Sacnderbeg A., Cicinelli P., Del Gratta C, Demartin M., Pizzella V., Traversa R., Romani G.L. (1998), Hand motor cortical area reorganization in stroke: a study with fMRI, Meg and Tcs maps. *Neuroreport, 9*(9): 2141–2146.

Rumelhart D.E. (1989), The architecture of mind: a connectionist approach. In: Posner M. (ed), *Foundations of cognitive science*, Cambridge (MA), MIT Press, 133–159.

Saab C. (2013), Visualizing the complex brain dynamics of chronic pain. *Journal of Neuroimmune Pharmacology, 8*(3): 510–517.

Sadato N., Pascual-Leone A., Grafman J., Ibañez V., Deiber M.P., Dold G., Hallett M. (1996), Activation of the primary visual cortex by Braille reading in blind subjects. *Nature, 380*(6574): 526–528.

Sandkühler J. (2009), Models and mechanisms of hyperalgesia and allodynia. *Physiological Reviews, 89*(2): 707–758.

Sawada M. and Sawamoto K. (2013), Mechanisms of neurogenesis in the normal and injured adult brain. *Keio Journal of Medicine, 62*(1): 13–28.

Schaechter J.D., Moore C.I., Connell B.D., Rosen B.R., Dijkhuizen R.M. (2006), Structural and functional plasticity in the somatosensory cortex of chronic stroke patients. *Brain, 129*(10): 2722–2733.

Schlaug G., Forgeard M., Zhu L., Norton A., Norton A., Winner E. (2009), Training-induced neuroplasticity in young children. *Annals of the New York Academy of Sciences, 1169*: 205–208.

Scholz J., Klein M.C., Behrens T.E., Johansen-Berg H. (2009), Training induces changes in white-matter architecture. *Nature Neuroscience, 12*(11): 1370–1371.

Sherrington C.S. (1906), *The Integrative Action of the Nervous System*, New York, Charles Scribner's Sons.

Seitz R.J., Huang Y., Knorr U., Tellmann L., Herzog H., Freund H.J. (1995), Large-scale plasticity of the human motor cortex. *Neuroreport, 6*(5): 742–744.

Semenza C. and Goodglass H. (1985), Localization of body parts in brain injured subjects. *Neuropsychologia, 23*(2): 161–175.

Somel M., Liu X., Khaitovich P. (2013), Human brain evolution: transcripts, metabolites and their regulators. *Nature Reviews Neuroscience, 14*(2): 112–127.

Spelke E. and Kinzler K. (2007), Core knowledge. *Developmental Science, 10*: 89–96.

Sporns O. (2012), The human connectome: a complex network. *Annals of New York Academy of Sciences, 1224*: 109–125.
Sur M. and Rubenstein J.L. (2005), Patterning and plasticity of the cerebral cortex. *Science, 310*: 805–810.
Swain R.A., Harris A.B., Wiener E.C., Dutka M.V., Morris H.D., Theien B.E., Konda S., Engberg K., Lauterbur P.C., Greenough W.T. (2003), Prolonged exercise induces angiogenesis and increases cerebral blood volume in primary motor cortex of the rat. *Neuroscience, 117*(4): 1037–1046.
Tanzi E. (1893), I fatti e le induzioni dell'odierna istologia del sistema nervoso. *Rivista Sperimentale di Freniatria e Medicina Legale, 19*: 419–472.
Toldi J., Farkas T., Völgyi B. (1994), Neonatal enucleation induces cross-modal changes in the barrel cortex of rat. A behavioural and electrophysiological study. *Neuroscience Letters, 167*(1–2): 1–4.
Tornero D., Wattananit S., Grønning Madsen M., Koch P., Wood J., Tatarishvili J., Mine Y., Ge R., Monni E., Devaraju K., Hevner R.F., Brüstle O., Lindvall O., Kokaia Z. (2013), Human induced pluripotent stem cell-derived cortical neurons integrate in stroke-injured cortex and improve functional recovery. *Brain, 136*(12): 3561–3577.
Twyman A.D. and Newcombe N.S. (2010), Five reasons to doubt the existence of a geometric module. *Cognitive Science, 34*(7): 1315–1356.
Ungerleider L.G., Doyon J., Karni A. (2002), Imaging brain plasticity during motor skill learning. *Neurobiology of Learning and Memory, 78*(3): 553–564.
Vallender E.J., Mekel-Bobrov N., Lahn B.T. (2008), Genetic basis of human brain evolution. *Trends in Neurosciences, 31*(12): 637–644.
Vallortigara G. (2012), Core knowledge of object, number, and geometry: A comparative and neural approach. *Cognitive Neuropsychology, 29*(1–2): 213–236.
Vargha-Khadem F., Carr L.J., Isaacs E., Brett E., Adams C., Mishkin M. (1997), Onset of speech after left hemispherectomy in a nine-year-old boy. *Brain, 120*(1): 159–182.
Verhaak P.F., Kerssens J.J., Dekker J., Sorbi M.J., Bensing J.M. (1998), Prevalence of chronic benign pain disorder among adults: a review of the literature. *Pain, 77*(3): 231–239.
Walker M.P., Brakefield T., Morgan A., Hobson J.A., Stickgold R. (2002), Practice with sleep makes perfect: sleep-dependent motor skill learning. *Neuron, 35*(1): 205–211.
Ward N.S., Brown M.M., Thompson A.J., Frackowiak R.S. (2003), Neural correlates of outcome after stroke: a cross-sectional fMRI study. *Brain, 126*(6): 1430–1448.
Weeks R., Horwitz B., Aziz-Sultan A., Tian B., Wessinger C.M., Cohen L.G., Hallett M., Rauschecker J.P. (2000), A positron emission tomographic study of auditory localization in the congenitally blind. *Journal of Neuroscience, 20*(7): 2664–2672.
Will B., Dalrymple-Alford J., Wol V. M., & Cassel J.-C. (2008), The concept of brain plasticity: Paillard's systemic analysis and emphasis on structure and function (followed by the translation of a seminal paper by Paillard on plasticity). *Behavioural Brain Research, 192*: 2–11.
Wiesel T.N. (1981), *Postnatal development of the visual cortex and the influence of environment.* Nobel Prize Lecture.

Wittmann B.C., Dolan R.J., Düzel E. (2011), Behavioral specifications of reward-associated long-term memory enhancement in humans. *Learning and Memory, 18*(5): 296–300.

Yang T.T., Gallen C.C., Schwartz B., Bloom F.E. (1993), Noninvasive somatosensory homunculus mapping in humans by using a large-array biomagnetometer. *Proceedings of the National Academy of Sciences USA, 90*: 3098–3102.

Yakovlev, P.I. and Lecours, A. (1967), The myelogenetic cycles of regional maturation of the brain. In: Minkowski, A., (ed), *Regional Development of the Brain in Early Life*, Oxford, Blackwell, 3–70.

SECTION 2
The role of specific factors on neural plasticity

3
THE IMPACT OF DEMOGRAPHIC FACTORS IN SHAPING NEURAL PLASTICITY

The influence of age on neural plasticity: development and aging

In the last few years, a bulk of converging data coming from different research fields has greatly influenced our conceptualization of brain changes and brain functions across the lifespan.

Until a few years ago, developing and aging were considered two distinct processes: the first, spanning from infancy to maturity and characterized by acquisition and consolidation through experience of specific skills and associated with a high degree of brain flexibility; the second, coinciding with an irreversible decline of learning through the aging process (Figure 3.1, line A). On the contrary, it is now widely believed that developing and aging evolve and influence each other across the entire lifespan: as a consequence, a continuous process of functional plasticity, although at slower pace, is thought to maintain sensitivity to environmental influence throughout life (Hensch, 2004, Figure 3.1, line B).

On the basis of these considerations, plastic changes in the developing and aging brain will be treated in the same chapter for a better understanding of the processes leading to the maturation and aging of the brain.

The critical period

The brain is particularly apt to acquire sensory information and develop particular skills during the first years of life. This period is critical because the

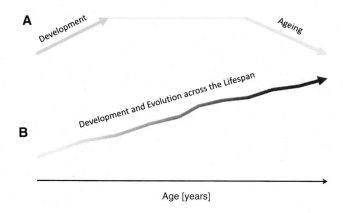

FIGURE 3.1 Schematic representations of two views of brain and cognition changes across the lifespan. From A. Pascual-Leone and M.J. Taylor. A Developmental Framework of Brain and Cognition from Infancy to Old Age. *Brain Topography* (2011) 24:183–186. With kind permission from Springer Science and Business Media.

absence of specific stimuli during this time interval can lead to irreversible deficits (Newport et al., 2002), which can have the effect of an acquired lesion in cognitively critical brain areas. While *experience-dependent* plasticity extends along the entire lifespan, *experience-expectant* and *experience-independent* plasticity occur only during development. The former requires the presence of specific types of experience for different brain systems to develop: Wiesel and Hubel (1963) showed that if one eye is kept closed after birth in kittens, their vision is compromised when the closed eye is eventually opened (see chapter 7). *Experience-independent* plasticity is also largely a developmental process: the postnatal pruning of the connections (see Innocenti and Price, 2005) allows the nervous system more precision in connectivity without requiring overwhelmingly complex genetic instructions (for a revision, see Kolb and Gibb, 2014).

The 'Sensitive' period has been defined by Daw (1998) as a time in development during which some property develops rapidly and is most susceptible to alteration by the environment. According to Bateson (1979), the critical period is similar to the brief opening of a window, with experience influencing development only when the window is open. This is a complex behavior that integrates many sensory modalities, including vision, taste, olfaction, and audition. The opening and closing of a critical period depends on many factors, ranging from specific features of sensory stimulus, to the type of experience, to the influence of attentional and motivational factors (Levelt and Hübener, 2012). Similarly, the length of the critical period varies according to species and systems, as does its way of concluding (rapid or gradual). In part, these variations are linked to the rate at which the organism develops: slowly developing organisms would be expected to have critical periods longer than quickly developing species.

The understanding of critical period plasticity derives from two sources: the effects of sensory deprivation and the superior ability of the developing brain to compensate for the effects of a perinatal brain injury.

The capacity of a cat's eye to activate neurons in the visual cortex depends on whether that eye has received visual input during the first three months of life (Freeman, 1996). Monocular deprivation leads to a permanent loss of the response in the deprived eye (Hubel and Wiesel, 1998), whereas rearing animals in the dark shifts the critical period for ocular dominance (OD) plasticity[1] (Mower, 1991). Shutting the eye of an adult cat does not lead to permanent effects, indicating that cells in the visual cortex are programmed during a key developmental window in the first few months of life. Similarly, the critical period for song learning in certain bird species (song sparrows) is not always tightly coupled to the time of hatching; instead, it can depend on external triggers, such as the seasons (Nulty et al., 2010).

Observations made in 3-month-old human babies show a gradual progressive specialization of the face-processing system through experience, stemming from general characteristics of the human visuo-perceptual system (Simion et al., 2007). Furthermore, and in analogy to the pattern described in visually deprived kittens, impoverished visual input in children (e.g. due to errors in refraction or strabismus) during the critical period causes amblyopia or loss of functional visual acuity (see Ganguly and Poo, 2013).

When other modalities have been examined, relatively similar results have been obtained. Within the motor system, a critical period is described: the primary motor cortex 'motor maps' develop after birth and undergo a process of refinement during a critical period analogous to that of the visual system (Anderson et al., 2010). The corticospinal tract (CST),[2] or pyramidal tract, is also refined through an activity-dependent process similar to the sensory system: the inactivation of CST during the postnatal period results in an alteration of axonal morphology and their topographical distribution, as well as long-term motor impairment (Martin, 2005).

A relevant human example in the auditory modality may be the loss of perceived phonemic boundaries if the language to which neonates are exposed does not utilize them (Werker and Tees, 1984). Similarly, the perception of some phonetic contrasts present in languages acquired at later age is difficult or sometimes impossible: the perception of English /r-l/ phonetic contrast, although easy for native English speakers, is extremely difficult for native Japanese speakers who learned English as a second language after childhood. Data from pre-verbally deaf children who have received cochlear implants show that the timing of implant can affect different levels of plasticity within the auditory system (Gordon et al., 2011; see also chapter 7).

In a wider perspective, the events occurring in the sensitive or even prenatal period can produce both negative and positive effects linked to the influence of epigenetic factors (see chapter 2, section 2.1.3): typically developing children institutionalized at birth have low intelligence quotients and future poor language development. This pattern, luckily, can be inverted by placing the children in high-quality foster care before the age of two (Nelson et al., 2007; Windsor et al., 2007).

The critical or sensitive period is a sort of 'window', mostly restricted to the first years of life, during which the brain is particularly apt to acquire sensory information and develop particular skills. This process is sustained by postnatal development and refinement of the anatomical and functional neural organization. Presence or absence of specific stimuli in this time interval can lead to irreversible motor, perceptual and cognitive changes. The length of the critical period is variable; in humans it extends longer than in other species, which is probably related to the amount of information and skill learning acquired after birth.

Brain changes following injury in the sensitive period

The search for the effect, of an early brain injury on the process of plasticity is a particularly thorny problem because the sensitive period coincides with brain development. The only available method is to observe, in laboratory animals, brain changes following injury in developing animals. If damage coincides with the period of neurogenesis, the brain can respond by increasing neurogenesis to replace lost neurons. Damage in the subsequent weeks leads to an increase of dendritic arborizations, probably reflecting an increased number of synapses (for a review, see Kolb and Gibb, 2007). In some cases, however, the changes are not beneficial, leading to a remodeling of cortical circuitry and apoptosis or programmed cell death (for a review, see Kolb and Teskey, 2012). In human infants, it has been found that synaptogenesis (Huttenlocher and Dabholkar, 1997) and metabolic changes (Chugani, 1998) differ with age across brain regions and correspond to the emergence of various behaviors in the first years of life. Furthermore, in comparison to other animals, the infancy period of humans extends longer and probably reflects the importance of incorporating that enormous amount of information and skill learning that characterizes the human species. It is only in the critical period that some structural and functional neural modification becomes essentially irreversible. Experimental evidence however, is mostly anedoctal, except for language acquisition (Fox et al., 2010). Lesions in the language areas of the language-dominant left hemisphere occurring in early infancy rarely result in severe speech and language disorders (Woods and Teuber, 1978; Woods and Carey, 1979; Vargha-Khadem et al., 1985; Thal et al., 1991). This gross sparing of speech and language functions has been attributed to the plasticity and reorganizational capacity of the immature brain, which may enable speech and language functions to develop in the right hemisphere. On the contrary, if language competence is not acquired or reacquired during the first year of life or if the lesion establishes in adulthood, language skills are in most cases (but see chapter 7) permanently affected.

A last problem to be discussed is the effects of sensory or cognitive enrichment delivered during the sensitive period. Rather than thinking that 'more is better', increasing evidence suggests that the 'expectable' environment during development requires not only the variation in light necessary for vision or tones heard for spoken language, but also an adequate degree of motivation and emotional support from care givers (for a review, see Fox et al., 2010). A *caveat* must be mentioned in evaluating the benefit of an enriched environment because the behavioral outcomes may be influenced by later experience, even though the neural circuits at lower level remain irreversibly altered, or by the unmasking of alternative pathways stemming from multisensory integration regions in the brain (Pascual-Leone et al., 2005).

> Brain injuries in developing animals have, in general, a better outcome than those occurring in adulthood. If damage coincides with the period of active neurogenesis, the brain can respond by increasing this process or by increasing synapses. Lesions in unilateral cognitive-dedicated areas in infancy do not prevent, in the majority of cases, an almost-normal development, which occurs via a process of take-over by the intact contralateral hemisphere.

Anatomical and functional changes in the aging brain

Asked to define time, Augustine wrote: "If no one asks me, I know what it is. If I wish to explain it to him who asks me, I do not know" (*Confessions, 11, XIV, 17*).

The same paradox applies in trying to define aging. Although distinguishing between old and young people may seem an easy task, there is no general agreement on the traits or age at which a person becomes old. At the moment, there is no standard numerical criterion, but the United Nations cut-off to refer to the older population is 60 years. While this definition is somewhat arbitrary, it is often associated with the age at which one can begin to receive pension benefits. Of course, this definition can be applied only to western or westernized countries; in Africa, for example, the definition of an elder or 'elderly' person correlates with the chronological ages of 50 to 65 years, depending on the environment, the region and the country. Conversely, in the West, the increasing life expectancy has postponed the age of retirement and the 'official' onset of aging to 65 years or older. From a different perspective, the onset of old age could coincide with the birth of the first grandchild: becoming a grandparent can be considered a mark of aging, since the generational task of parenting has been transferred to the sons and daughters.

A further subdivision classifies aged persons into three classes: elders (60–74), old (75–90), grand olds (90+). In addition, in cultures where life expectancy is generally high, the introduction of the concept of middle age, considered to be between about forty-five and sixty, has further increased the already fuzzy borders between these times of life. Lacking an accepted and acceptable criterion, the definition of aging reflects in many instances the social class differences or functional ability related to the workforce, but more often than not it is a reflection of the current political and economic situation. In Venice, for example, a reduced entrance fee to the museums is applied to people over 65, but in the water-buses, you must be over 70 to enjoy a reserved seat!

Aging is a universal and multifaceted phenomenon resulting from the combined effects of several processes (genetic, biological, and environmental) that affect, although at different degrees, all biological systems, including the cognitive system. Despite the growing number of studies aimed at understanding the nature and extent of age-related cognitive changes, the aging process remains, for several reasons, a complex subject. First and utmost is the question of distinguishing the possible effect of normal aging from those pathological processes that affect cognition. Most of these, such as Alzheimer's or Parkinson's disease, arise mostly, if not only, in older persons and can be characterized by years of a long preclinical stage, in which very subtle cognitive changes are the only symptoms. Second, since age is a variable that cannot be experimentally manipulated (participants cannot be randomly assigned to experimental conditions), most studies are correlational: comparisons are made among different age-groups. Only a minority are longitudinal, following cohorts of individuals from young adulthood to old age.

In the first part of this chapter, we will review the functional alterations of the cognitive processes that usually occur in normal aging and try to relate them to the morphological alterations either at cellular or neural connections.

The second part will be devoted to the description of the compensatory mechanisms that allow some of the best normal elders to perform some cognitive tasks at juvenile level, despite the 'normal' neural loss of their specific natural substrate.

Finally, this chapter will try to define, both in neurological and functional terms, the factors that differentiate normal aging from pathological aging, and tentatively indicate the signs that could be used to predict progression from normal to impaired cognition.

> As aging is difficult to define, so are the morphological and functional age-related neural modifications, since most pathological conditions, such as dementia of Alzheimer type, that affect old people have a long preclinical stage in which the effects of an initial pathological stage are difficult to disentangle from the effects of 'normal' aging.

Age-related neuronal changes

In contrast to the past prevailing opinion that the marker of neural aging was a diffuse loss of the neurons of the cerebral cortex, leading to a lower volume of the grey matter visible in post-mortem and *in vivo* through neuroimaging studies, more recent data show that in healthy aged humans, non-human primates and other animal species (for a review, see Pakkenberg and Gundersen, 1997 and West et al., 1994), a significant loss of neurons is confined mostly to cortical layers in area 8A of the dorsolateral prefrontal cortex (PFC), while the hippocampus and adjacent medial temporal lobe (MTL) neurons, which for many years were considered particularly sensitive to aging, do not show a significant loss in neuron numbers.

Similarly, the effect of aging on neuronal cell connections is not widespread across the cerebral cortex: a reduction with age of the dendritic branching, the fundamental determinant of neuronal wiring, as well as the extension of the dendritic spines[3] is region specific, and mostly confined to the PFC and medial temporal lobe structures (for a review, see Burke and Barnes, 2006). In analogy, studies of the biophysical properties of the aged neurons show that most electrical properties remain constant during normal aging; the alterations have been confined to the neurons of the PFC cortex.

It must be noted that widespread changes in the hemodynamic response (cerebral blood flow, oxygen metabolism and blood oxygenation level dependent (BOLD) response) have been recorded by Ances et al. (2009); analogously, changes in receptors, neurotransmitters and receptors have been reported in aging (for a review, see Cabeza, 2001).

> Age-related morphological alterations are not diffuse, but impinge only on some cortical structures; in particular, loss of neurons and decrease of connectivity are confined mostly to the prefrontal cortex.

The cognitive functions in the aging brain

As with most biological systems, the impact of normal and in most cases of pathological aging on cognitive skills is, at its beginning, subtle and in many ways usually unnoticed. In accordance with the morphological data, the effects are selective, impinging only on some cognitive functions.

A number of studies classify the age-related cognitive changes according to the onset of their decline. In particular, three categories of functions have been proposed: (1) life-long declining functions, (2) late-in-life declining functions and (3) life-long stable functions (see Hedden and Gabrieli, 2004, for a review).

As the speed of walking or running decreases with age, so does the rapidity to process or to react to internally or externally generated stimuli. According to Salthouse (1996), this reduction negatively affects specific skills because some cognitively relevant operations cannot be executed in a limited time and the products of early processing may no longer be available.

Life-long declining functions include processing speed, working memory (WM), inductive reasoning (Park et al., 2002; Park et al., 1996) and encoding and retrieval of information in the episodic memory system (see chapter 5). These skills are often covered by the umbrella term 'executive functions'. Executive functions are required to coordinate several processes in order to achieve a goal and are anatomically and functionally distinct from the modular functions such as language (for a review, see Shallice, 1988). A number of studies have tried to identify a potential common and unifying factor at the base of the above age-related deficits. Some authors (Craik and Byrd, 1982) favor a reduction of attentional resources along with a general slowing in information processing (Salthouse, 1996; Cona et al., 2013); in particular, older adults have a deficit in the ability to maintain goals of information in the episodic and WM systems, leading to a decrease in several cognitive functions.

Neuropsychological evidence suggests that executive processing is supported by the frontal lobes. These findings have led to the development of the 'frontal lobe hypothesis' of aging: the cognitive functions supported by the prefrontal cortex decline, for some unknown reason, at an earlier age than those supported by other brain regions, and the decline is reminiscent of the deficits observed in patients with frontal lobe acquired focal damage (for a review, see West, 1996.) Further support for this hypothesis derives from the application of non-invasive brain imaging studies, such the analysis of event-related potentials (ERP) or, more recently, of the event-related optical signal (EROS, for a review, see Gratton and Fabiani, 2010).[4] These methods, unlike fMRI or PET studies, allow high temporal resolution. It has been found that many ERP components related to attentional process can be affected by aging: for example, Daffner et al. (2011) in an ERP study found that older adults needed additional resource allocation in performing cognitive tasks at the same level of younger subjects, as measured by the amplitude of an ERP component, P3.

Unlike executive skills, other cognitive functions, such as lexical and numerical abilities and general semantic knowledge, are stable or even increase throughout life, slowly declining only in the very last decades of life (Lövden et al., 2004).

It can be concluded, according to Craick and Bird (1982), that age-related cognitive differences manifest in situations requiring large amounts of self-initiated processing or access to highly specific information, such as proper name retrieval or details of specific episodes.[5]

Compensatory strategies

Not only are age-related cognitive changes selective, but they are also not the same among similar age-matched individuals. General and specific factors are hypothesized to support inter-individual decline. Among them, educational level, health, cognitive and life style, and personality are all likely to modulate the age-related cognitive evolution. None of them, however, seems to play a decisive role.

As a possible reason at the base of such inter-individual difference, Stern (2002, 2012) has introduced the notion of cognitive reserve (CR). CR can act as a moderator between pathology and clinical outcome and is expressed as the mind's resistance to damage of the brain.

The CR notion stemmed from the hypothesis of a brain reserve, proposed by Katzman et al. (1989). They described an anatomo-clinical discordance shown by some elder people who were reported to enjoy a normal cognitive state, but were found, upon autopsy, to have massive deposits of amyloid plaques in the brain and numerous neurofibrillary tangles consistent with a pattern of advanced Alzheimer's disease (AD). According to Katzman et al., the AD-related cognitive impairment could not manifest itself, because the brains of these subjects were larger than average. In the following years, the concept of brain reserve has been modified and related to the weight of stimulating environment, such as educational and environmental experience. According to Stern (2012), CR can be separated into two distinct forms: brain or neural reserve and cognitive reserve. The neural implementation of CR can manifest in two forms: neural reserve (the ability to optimize or maximize normal performance) and neural compensation. This former mechanism consists of the recruitment of new networks in performing tasks by subjects not affected by brain pathology related to age or disease. Neural reserve is linked to the peculiarities of the brain structure, such as the number of neurons or synapses. A variety of factors, from genetics to education and leisure activities (see Stern, 2012), have been shown to have a role in shaping the neural reserve and explaining inter-individual differences.

In contrast, neural compensation consists of the often-successful attempt to combat the effect of normal or pathological aging by using compensatory mechanisms – a process of recruiting, in comparison to younger subjects, additional neurological space inside the same hemisphere or in the opposite hemisphere in performing cognitive operations. These mechanisms can be best shown by the following examples.

Despite the age-related anatomical changes in the PFC, most aged people perform at the same level of younger adults in attentional tasks. Functional neuroimaging studies (fRMI and PET) have shown a wider recruitment of brain areas in the older group when successfully performing similar tasks (Reuter-Lorenz et al., 2000; Schneider-Garces et al., 2010; Berlingeri et al., 2010). According to the compensation-related utilization of neural circuit hypothesis (CRUNCH, Cabeza et al., 2002; Cappell et al., 2010), a normal level of performance in some cognitive skills in older adults needs a wider cortical activation, whose level of load is, however, less than younger adults'. Similarly, Davis et al. (2012), in an fMRi study, found that, in comparison with the young, older adults showed a tendency to recruit prefrontal cortex (PFC) regions contralateral to those most active in the younger adults during a lateralized word-matching task. In addition, they found a positive correlation between fractional anisotropy (an MRI of myelination in the white matter, fiber density and axonal diameter) in the corpus callosum and both bilateral processing advantage and functional connectivity between contralateral PFC, indicating that older adults' ability to distribute processing across the hemispheres is constrained by white matter integrity. In conclusion, the deleterious effects of brain aging can be, in most cases, efficiently contrasted by the use of compensatory strategies both at neural and behavioral level. At single subject level, individuals who are provided with more efficient or wider neural networks could manifest more resilience to the effects of age-related 'normal' and pathological changes.

Normal and pathological aging

The effort of differentiating the effects of normal aging on cognitive skills from those related to neurodegenerative disorders, such as AD or Parkinson's disease, is far from being accomplished. While a full-fledged pattern of dementia is easily recognizable, the detection of its onset is subtle and the cognitive deficit can progress for years before being openly manifested. Similarly, the search of faultless biological markers (biochemical, neuro-radiological) in the early stages of degenerative dementia is far from being exhausted.

A comparative examination of the morphological and functional changes in normal and pathological aging has defined two components. The first is linked to a change, both morphological and functional, of the prefrontal regions in normal aging individuals, as described in the previous sections. The second component involves changes in the region of the medial temporal lobes and associative cortical areas, leading to a progressive loss of memory, both episodic and semantic, and of language, behavior and social skills.

On these premises, many efforts have been made to clinically differentiate the pattern of 'normal' cognitive decline from that of initial dementia. In 2011, The National Institute on Aging/Alzheimer's Association convened an international workgroup to review the biomarker, epidemiological, and neuropsychological evidence, and proposed conceptual frameworks as well as operational research to determine the factors that best predict the risk of progression from 'normal' cognition to mild cognitive impairment[6] and AD dementia. These recommendations are, however, intended for research purposes and do not have any clinical implications at this time (Sperling et al., 2011).

Living aging

Successful aging requires various forms of adaptations to respond to the changing demands across the life course (Negash et al., 2011).

Ulrich, the hero of Musil's book *The Man without Qualities*, realizes that, having reached a certain age, men think they will enjoy a stable state that will not change in the future. This feeling, recently called 'The End of History Illusion' (Quoidbach, Gilbert and Wilson, 2013) is present in every stage of adult life, but greater for young people than for older people. The removal of this illusion is often coincident in the older population with the beginning of subjective and objective aging.

Aging is not, however, only a consequence of brain changes. Although outside the specific scope of this book, several age-linked factors in style of life must be mentioned. While, for example, in comparison to young people, old people are more equipped with experience, they often show a decrease in specific competences, such as failing to acquire the specific knowledge linked to the development of new technologies. Loss of active work can make it difficult to keep and acquire friends and social contacts, leading to a loss of interests, curiosity and social insulation. This route is not, however, unavoidable; successful aging requires setting up new ways of living and researching new resources. The process is not easy; it requires strong motivation to overcome the neural fatigue needed to find and operate new neural and cognitive strategies.

In summary, physical and psychological factors equally contribute to both the onset of aging and its successful adaptation.

> Age-related cognitive decline is a multifaceted phenomenon. Interindividual variability and selective impairment or sparing of intellectual skills characterizes the process of human aging. Generally, attention, short term memory and planning are more sensitive to aging effects than language and numeric abilities. Semantic memory is more resistant than episodic memory. A potential common unifying factor at the base of these losses could be a deficit of executive functions, which are supported by the frontal structures. The deleterious effects of aging on cognition can

be, in most cases, successfully opposed by the adoption of compensatory strategies, such as the recruitment of additional brain areas, and the effects of cognitive reserve, related to experience and stimulating environment.

While a full-fledged dementia is easy to recognize, differentiating the effects of normal aging on cognitive skills from those related to the initial phase of a neurodegenerative disorder, such as AD or Parkinson's disease, is far from easy. Similarly, the search for specific biological markers (biochemical, neuro-radiological) in the early stages of degenerative dementia is far from being completed.

Neural plasticity and individual and gender differences

Inter-individual differences

Unless there is a developmental or acquired pathological deficit, all members of the human species share the same basic skills, such as vision and action, without noticeable inter-individual differences. On the other hand, one cannot fail to notice substantial inter-individual differences in a variety of domains, ranging from acquisition of motor and cognitive skills, to enhanced flexibility in decision making and in planning processes. This variability is evidenced in the capacity to learn a cognitive skill, in the rate at which the skill is learned, and in the highest performance in some skills.

In this chapter, we concentrate on two specific issues. The first is the structural basis of inter-individual differences in cognition in the light of the contribution of neuroimaging brain studies. Akin to the first issue is the second: how the study of the inter-individual differences can contribute to the question of cognitive and neural modularity. In addition, we will briefly report the result of some neural studies relating to sex/gender difference in behavior.

When, in the last couple of centuries, the notion became prevalent that human cognition supremacy was related to the anatomical specificities of the cerebral cortex, two different theories were offered to explain the neurobiological basis of inter-individual variation in intelligence and specific cognitive skills. The first was based on the notion that 'intelligence', however defined (for a review, see Gottfredson, 1997), was a unitary homogeneous ability (the *g factor*) that influences performance on all tests of mental ability. This notion led to the hypothesis in the neurosciences of intelligence, put forward by Galton (1888) among others, that individual differences in intelligence were associated with the notion that size matters (*bigger is better*).

In contrast, according to phrenologists like Gall and Spurzheim, the cognitive supremacy of the human species was seen as the result of the greater development in humans of the frontal lobes. These structures therefore came to constitute the 'site' of intelligence, with language being its highest expression. Eventually, Gall became convinced that the mind was composed of multiple distinct and innate faculties, whose physical sites were allocated in separate seats of the cortex. Accordingly, inter-individual cognitive differences derived from the size of the part of the brain dedicated to that specific faculty, intelligence being the sum of the integrated work of single faculties. Inter-individual variations were considered qualitative, rather than quantitative, reflecting the development of specific brain parts (faculty psychology, Fodor, 1983; multiple intelligence theory, Gardner, 1983).

Around the turn of the 20th century, a series of detailed necropsy studies of the brain of outstanding individuals was performed, with the aim of correlating their intellectual skill with brain anatomy. In general, the study concentrated on the weight of the brain or its lobes and on the patterns of gyral convolutions, both being usually reported within normal limits. As outlined by Witelson, Kigar, and Harvey (1999), this approach had several limitations: the observation was mostly anecdotal, the medical and cognitive status at the time of death was often not known and comparison with normal groups was not available. Finally, negative cases – individual cases showing the same brain characteristics of the exceptional people, but with a normal or even lower pattern of cognition – had not been reported.

The most famous single case report concerns Albert Einstein's brain. Upon his death, his brain was removed and sectioned. His brain was of normal size, but showed an extraordinary prefrontal cortex and an expansion of the left primary somatosensory and motor cortices near the regions that typically represent face and tongue. In addition, his parietal lobes were 'unusual', possibly providing some of the neurological underpinnings for his visuo-spatial and mathematical skills (Falk, Lepore and Noe, 2013).

It was only with the introduction of genetics (quantitative and molecular; for a review, see Deary, Penke and Johnson, 2010), and neuroimaging (morphological and functional) studies that the biological basis of inter-individual differences in cognitive skills enjoyed a renewed interest and acquired a more refined methodology. We will not review the studies of the genetic basis of intelligence; let it suffice to quote the conclusion of Payton (2009: 465) who, after a survey of more than 200 published studies on the 50 or so genes that have been implicated in differences in cognitive abilities, concluded that

> after 14 years of cognitive genetic research, there are no genes that we can conclusively say are responsible for the variation in cognition or its

decline with age in healthy normal individuals. Only consortia formed to produce genome-wide scans could, in the future, report genetic associations with cognitive functions based on samples of thousands of subjects.

Most neuroimaging studies on talents (for example, musicians, taxi drivers, etc.), some of them reviewed in chapter 2, are cross-sectional or longitudinal group studies, ignoring inter-individual differences within groups of experts and even controls. While in general it has been found that expertise in one particular field is associated with a more developed brain structure in the domain-specific brain zone, inter-individual differences have been underscored for different reasons. The interpretation of these results is, in most cases, clearly problematic, since it is difficult to differentiate, at the individual level, between the importance of training and that of inborn characteristics on modifying the brain architecture.

It is more useful, therefore, to explore inter-individual brain anatomy differences within a population of healthy non-expert individuals with regard to some basic skills (developed without specific training) and subsequently relate them to measures of behavioral and cognitive data.

Progress in neuroimaging techniques has allowed us to explore individual morphological characteristics in brain anatomy by comparing differences in brain shape or differences in the local composition of brain tissue (grey and white matter) after macroscopic differences in shape have been discounted. The methods most commonly used are voxel-based morphometry (VBM)[7] and diffusion tensor imaging (DTI). In a detailed review of the studies derived from functional (i.e. functional magnetic resonance imaging, fMRI; positron emission tomography, PET) and structural (i.e. magnetic resonance spectroscopy, diffusion tensor imaging, voxel-based morphometry) neuroimaging paradigms, Jung and Haier (2007) reported a striking consensus suggesting that variations in a distributed network predict individual differences found on intelligence and reasoning tasks. They named this the Parieto-Frontal Integration Theory (P-FIT). The P-FIT network includes the following: Brodmann areas (BAs), the dorsolateral prefrontal cortex (BAs 6, 9, 10, 45, 46, 47), the inferior (BAs 39, 40) and superior (BA 7) parietal lobule, the anterior cingulate (BA 32), and regions within the temporal (BAs 21, 37) and occipital (BAs 18, 19) lobes. This network implements control of behavior and thought across diverse contexts by a mechanism – global connectivity – by which components of this network might coordinate control of other networks. Cole et al. (2010) showed a highly selective relationship between the amount of global connectivity, as shown by fMRI images, and individual differences in fluid intelligence. They found that the lateral prefrontal cortex (LPFC) region's activity could predict performance in a high control demand WM task, exhibiting high global connectivity. This global connectivity, involving connections both within and outside the fronto-parietal network, shows a highly selective relationship with individual differences in fluid intelligence.[8] These findings, according to Cole et al., suggest LPFC is a sort of global neural hub with a wide influence that facilitates the ability to implement control processes central to human intelligence. The degree of connectivity is, however, not homogeneous. Mueller et al. (2013), in a recent functional connectivity study, found that connectivity was heterogeneous across the cortex, with significantly higher variability in hetero-modal association cortex and lower variability in unimodal cortices. A meta-analysis further revealed that regions predicting individual differences in cognitive domains are predominantly located in regions of high connectivity variability.

The issues of cognitive and neural modularity in the field of inter-individual differences are far from solved. For example, the question of how the weight of training and experience in one domain may trade off with a different neural and functional domain, leading to a positive or negative correlation, has yet to be clearly answered. One must remember that "the evidence coming from different sources points to positive correlations between ostensibly distinct cognitive abilities, positive manifold" (Carroll, 1993: 122), leaving, however, unresolved the issues of domain specific versus domain general modules. Finding that the same brain regions as specified above are activated and interconnected in the execution of different cognitive skills does not *per se* exclude a modular approach to the neural substrate of cognition. Rabaglia et al. (2011), relying on a careful meta-analysis of the available data and on computer simulation, tried to reconcile the global versus the modular approach. They posit that, from a fine-grained analysis of the properties of different cognitive modules, a common underlying mechanism could emerge, giving rise, at the individual level, to a positive correlation without excluding a modular approach; this positive manifold derives instead largely from between-task neural overlap, suggesting a potential way of reconciling individual differences with some form of modularity.

Some caution is needed, however, before concluding this chapter. First, it is widely recognized that a correlation between two variables does not necessarily imply that one causes the other: finding an association between structure – or degree of activation of a particular brain structure – and some cognitive performances does not always imply a causal relationship because it does not provide means to distinguish between response variables and covariates. From a neurological perspective, one must remember that differences in grey matter volume reflect synaptogenesis and dendritic arborizations, which are known, most of the times, to be experience-dependent, rather than inborn. Finally, the morphological data obtained with structural MRI and the functional results of fMRI studies often dissociate, suggesting that at present "understanding the relationship between inter-individual differences in brain structure and brain function may be a rich area for future research" (Kanai and Rees, 2011: 232).

> Inter-individual differences in cognition can reflect a specific neural organization – either inborn or experience related. From a meta-analysis of neuroimaging studies, the presence of a higher neural connectivity in a fronto-parietal network seems to be associated with a higher degree of intellectual performance.

Neural plasticity and sex/gender differences

Thanks to the presence of *la petite différence*, it is possible in the overwhelming majority of cases to sort individual bodies into male and female. The problem is much thornier when the brains and minds of people have to be distinguished, since brains and minds are far less dimorphic than genitalia.

Echoing Don Alfonso's statement in Mozart's *Così Fan Tutte*: *è la fede delle femmine come l'araba fenice, che ci sia ognun lo dice, dove sia nessun lo sa* (Women's constancy is like the Arabian Phoenix; everyone swears it exists, but no one knows where) and in spite of the number of papers that have been published on the anatomical and functional differences between male and female brains, a general consensus on the subject has still not been reached.

Inborn gender/sex brain morphology differences may depend, at least in part, on the level of steroid hormones at a critical level of fetal development. According to Jost (1953), it is the level of testosterone, an androgen hormone, that shifts the default female development pathway to a male phenotype. Following this paradigm, Phoenix et al. (1959) found that hormones have, at prenatal level, an organizing action on the neural tissues mediating mating behavior while, in adults, the same hormones mediate an 'activating' effect, which essentially determines the level of later activity or expression. These results, obtained in guinea pigs, were extended to many behaviors and species, including human and non-mating–related behavior. In this light, gender-related differences in cognition (males have better motor and spatial abilities, whereas females have superior memory and social cognition; for a review, see Andreano and Cahill, 2009), were related to the level of gonadal hormones.

The most characterized brain regions where functional and structural dimorphism have been studied are the hippocampus, amygdala, hypothalamus, and cortex cerebral areas associated with cognition and emotion. In addition to the anatomy, the neurochemistry and physiology have been found to differ in these areas. For example, dopamine, serotonin, and GABA, among others, have been found to exhibit significant sex differences in their metabolism (Andreano and Cahill, 2009), as well as various neuropeptidergic systems (Bielsky et al., 2005; Kauffman, 2010).

Following the exciting arrival of neuroimaging techniques in the field of neurosciences, a series of studies have been devoted to the issue of male/female brain anatomical differences, mostly focusing on the gender difference of single brain regions relative to the size of the entire cortex. Women, relative to cortex size, show greater cortical grey matter volume (Gur et al., 1999), larger volumes of regions associated with language functions, and larger volumes of the hippocampus and other cortical and subcortical regions (for a review, see Goldstein et al., 2001). Compared to women, men have been found to have larger volumes of total grey and white matter, relative to cortical size (Gur et al., 1999). Increased neuronal densities in some limbic and paralimbic regions – that is, the amygdala (Giedd et al., 1996), hypothalamus (Swaab and Fliers, 1985) and paracingulate gyrus (Paus et al., 1996) – have been reported in males, as well as larger genu of the corpus callosum (Witelson, 1989).

Rather than an analysis of gender-related differences between single cortical regions, most promising is an analysis of the differences of the brain on the whole, that is the human connectome, the large and complex network of elements and connections forming the human brain (Sporns, 2012). Ideally, this approach can provide fundamental insights into the organization and integration of brain networks. Ingalhalikar et al. (2013), using diffusion tensor imaging technique (DTI) in a large sample of young volunteers, found that males had greater within-hemispheric connectivity, whereas between-hemispheric connectivity and cross-module participation predominated in females. This effect was reversed in the cerebellar connections. The same pattern was observed in fMRI studies: females reported greater inter-hemispheric activation on a language task, while greater focal intra-hemispheric activation was found in males performing a spatial task (Gur et al., 2000).

These results are, however, still debatable. For a start, both behavioral and neuroimaging studies are group studies, not taking into account intra-group variability and also, more often than not, not taking into account occupational and educational interests, attainment, or sexual orientation (Hyde et al., 2008).

More important, it is tacitly assumed that the sex/gender differences are immutable. On the contrary, a short period of training can, for example, wipe out one of the most cited differences in cognitive skills, mental rotation ability. In a study conducted among female and male college undergraduates, Feng, Spence, and Pratt (2007) found that just 10 hours of training on an action video game virtually eliminated the sex/gender difference in spatial attention and simultaneously decreased the sex/gender disparity in mental rotation ability, a higher-level process in spatial cognition.

Also, gender-related studies fail to mention the notion that anatomical changes themselves are mostly experience and training related, rather than inborn (see chapter 2).

In an important review paper, not casually entitled, "Hardwired for Sexism? Approaches to Sex/Gender in Neuroscience", Jordan-Young and Rumiati (2012) suggest that studies aimed at finding gender-related neural differences may contribute to the effect of a society producing and often enhancing the differences. In two recently published fMRI papers, Wraga, Helt, Jacobs, and Sullivan (2007) and Krendl, Richeson, Kelley and Heatherton (2008) examined the role of positive and negative stereotypes on neural structure underlying shifts in women's performance of spatial reasoning and mathematical tasks, where a gender difference in favor of males has been repeatedly reported. In both studies, it was found that a prior exposure to a false but plausible stereotype of women's superior spatial or mathematical abilities not only improved their performance but also induced more efficient neural strategies.

Without ignoring the innate basis of such differences, an approach based on the role of experiential plasticity in shaping them, both at group and individual levels, would be that much more useful in understanding gender differences in cognition.

As already outlined, during the intrauterine period, a testosterone surge can masculinize the fetal brain; the absence of such a surge results in a feminine brain. According to Bao and Swaab (2011), a disturbance of the testosterone surge might be at the background of gender identity disorders (GID), at least in some cases. Transsexual individuals feel that their assigned biological gender is incongruent with their gender identity. Thanks to the availability of MRI, some authors have investigated the neuroanatomy and brain functions of transsexual individuals to better understand both the neuroanatomical features of transsexualism and the background of gender identity. In general, significant structural differences between transgender subjects and controls sharing the same biological gender have been reported. These differences involved both grey and white matter (for a review, see Simon et al., 2013). The number of studies are, at present, however, too scarce to draw any definite conclusion about how brain structural differences could impact the process of the disturbed evolution of gender identity or how disturbed gender identity could affect brain structure.

> Some gender-specific morphological and functional gender-related cortical differences have been reported. A better performance in linguistic tasks has been found in women, while men have been found superior in visuo-spatial tasks. These functional differences positively correlate with minor morphological gender-related differences. The majority of these studies do not, however, take into account inter-individual variability and the weight of education and prejudices in orienting the acquisition of specific skills.

A right brain for the left hand: similarities and differences in the left brain

Together with language, a lifelong preference of one limb for skilled work is a uniquely human trait. This characteristic had been thought to be present since the dawn of humankind: a high proportion of right-hand bias was in fact found by archaeologists to be present in prehistoric lithics, indicating that the first tool makers were primarily right-handed.

While hand preference is present in apes, no consistent right or left bias preference has been found: in a meta-analysis of more than 1000 captive and wild-born great apes, it was found that presence of right-hand specialization was around 50%; only if raised in captivity do great apes tend to show a right-hand preference, suggesting handedness is learned through imitation of caregivers (Corballis, 2003).

On the contrary, the right-hand preference is shared by the great majority of human beings, independent of gender and social or cultural background (around 70–80%, depending on the way of testing). This trait, however, is not universal: a consistent minority of humans (about 10%, Annett, 1985) show a left-hand preference, while a mixed preference was found in variable proportions (around 25–30%, Annett, 1985).

From ancient times, a number of hypotheses have flourished to explain the reason why a number of people, from early infancy, show a consistent and persistent use of their left hand in skilled activities. This stubbornness is very strong, despite the influence of the social environment in the past (and even today, in some groups) that considered the use of the left hand impolite, or even wrong (children were 'corrected' and forced to learn to write with the 'good' right hand). There are, of course, exceptions (e.g. Diego Maradona's left hand was the 'Hand of God' in the famous incident during the 1986 World Cup).

A strong genetic influence on handedness developing is firmly established and one of the favorite models is Annett's Right Shift Theory (Annett, 1985). This theory proposes that handedness in humans depends on chance, but that chance is weighted towards right-handedness in most people by an agent of right-hemisphere disadvantage. It argues for the existence of a single gene for right shift (RS+) that evolved in humans to aid the establishment of cerebral dominance for language and other lateralized functions in the left hemisphere. This bias explains the fact that in most right-handers the left hemisphere is dominant for language, praxis and hand preference.

Several lines of evidence support a genetic origin of handedness: left-handedness runs in families, and a child who has one left-handed parent has a greater chance of becoming left-handed than a child whose parents are both right-handed. Finally, hand preference manifests in early infancy, and an asymmetrical spontaneous head turn has been found in newborns.

In a minority of left-handers, there is no history of familial handedness and an environmental explanation has been claimed, such as perinatal damage to the left hemisphere with a consequent shift of the neural basis of hand preference to the right hemisphere. This concept derived from the studies of Bakan (quoted by McManus, 1996), who suggested an increased incidence of obstetric complications in non-familial left-handers, which caused asymmetrical minimal brain damage: although damage occurs randomly in the left or right hemisphere, the consequence is a necessarily increased left-handedness. More recently, Domielöff et al. (2011) reported a two-fold increase in left- and/or non-right-handedness in pre-term born children: this over-representation could be a consequence of a greater incidence of insult in the brain in pre-term born children.

More interesting in the present context is the research of anatomical and functional brain asymmetries in left-handers. For many years, following the 'Broca rule' (although Broca never explicitly postulated such a rule, Harris, 1993), it has been taught that the left-handers' cortical specialization mirrored that of right-handers. As a consequence, not only manual preference, but language and praxis (the process of programming actions and controlling performance by specifying how the appropriate movements must be selected and sequenced, De Renzi and Faglioni, 1999) neurological bases were located in the right hemisphere.

More recent studies have, however, questioned and refined this statement: it has been proposed that the left-hander brain differs from the typical right-hander brain organization not only in greater variability of the assignment of functions to the left or right hemisphere, but also in the strength of asymmetry, and that functions that are clearly lateralized in the typical right-hander brain may be distributed across both hemispheres in the left-hander brain. In the following section, two topics will be outlined: language and praxis.

Language representation

In the Naeser and Borod (1986) paper, aphasia followed left hemisphere lesion in 22 out of 31 left-handers; similarly, Basso et al. (1990) reported a higher incidence of language deficits following left rather than right hemisphere damage in non-right handers. Lack of significant difference from right-handers in type and severity of aphasia, as well as the prevalence of associated symptoms and type and rate of recovery following language rehabilitation, was reported by Basso et al. (1990).

Only recently the link between handedness and cerebral dominance for language has been investigated in healthy subjects, through non-invasive neuroimaging techniques, such as functional trans-cranial Doppler ultrasonography (Knecht et al., 2000): a right hemisphere dominance for language was found only in 4% of the strong right-handed subjects, while this proportion shifted to 15% and 27% in ambidextrous and strong left-handers.

Handedness and praxis

Since the pioneering study of Liepmann (1905), who reported an apraxic impairment only in left hemisphere damaged patients, a close relation between the representation of praxis skills and handedness was postulated, both in anatomical and functional terms. The same hemisphere that in right-handed people underlies the neural basis of handedness stores the processes at the basis of planning. Executions of learned movements are located in the left hemisphere. The dominant role of the left hemisphere for praxis was for many years unquestioned and only in recent times has a series of studies mitigated this claim with the report of apraxia following right hemisphere damage in right-handers (for a review, see De Renzi and Faglioni, 1999).

In a recent group study performed on a large group of left-handed patients affected by unilateral left or right hemisphere damage, Goldenberg (2013) reported that apraxia can be caused by lesions of the left hemisphere, which controls the non-dominant right hand, showing that the neurological basis of praxis can dissociate from that of handedness. A second important finding observed by Goldenberg was a dissociation between language impairment (aphasia) and apraxia, since some of the left handed patients affected by right hemisphere damage were apraxic, but not aphasic.

A last point must be finally mentioned. As for most minorities, the search of specific behavioral or pathological abnormalities associated with the most obvious differential trait has flourished: left-handedness has been linked to a greater susceptibility to dyslexia (van den Honert, 1977) or even schizophrenia (interpreted as a "result of a failure to establish cerebral asymmetry and that is a central feature of the pathophysiology of the illness"; for a review, see Dragovic and Hammond, 2005: 417).

When, however, these hypotheses were submitted to a rigorous experimental control, any difference linked to left- or right-handedness disappeared. Knecht et al. (2001) found that subjects with atypical lateralization did not differ significantly with respect to mastery of linguistic skills, academic achievement, artistic talent and intelligence. Deep-Soboslay et al. (2010) did not find that atypical handedness was associated with an increased risk of schizophrenia (Crow, 1997) or poorer neurocognition.

In summary, atypical cerebral localization for manual skills is, similarly to other *petite différences*, linked neither to a specific, invariable pattern of brain organization for cognitive skills nor to cognitive peculiarities.

Hand preference and language are human-specific traits. About 10% of humans show a left-hand preference, mostly of genetic origin. Their cerebral organization is not specular to that of right-handers: in right-handers, the neural bases of handedness and language are in the left hemisphere; in the majority of left-handers, they dissociate, with language mostly represented within the left hemisphere. In addition, left-handers show a lesser degree of lateralization: functions that are clearly lateralized in the typical right-hander brain may be distributed across both hemispheres in the left-hander brain.

SUMMARY

Brain plasticity is sensitive to many factors, including age, gender, and hand preference. Brain plasticity is enhanced in infancy up to adolescence (the critical period), during which time the process of acquiring information and developing specific skills reaches its peak. On the other hand, aging does not necessarily coincide with a global loss of cognitive functions. Only executive functions are particularly age dependent. One thorny problem is differentiating the effects of normal aging from those of pathological aging (e.g. Alzheimer's disease) at their onset, since the symptoms can coincide and no biological disease markers are at present available.

Inter-individual and gender-related cognitive differences have been repeatedly described, but no unanimous consensus has been reached about their nature – to what degree they are genetic or reflect the weight of experience or of motivational factors. A further variable impinging on neural plasticity is left-handedness, a trait shared by about 10% of the human population. In comparison to right-handers, left-handers have a more variable, diffuse lateralization of function across the cerebral hemispheres.

Notes

1. In mammals, the primary visual cortex is the first station along the visual pathway where information coming from both eyes converges at the level of single neurons, and many neurons in this area can be driven by stimulation through either eye. Typically, a neuron fires more action potentials when identical visual stimuli are presented to one eye versus the other, a receptive field property termed ocular dominance (OD) (Hubel and Wiesel, 1962).
2. The motor pathway that carries motor signals from the brain down the spinal cord and to the target muscle or organ.
3. Spines are neural protrusions of the dendrite, each of which receives input from one excitatory synapse. They contain neurotransmitter receptors and are essential for synaptic transmission and plasticity.
4. The concurrent recording of EROS with fRMI or other techniques provides further attempts to reach a more complete view of the functional and anatomical substrate of cognition and the impact of aging (for a review, see Fabiani, 2012).
5. Self-initiated processing describes cognitive operations that are neither habitual nor well supported by the environmental context; rather, they must be initiated and performed in a conscious, effortful manner, often using new processing operations directed at the specific task. They are considered to be, as said before, supported by the frontal lobes.

6   Mild neurocognitive disorder, or mild cognitive impairment, has been defined as a memory complaint corroborated by an informant, preserved general cognitive function and intact functional abilities (Petersen et al., 2014).
7   Voxel-based morphometry of MRI data involves spatially normalizing all the images to the same stereotactic space, extracting the grey matter from the normalized images, smoothing, and finally performing a statistical analysis to localize and make inferences about group differences. The output from the method is a statistical parametric map showing regions where grey matter concentration differs significantly between groups (Ashburner and Friston, 2000).
8   According to Cattell (1987), fluid intelligence is intelligence-as-process, and is typically assessed using tests that require on-the-spot processing. Fluid intelligence involves being able to think and reason abstractly and solve problems. This ability is considered independent of learning, experience, and education. Examples of the use of fluid intelligence include solving puzzles and coming up with problem-solving strategies. On the other hand, crystallized intelligence involves knowledge that comes from prior learning and past experiences.

Bibliography

Ances B.M., Liang C.L., Leontiev O., Perthen J.E., Fleisher A.S., Lansing A.E., Buxton R.B. (2009), Effects of aging on cerebral blood flow, oxygen metabolism, and blood oxygenation level dependent responses to visual stimulation. *Human Brain Mapping, 30*(4): 1120–1132.

Anderson C.T., Sheets P.L., Kiritani T., Shepherd G.M. (2010), Sublayer-specific microcircuits of corticospinal and corticostriatal neurons in motor cortex. *Nature Neuroscience, 13*(6): 739–744.

Andreano J.M. and Cahill L. (2009), Sex influences on the neurobiology of learning and memory. *Learning & Memory, 16*(4): 248–266.

Annett M. (1985), *Left, Right, Hand and Brain: The Right Shift Theory*, London: Erlbaum.

Annett M. (1998), Handedness and cerebral dominance: the right shift theory. *Journal of Neuropsychiatry and Clinical Neurosciences, 10*(4): 459–469.

Ashburner J. and Friston K.J. (2000), Voxel-based morphometry–the methods. *Neuroimage, 11*(6–1): 805–821.

Augustine. (1960), *The Confessions of St. Augustine*, New York: Image Books.

Bao A.M. and Swaab D.F. (2011), Sexual differentiation of the human brain: relation to gender identity, sexual orientation and neuropsychiatric disorders. *Frontiers in Neuroendocrinology, 32*(2): 214–226.

Basso A., Farabola M., Grassi M.P., Laiacona M., Zanobio M.E. (1990), Aphasia in left-handers. Comparison of aphasia profiles and language recovery in non-right-handed and matched right-handed patients. *Brain and Language, 38*(2): 233–235.

Bateson P. (1979), Issues concerning behavior. *Science, 203*(4378): 350.

Behrens T.E., Johansen-Berg H., Woolrich M.W., Smith S.M., Wheeler-Kingshott C.A., Boulby P.A., Barker G.J., Sillery E.L., Sheehan K., Ciccarelli O., Thompson A.J., Brady J.M., Matthews P.M. (2003), Non-invasive mapping of connections between human thalamus and cortex using diffusion imaging. *Nature Neuroscience, 6*(7): 750–757.

Berlingeri M., Bottini G., Danelli L., Ferri F., Traficante D., Sacheli L., Colombo N., Sberna M., Sterzi R., Scialfa G., Paulesu E. (2010), With time on our side? Task-dependent compensatory processes in graceful aging. *Experimental Brain Research, 205*(3): 307–324.

Bielsky I.F., Hu S.B., Ren X., Terwilliger E.F., Young L.J. (2005), The V1a vasopressin receptor is necessary and sufficient for normal social recognition: a gene replacement study. *Neuron, 47*(4): 503–513.

Bories C., Husson Z., Guitton M.J., De Koninck Y. (2013), Differential balance of prefrontal synaptic activity in successful versus unsuccessful cognitive aging. *Journal of Neuroscience, 33*(4): 1344–1356.

Burke S.N. and Barnes C.A. (2006), Neural plasticity in the ageing brain. *Nature Reviews Neuroscience, 7*(1): 30–40.

Cabeza R. (2001), Functional neuroimaging of cognitive aging. In: Cabeza R. and Kingstone A. (eds), *Handbook of functional neuroimaging of cognition*, Cambridge (MA), MIT Press, 331–377.

Cabeza R., Anderson N.D., Locantore J.K., Mcintosh A.R. (2002), Aging gracefully: compensatory brain activity in high-performing older adults. *Neuroimage, 17*(3): 1394–1402.

Cahill L. (2006), Why sex matters for neuroscience. *Nature Reviews Neuroscience, 7*: 477–484.

Cappell K.A., Gmeindl L., Reuter-Lorenz P.A. (2010), Age differences in prefontal recruitment during verbal working memory maintenance depend on memory load. *Cortex, 46*(4): 462–473.

Carroll J. (1993), *Human Cognitive Abilities: A Survey of Factor-Analytic Studies*, New York, Cambridge University Press.

Cattell R.B. (1963), Theory of fluid and crystallized intelligence: A critical experiment. *Journal of Educational Psychology, 54*: 1–22.

Cattell, R.B. (1987). *Intelligence: Its Structure, Growth, and Action.* New York: Elsevier.

Chugani H.T. (1998), A critical period of brain development: studies of cerebral glucose utilization with PET. *Preventive Medicine, 27*(2): 184–188.

Cole M.W., Pathak S., Schneider W. (2010), Identifying the brain's most globally connected regions. *Neuroimage, 49*(4): 3132–3148.

Cona G., Bisiacchi P.S., Amodio P., Schiff S. (2013), Age-related decline in attentional shifting: Evidence from ERPs. *Neuroscience Letters, 556*: 129–134.

Corballis M.C. (2003), From mouth to hand: gesture, speech, and the evolution of right-handedness. *Behavioral and Brain Sciences, 26*(2): 199–208.

Cowan N., Elliott E.M., Scott Saults J., Morey C.C., Mattox S., Himsjatullina A., Conway A.R. (2005), On the capacity of attention: its estimation and its role in working memory and cognitive aptitudes. *Cognitive Psychology 51*(1): 42–100.

Craik F.I.M. and Byrd M. (1982), Aging and cognitive deficits: The role of attentional resources. In Craik F.I.M. and Trehub S.E. (eds), *Aging and cognitive processes*, New York, Plenum Press, 191–211.

Crow T.J. (1997), Schizophrenia as failure of hemispheric dominance for language. *Trends in Neuroscience, 20*(8): 339–343.

Daffner K.R., Chong H., Sun X., Tarbi E.C., Riis J.L., Mcginnis S.M., Holcomb P.J. (2011), Mechanisms underlying age- and performance-related differences in working memory. *Journal of Cognitive Neuroscience, 23*(6): 1298–1314.

Davis S.W., Kragel J.E., Madden D.J., Cabeza R. (2012), The architecture of cross-hemispheric communication in the aging brain: linking behavior to functional and structural connectivity. *Cerebral Cortex, 22*(1): 232–242.

Daw N.W. (1998), Critical periods and amblyopia. *Archives of Ophthalmology, 116*(4): 502–505.

Deary I.J., Penke L., Johnson W. (2010), The neuroscience of human intelligence differences. *Nature Reviews Neuroscience, 11*(3): 201–211.

Deep-Soboslay A., Hyde T.M., Callicott J.P., Lener M.S., Verchinski B.A., Apud J.A., Weinberger D.R., Elvevåg B. (2010), Handedness, heritability, neurocognition and brain asymmetry in schizophrenia. *Brain, 133*(10): 3113–3122.

De Renzi E. and Faglioni P. (1999), Apraxia. In: Denes G. and Pizzamiglio L. (eds), *Handbook of clinical and experimental neuropsychology*, Hove (UK), Psychology Press, 421–441.

Domellöf E., Johansson A.M., Rönnqvist L. (2011), Handedness in preterm born children: a systematic review and a meta-analysis. *Neuropsychologia, 49*(9): 2299–2310.

Dragovic M. and Hammond G. (2005), Handedness in schizophrenia: a quantitative review of evidence. *Acta Psychiatrica Scandinavica, 111*(6): 410–419.

Fabiani M. (2012), It was the best of times, it was the worst of times: a psychophysiologist's view of cognitive aging. *Psychophysiology, 49*(3): 283–304.

Falk D., Lepore F.E., Noe A. (2013), The cerebral cortex of Albert Einstein: a description and preliminary analysis of unpublished photographs. *Brain, 136*(4): 1304–1327.

Feng J., Spence I., Pratt J. (2007), Playing an action video game reduces gender differences in spatial cognition. *Psychological Science, 18*(10): 850–855.

Fodor J.A. (1983), *The Modularity of Mind: An Essay in Faculty Psychology*, Cambridge (MA), Mit Press.

Fox S.E., Levitt P., Nelson C.A. 3rd (2010), How the timing and quality of early experiences influence the development of brain architecture. *Child Development, 81*(1): 28–40.

Freeman R.D. (1996), Studies of functional connectivity in the developing and mature visual cortex. *Journal of Physiology Paris, 90*(3–4): 199–203.

Galton F. (1888), Head growth in students at the University of Cambridge. *Nature, 38*: 14–15.

Ganguly K. and Poo M.M. (2013), Activity-dependent neural plasticity from bench to bedside. *Neuron, 80*(3): 729–774.

Gardner H. (1983, 1993), *Frames of Mind: The Theory of Multiple Intelligences*, New York, Basic Books.

Giedd J.N., Vaituzis A.C., Hamburger S.D., Lange N., Rajapakse J.C., Kaysen D., Vauss Y.C., Rapoport J.L. (1996), Quantitative Mri of the temporal lobe, amygdala, and hippocampus in normal human development: ages 4–18 years. *Journal of Comparative Neurology, 366*(2): 223–230.

Goldenberg G. (2013), Apraxia in left-handers. *Brain, 136*(8): 2592–2601.

Goldstein J.M., Seidman L.J., Horton N.J., Makris N., Kennedy D.N., Caviness V.S. Jr., Faraone S.V., Tsuang M.T. (2001), Normal sexual dimorphism of the adult human brain assessed by in vivo magnetic resonance imaging. *Cerebral Cortex*, 11(6): 490–497.

Gordon K.A., Wong D.D., Valero J., Jewell S.F., Yoo P., Papsin B.C. (2011), Use it or lose it? Lessons learned from the developing brains of children who are deaf and use cochlear implants to hear. *Brain Topography*, 24(3–4): 204–219.

Gottfredson L.S. (ed) (1997), Intelligence and social policy. *Intelligence*, 24(1), (Special issue).

Gratton G. and Fabiani M. (2010), Fast optical imaging of human brain function. *Frontiers in Human Neuroscience*, 4: 52.

Gur R.C., Alsop D., Glahn D., Petty R., Swanson C.L., Maldjian J.A., Turetsky B.I., Detre J.A., Gee J., Gur R.E. (2000), An fMri study of sex differences in regional activation to a verbal and a spatial task. *Brain and Language*, 74(2): 157–170.

Gur R.C., Turetsky B.I., Matsui M., Yan M., Bilker W., Hughett P., Gur R.E. (1999), Sex differences in brain gray and white matter in healthy young adults: correlations with cognitive performance. *Journal of Neuroscience*, 19(10): 4065–4072.

Harris L.J. (1993), Broca on cerebral control for speech in right-handers and left-handers: a note on translation and some further comments. *Brain and Language*, 45(1): 108–120.

Hedden T. and Gabrieli J.D. (2004), Insights into the ageing mind: a view from cognitive neuroscience. *Nature Reviews Neuroscience*, 5(2): 87–96.

Hensch T.K. (2004), Critical period regulation. *Annual Review of Neuroscience*, 27: 549–579.

Hubel D.H. and Wiesel T.N. (1962), Receptive fields, binocular interaction and functional architecture in the cat's visual cortex. *Journal of Physiology*, 160: 106–154.

Hubel D.H. and Wiesel T.N. (1998), Early exploration of the visual cortex. *Neuron*, 20(3): 401–412.

Huttenlocher P.R. and Dabholkar A.S. (1997), Regional differences in synaptogenesis in human cerebral cortex. *Journal of Comparative Neurology*, 387(2): 167–178.

Hyde J.S., Lindberg S.M., Linn M.C., Ellis A.B., Williams C.C. (2008), Diversity. Gender similarities characterize math performance. *Science*, 321(5888): 494–495.

Ingalhalikar M., Smith A., Parker D., Satterthwaite T.D., Elliott M.A., Ruparel K., Hakonarson H., Gur R.E., Gur R.C., Verma R. (2013), Sex differences in the structural connectome of the human brain. *Proceedings of the National Academy of Sciences USA*, 111(2): 823–828.

Innocenti G.M. and Price D.J. (2005), Exuberance in the development of cortical networks. *Nature Reviews Neuroscience*, 6: 955–965.

Jordan-Young R. and Rumiati R. (2012), Hardwired for Sexism? Approaches to Sex/Gender in Neuroscience. *Neuroethics*, 5(3): 305–315.

Jost A. (1953), Problems of fetal endocrinology: the gonadal and hypophyseal hormones. *Recent Progress in Hormone Research*, 8: 379–418.

Jung R.E. and Haier R.J. (2007), The Parieto-Frontal Integration Theory (P-FIT) of intelligence: converging neuroimaging evidence. *Behavioral and Brain Sciences*, 30(2): 135–154.

Kanai R. and Rees G. (2011), The structural basis of inter-individual differences in human behavior and cognition. *Nature Reviews Neuroscience, 12*(4): 231–242.

Katzman R., Aronson M., Fuld P., Kawas C., Brown T., Morgenstern H., Frishman W., Gidez L., Eder H., Ooi W.L. (1989), Development of dementing illnesses in an 80-year-old volunteer cohort. *Annals of Neurology, 25*(4): 317–324.

Kauffman A.S. (2010), Gonadal and nongonadal regulation of sex differences in hypothalamic Kiss1 neurons. *Journal of Neuroendocrinology, 22*: 682–691.

Knecht S., Dräger B., Deppe M., Bobe L., Lohmann H., Flöel A., Ringelstein E.B., Henningsen H. (2000), Handedness and hemispheric language dominance in healthy humans. *Brain, 123*(12): 2512–2518.

Knecht S., Dräger B., Flöel A., Lohmann H., Breitenstein C., Deppe M., Henningsen H., Ringelstein E.B. (2001), Behavioural relevance of atypical language lateralization in healthy subjects. *Brain, 124*(8): 1657–1665.

Kolb B. and Gibb R. (2007), Brain plasticity and recovery from early cortical injury. *Developmental Psychobiology, 49*(2): 107–118.

Kolb B. and Gibb R. (2014), Searching for the principles of brain plasticity and behavior. *Cortex, 58*: 251–260.

Kolb B. and Teskey G.C. (2012), Age, experience, injury, and the changing brain. *Developmental Psychobiology, 54*(3): 311–325.

Krendl A.C., Richeson J.A., Kelley W.M., Heatherton T.F. (2008), The negative consequences of threat: a functional magnetic resonance imaging investigation of the neural mechanisms underlying women's underperformance in math. *Psychological Science, 19*(2): 168–175.

Levelt C.N. and Hübener M. (2012), Critical-period plasticity in the visual cortex. *Annual Review of Neuroscience, 35*: 309–330.

Liepmann H. (1905), The left hemisphere and action. In: Kimura D. (1980), *Translations from Liepmann's essays on apraxia*, Research Bulletin, London (Ont), Department of Psychology, University of Western Ontario, 506.

Lövdén M., Rönnlund M., Wahlin A., Bäckman L., Nyberg L., Nilsson L.G. (2004), The extent of stability and change in episodic and semantic memory in old age: demographic predictors of level and change. *Journals of Gerontology B Psychological Sciences Social Sciences, 59*(3): 130–134.

Marcotte K. and Ansaldo A.J. (2014), Age-related behavioural and neurofunctional patterns of second language word learning: Different ways of being successful. *Brain and Language, 135*: 9–19.

Martin J.H. (2005), The corticospinal system: from development to motor control. *The Neuroscientist, 11*(2): 161–173.

Mcmanus I.C. (1996), Handedness. In: Beaumont J.G., Kenealy P.M., Rogers M.J.C. (eds), *The Blackwell dictionary of neuropsychology*, Oxford, Blackwell, 367–376.

Mower G. D. (1991), The effect of dark rearing on the time course of the critical period in cat visual cortex. *Brain Research Developmental Brain Research, 58*(2): 151–158.

Mueller S., Wang D., Fox M.D., Yeo B.T., Sepulcre J., Sabuncu M.R., Shafee R., Lu J., Liu H. (2013), Individual variability in functional connectivity architecture of the human brain. *Neuron, 77*(3): 586–595.

Naeser M.A. and Borod J.C. (1986), Aphasia in left-handers: lesion site, lesion side, and hemispheric asymmetries on CT. *Neurology, 36*(4): 471–488.

Negash S., Smith G.E., Pankratz S., Aakre J., Geda Y.E., Roberts R.O., Knopman D.S., Boeve B.F., Ivnik R.J., Petersen R.C. (2011), Successful aging: definitions and prediction of longevity and conversion to mild cognitive impairment. *American Journal of Geriatric Psychiatry, 19*(6): 581–588.

Nelson C.A. 3rd., Zeanah C.H., Fox N.A., Marshall P.J., Smyke A.T., Guthrie D. (2007), Cognitive recovery in socially deprived young children: the Bucharest Early Intervention Project. *Science, 318*(5858): 1937–1940.

Newport E.L., Bavelier D., Neville H.J. (2002), Critical thinking about critical periods: Perspectives on a critical period for language acquisition. In: Dupoux E. (ed), *Language, brain and cognitive development*, Cambridge (MA), Mit Press, 481–502.

Nulty B., Burt J.M., Akçay Ç., Templeton C.N., Campbell S.E., Beecher M.D. (2010), Song learning in song sparrows: Relative importance of autumn vs. spring tutoring. *Ethology, 116*: 653–661.

Pakkenberg B. and Gundersen H.J. (1997), Neocortical neuron number in humans: effect of sex and age. *Journal of Comparative Neurology, 384*(2): 312–320.

Park D.C., Lautenschlager G., Hedden T., Davidson N.S., Smith A.D., Smith P.K. (2002), Models of visuospatial and verbal memory across the adult life span. *Psychology and Aging, 17*(2): 299–320.

Park D.C., Smith A.D., Lautenschlager G., Earles J.L., Frieske D., Zwahr M., Gaines C.L. (1996), Mediators of long-term memory performance across the life span. *Psychology and Aging, 11*(4): 621–637.

Pascual-Leone A., Amedi A., Fregni F., Merabet L.B. (2005), The plastic human brain cortex. *Annual Review of Neuroscience, 28*: 377–401.

Paus T., Tomaiuolo F., Otaky N., Macdonald D., Petrides M., Atlas J., Morris R., Evans A.C. (1996), Human cingulate and paracingulate sulci: pattern, variability, asymmetry, and probabilistic map. *Cerebral Cortex, 6*(2): 207–214.

Payton A. (2009), The impact of genetic research on our understanding of normal cognitive ageing: 1995 to 2009. *Neuropsychology Review, 19*(4): 451–477.

Petersen R.C., Caracciolo B., Brayne C., Gauthier S., Jelic V., Fratiglioni L. (2014), Mild cognitive impairment: a concept in evolution. *Journal of Internal Medicine, 275*(3): 214–228.

Phoenix C.H., Goy R.W., Gerall A.A., Young W.C. (1959), Organizing action of prenatally administered testosterone propionate on the tissues mediating mating behavior in the female guinea pig. *Endocrinology, 65*: 369–382.

Quoidbach J., Gilbert D.T., Wilson T.D. (2013), The end of history illusion. *Science, 339*(6115): 96–98.

Rabaglia C.D., Marcus G.F., Lane S.P. (2011), What can individual differences tell us about the specialization of function? *Cognitive Neuropsychology, 28*(3–4): 288–303.

Reuter-Lorenz P.A., Jonides J., Smith E.E., Hartley A., Miller A., Marshuetz C., Koeppe R.A. (2000), Age differences in the frontal lateralization of verbal and spatial working memory revealed by PET. *Journal of Cognitive Neuroscience, 12*(1): 174–187.

Salthouse T.A. (1996), The processing-speed theory of adult age differences in cognition. *Psychological Review, 103*(3): 403–428.

Schneider-Garces N.J., Gordon B.A., Brumback-Peltz C.R., Shin E., Lee Y., Sutton B.P., Maclin E.L., Gratton G., Fabiani M. (2010), Span, Crunch, and beyond: working memory capacity and the aging brain. *Journal of Cognitive Neuroscience*, 22(4): 655–669.

Shallice T. (1988), *From Neuropsychology to Mental Structure*, Cambridge (UK), Cambridge University Press.

Simion F., Leo I., Turati C., Valenza E., Dalla Barba B. (2007), How face specialization emerges in the first months of life. *Progress in Brain Research*, 164: 169–185.

Simon L., Kozák L.R., Simon V., Czobor P., Unoka Z., Szabó Á., Csukly G. (2013), Regional grey matter structure differences between transsexuals and healthy controls–a voxel based morphometry study. *PLoS One*, 8(12): e83947.

Sperling R.A., Aisen P.S., Beckett L.A., Bennett D.A., CRAFT S., Fagan A.M., Iwatsubo T., Jack C.R. JR., Kaye J., Montine T. J, PARK D.C., Reiman E.M., Rowe C.C., Siemers E., Stern Y., YAFFE K., Carrillo M.C., Thies B., MORRISON-Bogorad M., WAGSTER M.V., Phelps C.H. (2011), Toward defining the preclinical stages of Alzheimer's disease: Recommendations from the National Institute on Aging-Alzheimer's Association workgroups on diagnostic guidelines for Alzheimer's disease. *Alzheimers Dement.* 7(3): 280–292.

Sporns O. (2012), The human connectome: a complex network. *Annals of New York Academy of Sciences*, 1224: 109–125.

Stern Y. (2002), What is cognitive reserve? Theory and research application of the reserve concept. *Journal of the International Neuropsychological Society*, 8(3): 448–460.

Stern Y. (2012), Cognitive reserve in ageing and Alzheimer's disease. *Lancet Neurology*, 11(11): 1006–1012.

Sternberg S. (1966), High-speed scanning in human memory. *Science*, 153(3736): 652–654.

Swaab D.F. and Fliers E. (1985), A sexually dimorphic nucleus in the human brain. *Science*, 228(4703): 1112–1115.

Thal D.J., Marchman V., Stiles J., Aram D., Trauner D., Nass R., Bates E. (1991), Early lexical development in children with focal brain injury. *Brain and Language*, 40(4): 491–527.

Van Den Honert, D. (1977), A neuropsychological technique for training dyslexics. *Journal of Learning Disabilities*, 10: 21–27.

Vargha-Khadem F., O'Gorman A.M., Watters G.V. (1985), Aphasia and handedness in relation to hemispheric side, age at injury and severity of cerebral lesion during childhood. *Brain*, 108(3): 677–696.

Werker J.F. and Tees R.C. (1984), Phonemic and phonetic factors in adult cross-language speech perception. *Journal of the Acoustical Society of America*, 75(6): 1866–1878.

West M.J., Coleman P.D., Flood D.G., Troncoso J.C. (1994), Differences in the pattern of hippocampal neuronal loss in normal ageing and Alzheimer's disease. *Lancet*, 344(8925): 769–772.

West R.L. (1996), An application of prefrontal cortex function theory to cognitive aging. *Psychological Bulletin*, 120: 272–292.

Wiesel T.N. and Hubel D.H. (1963), Single-cell responses in striate cortex of kittens deprived of vision in one eye. *Journal of Neurophysiology*, 26: 1003–1017.

Windsor J., Glaze L.E., Koga S.F., the Beip Core Group (2007), Language acquisition with limited input: Romanian institution and foster care. *Journal of Speech Language and Hearing Research, 50*: 1365–1381.

Witelson S.F. (1989), Hand and sex differences in the isthmus and genu of the human corpus callosum. A postmortem morphological study. *Brain, 112*(3): 799–835.

Witelson S.F., Kigar D.L., Harvey T. (1999), The exceptional brain of Albert Einstein. *Lancet, 353*(9170): 2149–2153.

Woods B.T. and Carey S. (1979), Language deficits after apparent clinical recovery from childhood aphasia. *Annals of Neurology, 6*(5): 405–409.

Woods B.T. and Teuber H.L. (1978), Changing patterns of childhood aphasia. *Annals of Neurology, 3*(3): 273–280.

Wraga M., Helt M., Jacobs E., Sullivan K. (2007), Neural basis of stereotype-induced shifts in women's mental rotation performance. *Social Cognitive and Affective Neuroscience, 2*(1): 12–19.

SECTION 3
Specific skills

4
LANGUAGE AND NEURAL PLASTICITY

Functional and structural processes of language: typical and atypical development

In his seminal work, Eric Lenneberg (1967) made some fundamental assumptions on language development: language is innately determined and its normal acquisition is dependent on the integrity of specific neural networks and on exposure to spoken language in a critical period that extends from infancy to puberty. Only perinatal bilateral brain damage, preverbal deafness (see chapter 7) or extreme social isolation can impair a normal and faultless emergence of it.[1] Several lines of evidence suggest the presence of a strict relation between proficiency in language – from phonology to grammar – and the time of exposure. Peak proficiency in language acquisition is reached by children exposed to language from birth or very early childhood. Not being exposed to language before the age of 4 years significantly impairs its acquisition. In addition, in contrast with the native language (L1) that develops without explicit learning, the process of later acquisition of a second language often requires specific learning – in particular, if it is learned after the end of the critical period (see chapter 3). According to Newport (1990), two possible mechanisms can be considered for the decay of language development over age. The first refers to Chomsky (1965, 1981), who considers language a special faculty that includes inborn knowledge of constraints on the form that language may take. In this case, it may be assumed that language faculty is intact at birth, but decays or deteriorates as maturation continues.

A second hypothesis suggests that language learning declines because of the further development of other, non-verbal, cognitive skills.

Language processing is not, however, limited to the oral-auditory channel. It may be expressed through the written modality or through sign language, which is a natural language not derived, and independent of, the spoken language (see section 4.3.4).

After a brief introduction to the neural mechanisms subserving the processing of language in typically developed subjects, this chapter will illustrate the functional and neurological architecture of language processing in atypical populations and through different modalities.

The anatomo-functional basis of language

Human language coexists alongside other forms of communication. It can be attributed to a genetic mutation that supported the emergence of independent systems or modules that were shared with other species and were applied to the communicative faculty, allowing the emergence of language in its entirety (for a review, see Hauser et al., 2002).

Among the first to experimentally confirm that language could be considered a biological faculty or system with anatomical and functional substrates, were Broca (1861, 1864) and Wernicke (1876). This concept arose from the observations of patients affected by a loss of specific components of speech and language, roughly concerning production (Broca) and comprehension (Wernicke), following focal brain lesion of the left hemisphere. On the basis of these early anatomo-clinical observations,[2] a neurological model of language was established in which language comprehension is possible through the activation of the acoustic images of the words, located in the posterior part of the left superior temporal gyrus. Once processed, the acoustic images activate a set of motor and sensory images that form the specific conceptual representation of the words. Spontaneous speech stems from the activation of a conceptual representation, which in turn activates the motor and sensory images associated with the corresponding concepts. Sensory and motor centers are interconnected by a dorsal connection (the arcuate fasciculus, AF), forming a neural network that when lesioned determines the appearance of specific forms of aphasia (Lichtheim, 1885).

Thanks to the progress of neuroimaging technology, the functional and neurological basis of language are at present accessible *in vivo*, attesting that the Wernicke-Lichtheim model of language processing was essentially correct, but needed some refinement. The modifications essentially involved the connections between the temporal and frontal language centers, one dorsal

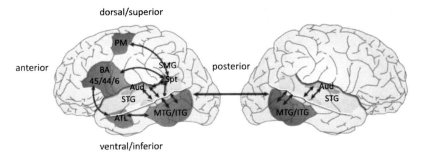

FIGURE 4.1 The functional neuroanatomy of language. Reprinted from G. Hickok. 2009. The functional neuroanatomy of language. *Physics of Life Reviews* 6(3), 121–143 with permission from Elsevier.

and one ventral, each consisting of several bundles of fibers, fulfilling independent roles in language processing (Figure 4.1). The ventral pathway connections have been related to semantic and lexical processing. The dorsal pathway main function supports the auditory-motor mapping and the processing of syntactically complex sentences (for a review, see Friederici, 2011; Hickock and Poeppel, 2007). The above model can be applied to the processing of segmental language abilities, such as phonetics and phonology, syntax and lexicon. Language, however, carries also supra-segmental information such as prosody and stress, which create sentence intonation. Clinical studies and functional neuroimaging data propose that prosody carrying linguistic information (e.g. distinguishing an indicative from an interrogative sentence) is processed by the left hemisphere, while the right hemisphere processes the affective contents of prosody (Gandour et al., 2004).

> Language is a species-specific human skill that develops following exposure to spoken language in infancy (the critical period) and without specific learning. Language is a biological faculty, provided with a specific neurological substrate, usually located within the left hemisphere. The first neurological models of language located language comprehension and production centers in specific parts of the left hemisphere, connected by a bundle of fibers. More recent models posit the existence of specific anatomo-functional systems processing the different components of language faculty – phonology, syntax, lexicon and prosody – this last calling for a specific role of the right hemisphere.

The neurological basis of language development

Only humans have the ability to acquire language (see Denes, 2011, for a review), and already at birth neonates show a variety of linguistic capacities. Even premature babies, whose cortical organization is not completed at birth, show a left frontal region reaction in a syllabic discrimination task, while discrimination responses to a change in human voice (e.g. male vs. female) activate both frontal areas (Mahmoudzadeh et al., 2013). The neurological language-related network of 2-day-old infants was investigated by Perani et al. (2011) using fMRI to determine differences of brain activation as a function of different speech conditions (normal speech or speech from which the segmental information was removed, 'hummed' speech). They were able to show that the brain regions triggered by speech in neonates are similar to those that became active in children and adults, although with a less left lateralized pattern of activation and not fully myelinated. Along the same lines, Brauer et al. (2013) found that the dorsal pathway connecting the temporal regions to the left inferior frontal gyrus (part of the Broca's area in the adult) matures at later stages (as expressed by a delayed myelination), suggesting that more complex linguistic functions, such as syntax, should rely on the maturation of this pathway. The process of maturation of the auditory cortex lasts for several years: synaptic densities rise steeply during the first 4–6 months after birth, resulting in a maximum synaptic density at the age of 0.5–4.0 years (Huttenlocher and Dabholkar, 1997). Afterwards, synaptic density decreases from 2 to 4 years of age until adolescence.

At birth, babies are world citizens, able to discriminate the prosodic elements and phonemic contrasts of every language (Mehler et al., 1988; Friederici, 2006). It is only at around 2 years old that children adjust to their linguistic environment so that they discriminate only between contrasts specific to their native language (cultural bound listening). Specific neural patterns are thus established through the use of computational strategies that allow identification of the characteristics of the native language (Kuhl, 2004). In some people, as in the case of long-trained expert phoneticians (e.g. speech and language therapists, radio announcers), this ability is particularly pronounced: Golestani et al. (2011) found a positive correlation between the size of left pars opercularis (Broca's area) and years of phonetic transcription training experience. Phoneticians were also more likely to have multiple or split left transverse gyri in the auditory cortex in the left temporal lobe than non-expert controls, without correlation with the amount of phonetic transcription training. The interpretation of these findings is open; although the extensive training with speech sound analysis, and maybe even with articulation-based approaches, can lead to plastic changes in Broca's area, the temporal lobe asymmetries could be of genetic origin. The maturation of temporal lobe structures is in fact stabilized by the age of 7 years (Yakovlev and Lecours, 1967). It is therefore possible that the presence of such a morphological feature may make it more likely for individuals to become phoneticians or to work in domains requiring detailed auditory processing.

Similarly, neural circuits specific for word recognition develop at very early stages in life: detailed information about prosodic information, such as lexical stress, is encoded by 1-month-old infants (see Werker and Curtin, 2005, for a review). Thierry et al. (2003) have shown, in an event-related potential (ERP) study, that already at the age of 11 months, listening to unknown words leads to the occurrence of specific neural events (greater width of a negative peak at the level of the hemispheres, which tends to concentrate in the left cerebral hemispheres). Finally, Friedrich et al. (2004), using the same technique, demonstrated that towards 1 year of age, the simultaneous presentation of a word and its corresponding image activates a specific electrical response in fronto-temporal areas, which is not present when the heard word does not coincide with the image.

At birth, babies can discriminate the prosodic elements and phonemic contrasts of every language. It is only at around 2 years old that children adjust to their linguistic environment so that they discriminate only between contrasts specific to their native language. Specific neural patterns are thus established that allow identification of the characteristics of the native language.

The acquisition of language beyond the critical period and the role of the right hemisphere

The left hemisphere dominance in the neural organization of language is shared by the vast majority of humans: not only are most people right-handed, but also a consistent minority of left-handed subjects (see chapter 3) activate their left hemisphere in language processing tasks. The right hemisphere, on the other hand, seems to be better suited for mediating a variety of paralinguistic phenomena that accompany the production of words and sentences (see Denes, 2011). In addition, these language-specific neural circuits are present at birth, but their activation depends on the time of exposure of language. The question, however, of the possibility of activation of these or alternative language circuits in absence of exposure in the critical period or in the presence of perinatal left hemisphere damage is far to be settled. A review of the available data will follow.

Social isolation and development of language: the case of Genie

Few cases of children reared in extreme social isolation have been described. In the context of the nature/nurture debate on the origin of language, the most well known is Victor, the 'Wild Boy of Aveyron' (Itard, 1962). These reports are anecdotal and the only consistent report is that lack of language experience in infancy leads to impaired language development.

The study of the language development of a girl, 'Genie' (a fictitious name) (Curtiss, 1977; Fromkin et al., 1974), who, until the age of 13, was reared in social isolation and not exposed to language, is relevant for two reasons. First, it gives an experimental support to the Lenneberg hypothesis (1967) on the role of critical period exposure for normal language development. In addition, it can provide some experimental data on how a delayed speech exposure can impinge on the innate neural organization of language.

From the little medical information available, we know that Genie was delivered by Caesarian section. No neurological abnormalities were recorded, and at the age of 1 year her weight was normal. She failed to walk at a normal age because of a congenital hip dislocation. Her father was convinced that the child was hopelessly retarded and convinced his wife to lock Genie in a small closet-like room at the age of 18 months, tied to a small potty chair. She lived in extreme visual and acoustic isolation: her father and older brother never spoke to her, their vocal utterances being limited to sounds like dogs barking. Her blind mother was allowed to spend no more than a few minutes a day with Genie during feeding. After her father died, Genie was finally freed from the closet. She was 13 years old.

When admitted to a hospital, her neurological examination was normal and it did not show any sign of autistic disorder; she readily engaged in social play.

She was completely mute apart from some 'throaty whimpers' but could communicate her needs, although to a limited extent, nonverbally. In the following months, she started to produce and understand some words, but the examiners had to wait about one year after Genie's emergence from isolation before some formal linguistic tests could be administered. Genie's linguistic skills were mostly based on comprehension tests, since her production, despite a sound improvement from the beginning, was severely defective, perhaps consequent to a defective neuromuscular control of the speech apparatus.

Whereas comprehension of some words was already present at the beginning of the testing period, comprehension of grammatical structures was practically nonexistent. In the following months, she showed a remarkable improvement in her lexicon. However, her grammatical competence, even after years, was still defective. She acquired the word order rules but did not control morphology.

Genie's progress was slower and deviant from that of typically developing children: while her lexicon was much larger than that of normally developing children exhibiting syntactic skills similar to hers, her grammatical performance was similar to that shown by 2 to 2.5-year-old children. However, that Genie was able to acquire language, even if in a deviant way, after the critical period raised the interest of researchers keen to discover the neural mechanisms underlying her language.

Neuroimaging methods, such as CT scan or MRI, were not available in the mid-1970s. The only non-invasive method available to infer about which of the two hemispheres was 'dominant' for language processing was dichotic listening testing. In this procedure, two different sets of digits or words of the same length are presented simultaneously to the two ears through earphones, and the subject's task is to report them. In right-handed people, the digits presented to the right ear are reported more accurately. This right-ear advantage has been attributed to the anatomical structure of the auditory system, whose crossed pathways are more efficient than unilateral ones: it follows that stimuli presented to the right ear have preferential access to the left, language-dominant hemisphere. On the contrary, non-verbal stimuli, such as musical chords or environmental sounds, show a left ear preference, revealing a right-hemisphere dominance for processing this type of stimuli (Kimura, 1963).

In the case of Genie, the results showed that, in spite of being right-handed, she showed a consistent and extreme left-ear advantage, suggesting a right-hemisphere dominance. This pattern is unusual because cases of right-hemisphere dominance for language in right-handed subjects are rare[3] and even most left-handers have a left-hemisphere language preference.

These findings tentatively suggest that, in order to became language dominant, the left hemisphere has to be 'prompted' by language exposure in the critical period. If such stimulation does not take place, the right hemisphere can take its place, but less efficiently: while lexicon can be acquired at normal level, syntax development remains poor, suggesting that the syntactic computational rules are essentially inborn and located in the left hemisphere.

> In order to fully develop, inborn language circuits within the left hemisphere must be activated by language exposure in the critical period. In cases of absence of exposure during the critical period, language development and use remain poor, with syntactic abilities being the most impaired. Language acquisition after the end of the critical period, as in the case of socially isolated children, is poor; it may be accomplished through compensatory activity of the right hemisphere.

The missing left hemisphere and language development

The occurrence of a severe left hemisphere lesion in early infancy does not prevent language development, provided that the right hemisphere is undamaged. Analysis of these cases is particularly important in trying to clarify two points: the potentiality of the right hemisphere to develop and use language and the comparison of the right hemisphere language network with that of the inborn left hemisphere. Some children who sustained left congenital or perinatal damage, characterized by right sided hemiplegia and severe epilepsy, had their hemisphere removed in early, middle or late childhood (for a review, see Vanlancker-Sidtis, 2004). In comparison to normal children and right-hemispherectomized children, their language was, however, found defective in mastering syntactic contrasts and morphology.

Vargha-Khadem et al. (1997) reported the case of a boy (Alex) affected by Sturge-Weber syndrome[4] whose linguistic development was practically absent until the age of 8.5 years, when he was submitted to left hemispherectomy for relieving his intractable epilepsy.

Before the operation, his expressive language was limited to one word and some sounds he used to refer to objects. On the other hand, language comprehension was better, equivalent to that of a 4-year-old child. The operation was successful, and Alex was seizure free; the anticonvulsant therapy was withdrawn at the age of 9. One month after the therapy withdrawal, he, started uttering syllables and words almost suddenly, with a strong progression over the years. Similar progress was present in language comprehension, reaching, at the age of 14, a language score of 70, equivalent to the level of a typically developed boy of 8.5 years of age. In parallel with his language progress, Alex's IQ improved, although less dramatically, from a level of less than 40 at age 11 to an IQ of 52 at age 14.

However, his language progression was not uniform. While his word and sentence production increased to the uttering of sentences of up to 11 words, his performance on expressive tasks involving non-word processing was limited: his level on morphological and phonological awareness tasks (rhyme detection, phoneme segmentation and blending) corresponded to that of a 5-year-old child (≥3 years below his level in processing real words). Similarly, his language comprehension was selectively impaired in processing complex grammatical sentences that require storing a sequence of order in the verbal short term memory.

Alex's case is important in showing that language can develop beyond the critical period. The right hemisphere can support this process, although with some limits: Alex's language was selectively defective in mastering complex linguistic skills involving syntax and phonology, suggesting that these operations could rely on some inborn neural mechanisms located in the left hemisphere. Alternatively, as Vargha-Khadem et al. suggest, the above deficit could be a consequence of a poor verbal memory deficit, secondary to Alex's delayed IQ development.

Alex's case, and those of other children affected by early or developmental left hemisphere damage described by Liégeois et al. (2004), confirms the possibility of the right hemisphere taking over language skills, but does not specify the structural and functional organization of a language network in the isolated right hemisphere. Danelli et al. (2013) reported, in an fMRI study, the linguistic profile and neurolinguistic organization of a 14-year-old adolescent who underwent a left hemispherectomy at the age of 2.5 years. His language examination was essentially within normal limits, apart from a slight impairment in lexical tasks. Reading and writing were within the normal range. His only difficulty emerged with loan words processing, whose nature was difficult to interpret on a linguistic basis, given his relative poor performance on the verbal part of the Wechsler IQ test (full scale IQ 78). fMRI patterns for several linguistic and metalinguistic tasks were similar to those observed in the left hemisphere of right-handed controls, suggesting that the language areas of the language-processing right hemisphere conformed to a left-like linguistic neural blueprint, including the areas specific to written language. The only significant difference was a pattern of stronger recruitment, in comparison to controls, of the prefrontal cortex in most of the controlled linguistic processes investigated (e.g. controlled word retrieval vs. automatic production) or word listening: a sign that right-hemisphere processing language tasks are more demanding and need additional neural resources.

A severe left-hemisphere lesion in early infancy does not prevent language development, provided that the right hemisphere is undamaged. Some children who sustained left congenital or perinatal damage, characterized by right-sided hemiplegia and severe epilepsy, have had their hemisphere removed in the early, middle or late childhood. In comparison to normal children and right-hemispherectomized children, their language competence was good, being only defective in mastering syntactic contrasts and morphology. Neuroimaging studies in left-hemisphere surgically deprived children show a neurological organization of language in the right hemisphere similar to that in the left hemisphere of normal right-handed children. In addition to the activation of right-hemisphere language area, a strong recruitment of prefrontal cortex areas has been found, suggesting the linguistic skills supported by the right hemisphere need more attentional control.

Culturally acquired language modalities: reading and writing

In contrast to the spoken language, whose neurological bases are inborn and develop without explicit learning, written language is a recently developed, culturally derived skill. (The first examples date back about 5000 years.) Mastering this ability develops only after explicit learning; even in present times, a consistent minority of people with normal cognitive skills are still illiterate.

These considerations rule out the possibility that the brain contains built-in mechanisms designed for reading. As a consequence, the development of this process must involve parts of the existing visual system and its conversion to the task of processing single letters and words. An experimental proof of the specificity of reading mechanisms derives from two sources. The first is the study of patients who, following a focal brain lesion, present an isolated reading (pure alexia) and/or writing disorder (alexia and agraphia), without accompanying deficits in processing spoken language. The second is the more recent neuroimaging findings that have confirmed and partially modified the previous neurological models of processing written language.

The first neurological model of reading, based on two anatomo-clinical observations of two patients, one alexic and the other alexic and agraphic but without any problem in processing spoken language, was made by Déjérine (1891, 1892). He proposed that recognition of single letters comes about in the occipital cortex visual areas, with the product transmitted to a specific area, localized in the angular gyrus of the left parietal lobe (considered by Dejérine the center for the written images of the words) and finally to the motor center for word articulation. Reading comprehension was possible through a conversion process from the visual image of a word to its auditory image. During writing to dictation, the opposite process occurs: the centers for auditory memory and/or articulatory memory activate the angular gyrus and thereafter the corresponding motor programmers for graphic realization. According to Dejérine, both processes come about through a sub-lexical mechanism: in reading, the letters making up the single words are processed serially, one by one, with each letter transformed into a phoneme. Thereafter, they are assembled to be converted into heard words. The opposite process occurs in writing, so that words are broken down into their constituent phonemes and are then transformed into letter strings. The *post-mortem* examination of the pure alexic patient revealed a lesion of the left occipital cortex and the posterior part of the corpus callosum, thus preventing the connection between visual cortices and the left angular gyrus. The alexic–agraphic patient had a lesion at the level of the left angular gyrus, leading to an inability to read and write because visual word images have to be retrieved before the activation of the corresponding oral spelling pattern or graphic motor patterns. The validity of the Dejérine model, based solely on the work of sub-lexical mechanisms, was later challenged by the appearance of new models underlying normal reading and writing processes, which, in turn, were developed, expanded and verified on the basis of results obtained from the study of dyslexic patients and neuroimaging studies.

At the present time, the most frequently used models of reading are dual route models (for a review, see Denes, 2011), which postulate the existence of at least two separate mechanisms involved in the processing of strings of letters, one lexical and one sub-lexical. The first procedure, specific for known words, works through a process of direct mapping between the visual characteristics of the string of letters and the previously stored lexical representation. Orthographic representations are functionally separate from the phonological input lexicon and have access to an amodal semantic system, which is, in turn, connected to the phonological output lexicon. Alongside the lexical procedure, the two-route model postulates the existence of a procedure that allows new words or non-words to be read through phonological recording of letter strings. This operation uses abstract rules of writing-to-sound conversion, which allows the graphemic information of the written string to be translated into the corresponding phonological code, avoiding passage through the semantic system. Once the abstract phonological representation has been obtained through the lexical or non-lexical route, the information passes into a short term memory store that holds the abstract representation processed in the preceding stages during planning of the articulation processes necessary for the word to be produced out loud.

A fundamental step for accessing both routes is the computation of the visual word representation that serves as input for subsequent processing: a word is recognized as such, independently from changes in position, case and font (Deahene et al., 2005). Several neuroimaging studies (Cohen and Dehaene, 2004) have reported a consistent activation of a cerebral area, located in the left occipito-temporal sulcus, lateral to fusiform gyrus, in identifying visual letter strings. This area, dubbed by Cohen et al. (2000) the visual word form area (VWFA), is specifically activated by letter strings, as opposed to abstract graphic patterns or faces. This localization has been found to be the same among readers adopting different reading directions or script systems (alphabetic, syllabic as in Japanese Kana or morphosyllabic as in Chinese, Bolger et al., 2005).

Reading is not a self-sustained process, but its acquisition leads to an increased mastery of spoken language. In comparison to illiterates, expert readers develop better metaphonological capabilities (e.g. phonemic segmentation and blending tasks) and verbal short term memory (Morais and Kolinski, 2005). Similarly, a higher activation of VWFA in spoken language tasks was found in literate versus illiterate adults or in dyslexic versus normal child readers. In a recent fMRI study, Monzalvo and Dehaene-Lambertz (2013) found that, after one year of reading practice, children showed an increased activation of the brain regions involved in phonological representation. Three years of reading practice led to a further cortical activation in a region close to VWFA when children were listening to their native language.

In conclusion, it can be safely admitted that a culturally derived skill such as reading can positively influence most linguistic abilities. Such change can be sustained by a functional modification of the inborn language system through the development of culturally derived visual processing modules, widely interconnected with the spoken language systems.

Written language is a culturally derived skill that needs specific learning to develop. The first neurological models of written language processing were based on sub-lexical processes, by which reading occurs through a process of conversion of written letters into phonemes, while the opposite process is at work for writing. This model was supported by the activity of the left hemisphere, through connections of visual and

> language areas. The model, however, was found to be only partially adequate to fully understand the written word processing and deficits. At the present time, the most frequently used models of reading are dual route models, which postulate the existence of at least two separate mechanisms involved in the processing of strings of letters, one lexical and one sub-lexical.
>
> Since mastering written language is not an inborn skill, its specific neural mechanisms develop through a process of cultural recycling of inborn neural circuits.

Many languages, one brain
Cross-linguistic differences

Language is a universal species-specific capability, and languages are the various manifestations of that capability. As of 2009, 6,909 distinct languages were spoken, according to the ethnologue of M.P. Lewis (2009, published by SIL International).

Languages can differ in phonetics, phonology, morphology, lexicon, syntax, prosody and written form (for example, alphabetic and ideographic). In most languages of Indo-European origin, such as English or French, tone differences in syllable pronunciation do not correspond to a change of meaning (atonal languages). On the other hand, many languages, such as Mandarin-Chinese and Thai, use pitch to distinguish lexical or grammatical meaning – that is, to distinguish or to inflect words (tonal languages). It is therefore not surprising that a number of recent studies have tackled the problem of cross-linguistic variations, in particular, to what extent a functional neuro-anatomic model of language processing, based on data mostly from Indo-European languages such German, English or French, can be taken as valid in other languages, such as Chinese. A reliable source for exploring this field derives from the availability of neuroimaging or electrophysiological studies, such as event-related potentials (Kaan, 2007).

Recently, several studies have compared neural mechanisms of tone processing in speakers of a tonal language (Chinese) with those of an atonal language (English) and found that speakers of a tonal language showed more left-lateralized activations in the fronto-temporal regions, in contrast with atonal language speakers (Gandour et al., 2003; Xu et al., 2006). Evidence was also reported that the left hemisphere is more effective in learning lexical tones than the right hemisphere (for a review, see Chen et al., 2009).

A number of studies have, in addition, examined whether less-studied languages, such as Chinese, show similar electrophysiological or neuroanatomical processing signatures for particular types of linguistic processing. In speakers of English and other Indo-European languages, verbs are represented in the frontal region (e.g. the left prefrontal cortex, including Broca's area), whereas nouns are represented in the posterior regions (the temporal–occipital regions, outside Broca's area) (Petersen et al., 1989). Nouns and verbs in Chinese, however, activate a wide range of overlapping brain areas in distributed networks, in both the left and the right hemispheres (Li et al., 2004). The reason for this cross-cultural difference is probably that categorization of words into different grammatical classes is less clear-cut in Chinese than in English. Many individual words in Chinese cannot be easily distinguished as nouns or verbs, mainly due to a lack of inflectional morphology in Chinese. Most words play multiple grammatical roles, resulting in an abundance of class-ambiguous words that can be used as either nouns or verbs.

Cross-linguistic differences in processing written language

In the alphabetic system, the correspondence between letters or graphemes (made of one or more letters) is variable. In some languages – for example, Serbo-Croatian and partially in Italian – the application of written-sound transcoding rules allows the phonology and orthography to be obtained for any string of letters or phonemes (transparent or shallow orthographies). Other languages, such as French or English, may have multiple correspondences between grapheme and phoneme (opaque orthographies). In English, for example, not only do different letter groups represent the same sound, but often a grapheme maps onto several phonemes (e.g. the grapheme *ea* in *mean*, *head* and *steak* is pronounced as the phonemes /i/, /e/ and /ei/, respectively). In addition, different orthographic forms can represent the same sound. Finally, Chinese and Japanese adopt a logographic system, without any grapheme to phoneme correspondence. In a PET study, Paulesu et al. (2000) found that reading Italian induced more activation in the left posterior superior temporal gyrus than reading English (a quasi-transparent orthography), whereas reading English elicited more activation in the left posterior inferior temporal region and the left inferior frontal gyrus. When comparing English with Chinese, researchers have found that reading English activates the posterior superior temporal gyrus and adjacent supra marginal cortex, whereas reading Chinese activated the dorsal extent of the inferior parietal lobule (perhaps because this area is also involved in visuo-spatial analysis of Chinese characters) (see Tan et al., 2005, for a review).

Despite the above-described differences, it is worth stressing that a common activation in the fronto-temporal, occipito-temporal and occipital region is shared across all languages. In conclusion, we fully agree with the statement expressed in the 11th edition of the Encyclopedia Britannica: "all existing human speech is one in the essential characteristics which we have thus far noted or shall hereafter have to consider, even as humanity is one in its distinction from the lower animals; the differences are in nonessentials".

The bilingual brain

More than half of the world's population are actively learning or speaking a second language in addition to their native tongue (Grosjean and Li, 2013). The degree of competence, amount of daily use, and age of acquisition of the second language (L2) in comparison to the native language (L1) can vary. On these premises, it is not surprising that an increasing number of studies, from the observation of aphasic impairment in polyglots to more recent neuroimaging studies in non-brain-damaged populations, examine the organization of the brain structures of bilinguals relative to monolinguals.

Following the first description of polyglot aphasia by Pitres (1895), a number of cases of polyglot aphasics have been reported (for a review, see Paradis, 1995; Denes, 2011). The interest of the clinicians was focused on the issue of whether the learning and use of L2 involves the same neurological and functional mechanisms as those involved in L1; as a consequence, they concentrated on the differences in the types of linguistic deficits across the languages spoken by the polyglot patients and their pattern of recovery. The results were, however, quite disappointing, for reasons including the limited availability of aphasic polyglots and the many methodological flaws, which involved the insufficient linguistic competence of the part of the examiner and the lack of precise information about the age of acquisition, the frequency of use, and the degree and difference in the mastery of the different languages spoken by the patient. In a nutshell, the results of these clinical studies concurred in ascribing to the same hemisphere (usually the left) the neurological basis of L1 and L2. At the same time, the differences in aphasic impairment found in the languages used by the aphasic patient (for example, a patient with a pattern of Broca aphasia in Hebrew and Wernicke's aphasia in English, Albert and Obler, 1978) have been ascribed either to the different degree of linguistic competence or to the different structure of the two languages.

Similarly puzzling are the observations relating to the pattern of recovery, ranging from selective, to parallel, to differential. Rather than thinking that recovery is the result of a structural process that moves around different cerebral areas producing alternate or different effects, Paradis (1989) interprets the above findings as the result of a deficit in the control mechanisms that, in non-brain-damaged polyglots, allow transition from one language to another and the continuation of use of one language without interference from the other.

A big step in providing a set of reliable data about the processes of learning and using more than one language has been provided by the application of functional neuroimaging techniques (PET, fMRI) in normal bilingual participants, offering the chance to consider the weight of independent variables, such as age of acquisition, linguistic competence, and exposure to and familiarity with the different languages.

Age-of-acquisition effects are seen in the functional organization of the brains of native and second language speakers (Fabbro, 2001; Perani et al., 1996). Simultaneous acquisition of different languages in early childhood leads to greatest proficiency, without modifying the brain structure relative to monolingual speakers. On the other hand, later acquisition not only leads to a lesser proficiency, but also needs additional neural resources, with higher activation of several left hemisphere areas. Wartenburger et al. (2003) carried out an fMRI study in which bilingual subjects (Italian-German) performed tasks involving syntactic and semantic processing. The first group was made up of subjects who were bilingual from birth; the second group contained subjects with the same proficiency in both languages but who had acquired L2 after 6 years of age. A third group was made up of subjects who had acquired L2 after 6 years of age with less competence in the language. Critical factors were found to be both the degree of linguistic proficiency and the age of acquisition. In syntactic tasks, an overlapping activation of the cerebral areas dedicated to syntactic processing (Broca's area and basal ganglia) was revealed only in the subjects who were bilingual from an early age. Late L2 learners showed a greater degree of activation in the adjacent areas, suggesting additional neural involvement. No significant difference between these groups was found, on the other hand, in lexical-semantic tasks; in these tasks, there was similar activation of the perisylvian areas of the left hemisphere, independent of age of acquisition or linguistic competence.

Structural changes of the language-related areas in bilingual subjects have been reported in several neuroimaging studies; these changes include increased grey matter density, increased cortical thickness, or enhanced white matter integrity (for a review, see Li, Legault and Litcofsky, 2014). Mechelli et al. (2004) found that learning a second language increases the density of grey matter in the left inferior parietal cortex and that the degree of structural reorganization in this region is modulated by the proficiency attained and the age at acquisition. Klein et al. (2014) recently confirmed the lack of structural difference in language processing areas in early bilinguals in comparison with monolinguals; the researchers measured cortical thickness in bilingual subjects whose second language learning was simultaneous to first language (0–3 years of age) or later (either in early or late childhood). Only later acquisition of L2 was associated with significantly thicker cortex in the left inferior frontal gyrus and thinner cortex in the right inferior frontal gyrus.

The effects of language exposure have been investigated recently by Perani et al. (2003) in an fMRI study of bilingual subjects (Spanish-Catalan) living in Barcelona (and therefore with greater exposure to Catalan than to Spanish). The subjects were divided into two groups (L1 Spanish, L1 Catalan). In a word generation task, carried out with the same degree of competence by both groups, the Spanish-native language subjects displayed a smaller degree of neural activation in a task of generating words in Catalan compared to the degree of activation observed in Catalan-as-L1 subjects carrying out the same task in Spanish. These data confirm that exposure as well as linguistic competence play a role in modulating a specific neural involvement in the different languages spoken by the polyglot individual.

Finally, a further advantage of early bilingualism was reported in a number of recent studies. Bilingual children and infants need a precocious development of control and selection abilities to master different speech structures (for a review, see Kovács and Mehler, 2009). This ability has been found to extend to a variety of tasks that measure non-linguistic executive functioning, suggesting that some facets of the bilingual experience give rise to generalized improvements in cognitive performance. This flexible behavior may strengthen the functioning of the neural circuits involved in sustained attentional processes. Stocco and Prat (2014), through an fMRI study, investigated the changes of the fronto-striatal loop that directs signals to the prefrontal cortex. They examined a group of healthy bilinguals and monolinguals performing a Rapid Instructed Task Learning paradigm, which requires behaving according to ever-changing rules. Bilinguals were faster than monolinguals when executing novel rules, and this improvement was associated with greater modulation of activity in the basal ganglia. These structures are strongly interconnected with the prefrontal cerebral cortex, an area critical for executive functions such as rule learning, decision making and sustained attention.

Individual differences in L2 learning

Regardless of motivation, educational, cognitive and socio-cultural levels, it is commonly recognized that there is a huge variability in the ability to learn a second language, particularly at the phonetic-phonological and syntactic levels.

Golestani et al. (2007) used fMRI neuroimaging techniques to explore the possibility of this difference being conditioned to some extent by a particular neural organization. Their study was carried out on normal subjects and involved the production and identification of phonemes that differed from the phonemes belonging to the subjects' L1. The authors found that the subjects who performed the task with the greatest speed and efficiency demonstrated a high degree of cerebral asymmetry (left > right) between the parietal lobes. Golestani and Pallier (2007) also examined whether structural differences were associated with the accurate pronunciation of non-native phonemes and they identified increased white matter density when comparing accurate to non-accurate speakers. Further RM studies have also evidenced a greater neural volume at the level of the left inferior parietal lobe (Mechelli et al., 2004) and a greater density of white matter in the left primary auditory cortex (gyrus of Heschl). These data seem to suggest that subjects more skilled in acquiring the phonetic characteristics of L2 possess a relatively greater development of the cerebral areas linked to the phonological processing of acoustic stimuli or a greater degree of neural plasticity in specific cerebral structures as the result of learning a second language.

It is possible to conclude that, in polyglots, there is an overlap of functional and structural neural substrate for both languages that is more evident when the competence in both languages tends to coincide. The paramount importance of the age of acquisition fits nicely with the notion that the brain's neural plasticity is enhanced by early sensory experience, such as simultaneous exposure to different languages.

Language is a universal ability expressed in many different spoken languages. Several studies have been devoted to the similarities and differences in language cerebral representation of polyglots and the factors influencing it.

Neural representation of language does not depend upon the number and types of languages used. In polyglots, there is an overlap of functional and structural neural substrate in the left hemisphere for the two or more languages spoken, which is more evident when the competence in both languages tends to coincide. Age of acquisition is the most important factor for being a highly proficient polyglot, a fact that fits with the notion that the brain's neural plasticity is enhanced by early sensory experience.

Inter-individual differences in the ability to learn a second language have been tentatively attributed to a greater development of cerebral areas linked to phonological processing.

The neural basis of signed language

Signed language is a natural language used by a preverbal deaf population; it is not derived from spoken language, and it is characterized by a specific lexicon and grammar, with its own rules at segmental and morphological levels. The sign languages used by different hearing-impaired communities may differ, although usually to a lesser extent in comparison to spoken languages. If deaf children acquire sign language as their native language from the onset, its development follows the same rules and time frame as spoken language. Later exposure, after the closing of the critical period, requires specific learning that can be less proficient (also similar to the learning of a second language in the hearing population).

The investigation of the neurological basis of signed language derives from the observation of cases of aphasia in the signing population: in a nutshell, they mirror, both at linguistic and lesion level, the aphasic pattern of hearing people. Patients have been described with the same patterns of aphasia (Broca's, Wernicke's) as those observed in hearing subjects; similarly, the lesion localization was confined to the left hemisphere, with further specification according to the type of aphasia (for a review, see Corina, 1998). These data confirm that, despite differences in the input and output modality of language, core left perisylvian regions universally serve linguistic function. Neuroimaging studies of deaf signers have generally provided support for this claim. However, more fine-tuned studies suggest that left and right-parietal regions may play a special role in the mediation of signed language (Bavelier et al., 1998; Newman et al., 2002). In particular, the role of the parietal lobes has been found to be crucial in some aspects of sign processing that require a 'referential use' of the space. Compared to the processing of 'non-topographical sentences', in which the designated space is used as the sole area for the realization of signs and where the movement or the position of the sign is purely phonological (for example, "the flower is red"), in the production of a sentence such as "the teacher criticized the student", the sign corresponding to 'teacher' is placed in a higher position, with the verb pointing down towards the student. It is not, surprising, therefore, that MacSweeney et al. (2002) found a left parietal lobe activation in processing sentences where the precise configuration and location of the hands in space represent objects, agents and actions. When further spatial processing is required, such as mapping between real-world spatial relationships and an internal representation of sign space during production, right parietal mechanisms are further engaged (see Mac-Sweeney et al., 2008, for a revision). Some doubts, however, must be raised about the role of the right parietal lobe in processing the above tasks: is the processing purely linguistic, pointing to a linguistic role of the right parietal lobe in processing sign language? Or does the interpretation of sentences heavily weighted with spatial information require the building of a spatial representation carried out by the right hemisphere?

> Signed language is a natural language expressed by signs. Clinical observations of aphasic signers and neuroimaging studies in healthy signers show that deaf signers and hearing subjects share the same brain areas for language processing.

Reading by hand: the Braille system

The Braille system is a tactile code for reading and writing introduced by Braille (1839) that allows blind people to read and write. It is based on the positions of six raised dots, which are arranged in two columns and three rows to form a Braille cell (for a total of 64 different combinations). These 64 tactile signs represent the letters of the alphabet, as well as numbers, punctuation, mathematical symbols and musical notes.

Braille reading is dependent on tactile perception, which is mediated by the sensory-motor cortex situated in the parietal lobe. Consequently, there must be a complex process of functional reorganization of the cerebral cortex to allow tactile patterns to be transformed into linguistic stimuli.

Pascual-Leone and Torres (1993) have shown that Braille readers possess a greater neuronal representation of the 'reading' fingers in comparison to the neural representation of the other fingers, hypothesizing a relationship between the use of a cerebral circuit and its neurological representation.

Braille reading involves, however, not only tactile sensory processing but also higher-level cognitive, especially linguistic, operations. A PET study found selective activation for words compared to non-words in a left occipito-temporal region, whether during visual presentations to sighted subjects or during Braille presentations to blind subjects (Büchel et al., 1998).

Similarly, covert verb generation in response to Braille nouns or heard nouns was shown to yield essentially identical activations in occipital and occipito-temporal visual cortical areas, including primary visual areas (for a review, see Burton et al., 2003). TMS over medial occipital cortex is, moreover, disruptive to verb generation performance in the congenitally blind (Amedi et al., 2004). Visual cortical activation in the visual cortex in blind people is engaged in auditory language processing. This activity may be related to semantic processing (Burton et al., 2003) and the magnitude of fMRI activation scales with both semantic and syntactic complexity (Röder et al., 2002). The congenitally blind were reported to recruit the occipital cortex even during a verbal memory task lacking sensory stimulation, with a preference for posterior occipital regions, including visual areas whose activation magnitude correlated with verbal memory performance (Amedi et al., 2003).

From a clinical perspective, Hamilton et al. (2000) described the case of an expert Braille reader, blind from birth, who developed an alexia for Braille with no other neuropsychological deficit following a bilateral occipital lesion. On the other hand, the patient's ability to recognize and name objects through the tactile modality was normal.

In conclusion, it can be stated that Braille reading represents a model of neuronal plasticity, in which the occipital cerebral cortex, genetically destined for the processing of visual stimuli, is involved in the task of transforming tactile stimuli into linguistic stimuli in order to allow reading through touch.

> Braille reading is supported by a process that involves connections between somatosensory and visual areas that allow the conversion of tactile stimuli into linguistic stimuli. Experimental evidence suggests that, in blind persons, brain areas commonly associated with the processing of visual information are recruited in a compensatory cross-modal manner; the primary visual cortex is activated in blind subjects performing a Braille reading task.

SUMMARY

Language is a species-specific human skill supported by a dedicated neural substrate, usually located in the left hemisphere. Exposure to language in the critical period is a *sine qua non* for its development. In those who lack early language exposure, its development is not adequate, syntactic abilities being the most impaired.

Acquisition of written skills requires specific learning. Specific culturally derived neural networks develop when written language is mastered.

In polyglots, there is an overlap of functional and structural neural substrate in the left hemisphere for the two or more languages spoken, which is more evident when the competence in both languages tends to coincide.

Signed language is a natural language expressed by signs. Its neurological bases overlap with those of spoken language. Braille reading is supported by a process that involves connections between somatosensory and visual areas that allow the conversion of tactile stimuli into linguistic stimuli.

Notes

1. Notice that Down syndrome, or trisomy of chromosome 21, the most common cause of intellectual disability, does not involve severe impairment of the capacity of acquiring language, while in Angelman syndrome, also genetically determined, the lack of speech is disproportionate to degree of impairment.
2. The anatomo-clinical method is based on the observation of the patient's clinical picture combined with the results of micro- or macroscopic examination of the brain post-mortem.
3. Cases of aphasia in right-handers following a right hemisphere lesion (crossed aphasia) are extremely rare (Denes and Caviezel, 1981).
4. Sturge-Weber syndrome is a rare neurocutaneous disorder with angiomas that involves the leptomeninges and the skin of the face. In most cases, it is characterized by the presence of seizures, which progress to frequent, secondarily generalized seizures that are not sensitive to the usual antiepileptic medications.

Bibliography

Albert M.L. and Obler L.K. (1978), *The Bilingual Brain: Neuropsychological and Neurolinguistic Aspects of Bilingualism*, New York, Academic Press.

Amedi A., Floel A., Knecht S., Zohary E., Cohen L.G. (2004), Transcranial magnetic stimulation of the occipital pole interferes with verbal processing in blind subjects. *Nature Neuroscience*, 7(11): 1266–1270.

Amedi A., Raz N., Pianka P., Malach R., Zohary E. (2003), Early 'visual' cortex activation correlates with superior verbal memory performance in the blind. *Nature Neuroscience*, 6(7): 758–766.

Bavelier D., Corina D.P., Neville H.J. (1998), Brain and language: a perspective from sign language. *Neuron*, 21(2): 275–278.

Bolger D.J., Perfetti C.A., Schneider W. (2005), Cross-cultural effect on the brain revisited: universal structures plus writing system variation. *Human Brain Mapping, 25*(1): 92–104.

Braille L. (1839), *Nouveau procédé pour representer des points la forme meme des letters, les cartes de geographie, les figures de geometrie, les caracteres de musiques, etc., a l'usage des aveugles*. Institution royale des jeunes aveugles.

Brauer J., Anwander A., Perani D., Friederici A.D. (2013), Dorsal and ventral pathways in language development. *Brain and Language, 127*(2): 289–295.

Broca P. (1861), Nouvelle observation d'aphémie produite par une lésion de la troisième circonvolution frontale. *Bulletins de la Societe d'anatomie, 6*: 398–407.

Broca P. (1864), Sur les mots aphemie, aphasie et aphrasie, Lettre a M. le Professeur Trousseau. *Gazette des hopitaux, 23*.

Büchel C., Price C., Friston K. (1998), A multimodal language region in the ventral visual pathway. *Nature, 394*(6690): 274–277.

Burton H., Diamond J. B., Mcdermott K. B. (2003), Dissociating cortical regions activated by semantic and phonological tasks: a Fmri study in blind and sighted people. *Journal of Neurophysiology, 90*(3): 1965–1982.

Burton H., Snyder A.Z., Diamond J.B., Raichle M.E. (2002), Adaptive changes in early and late blind: a Fmri study of verb generation to heard nouns. *Journal of Neurophysiology, 88*(6): 3359–3371.

Chen C., Xue G., Mei L., Chen C., Dong Q. (2009), Cultural neurolinguistics. *Progress in Brain Research, 178*: 159–171.

Chomsky N. (1965), *Aspects of the Theory of Syntax*, Cambridge (MA), Mit Press.

Chomsky N. (1981), *Lectures on Government and Binding: The Pisa Lectures*. Holland, Foris Publications.

Cohen L. and Dehaene S. (2004), Specialization within the ventral stream: the case for the visual word form area. *Neuroimage, 22*(1): 466–476.

Cohen L., Dehaene S., Naccache L., Lehéricy S., Dehaene-Lambertz G., Hénaff M.A., Michel F. (2000), The visual word form area: spatial and temporal characterization of an initial stage of reading in normal subjects and posterior split-brain patients. *Brain, 123*(2): 291–307.

Corina D. (1998), Studies of neural processing in deaf signers: toward a neurocognitive model of language processing in the deaf. *Journal of Deaf Studies and Deaf Education, 3*(1): 35–48.

Curtiss S. (1977), *Genie: A Psycholinguistic Study of a Modern-Day "Wild Child"*, Perspectives in Neurolinguistics and Psycholinguistics, Boston, Academic Press.

Danelli L., Cossu G., Berlingeri M., Bottini G., Sberna M., Paulesu E. (2013), Is a lone right hemisphere enough? Neurolinguistic architecture in a case with a very early left hemispherectomy. *Neurocase, 19*(3): 209–231.

Dehaene S., Cohen L., Sigman M., Vinckier F. (2005), The neural code for written words: a proposal. *Trends in Cognitive Sciences, 9*(7): 335–341.

Déjerine J. (1891), Sur un cas de cécité verbale avec agraphie, suivi d'autopsie. *Comptes Rendus des Séances et Mémoires de la Société de Biologie, 3*: 197–201.

Déjerine J. (1892), Contributions à l'étude anatomo-pathologique et clinique de différentes variétés de cécité verbale. *Comptes Rendus des Séances et Mémoires de la Société de Biologie, 4*: 61–90.

Denes G. (2011), *Talking Heads: The Neuroscience of Language*, East Sussex, UK: Psychology Press.
Denes G. and Caviezel F. (1981), Dichotic listening in crossed aphasia: "paradoxical" ipsilateral suppression. *Archives of Neurology*, 38(3): 182–185.
Fabbro F. (2001), The bilingual brain: bilingual aphasia. *Brain and Language*, 79(2): 201–210.
Friederici A.D. (2006), The neural basis of language development and its impairment. *Neuron*, 52(6): 941–952.
Friederici A.D. (2011), The brain basis of language processing: from structure to function. *Physiology Review*, 91(4): 1357–1392.
Friedrich M. and Friederici A.D. (2004), N400-like semantic incongruity effect in 19-month-olds: processing known words in picture contexts. *Journal of Cognitive Neuroscience*, 16(8): 1465–1477.
Fromkin V., Krashen S., Curtiss S., Rigler D., Rigler, M. (1974), The development of language in Genie: A case of language acquisition beyond the "Critical Period". *Brain and Language*, 1: 81–107.
Gandour J., Tong Y., Wong D., Talavage T., Dzemidzic M., Xu Y., Li X., Lowe M. (2004), Hemispheric roles in the perception of speech prosody. *Neuroimage*, 23(1): 344–357.
Gandour J., Wong D., Dzemidzic M., Lowe M., Tong Y., Li X. (2003), A cross-linguistic fmri study of perception of intonation and emotion in Chinese. *Human Brain Mapping*, 18(3): 149–157.
Golestani N., Molko N., Dehaene S., Lebihan D., Pallier C. (2007), Brain structure predicts the learning of foreign speech sounds. *Cerebral Cortex*, 17(3): 575–582.
Golestani N. and Pallier C. (2007), Anatomical correlates of foreign speech sound production. *Cerebral Cortex*, 17(4): 929–934.
Golestani N., Price C.J., Scott S.K. (2011), Born with an ear for dialects? Structural plasticity in the expert phonetician brain. *Journal of Neuroscience*, 31(11): 4213–4220.
Grosjean F. and Li P. (eds) (2013), *The Psycholinguistics of Bilingualism*, Oxford, Wiley-Blackwell.
Hamilton R., Keenan J.P., Catala M., Pascual-Leone A. (2000), Alexia for Braille following bilateral occipital stroke in an early blind woman. *Neuroreport*, 11(2): 237–240.
Hauser M.D., Chomsky N., Fitch W.T. (2002), The faculty of language: what is it, who has it, and how did it evolve? *Science*, 298(5598): 1569–1579.
Hickok G. (2009), The functional neuroanatomy of language. *Physics of Life Reviews*, 6(3): 121–143.
Hickok G. and Poeppel D. (2007), The cortical organization of speech processing. *Nature Reviews Neuroscience*, 8(5): 393–402.
Huttenlocher P.R. and Dabholkar A.S. (1997), Regional differences in synaptogenesis in human cerebral cortex. *Journal of Comparative Neurology*, 387(2): 167–178.
Itard J.M.G. (1801, 1962), *The Wild Boy of Aveyron*, New York, Appleton-Century-Crofts.
Kaan E. (2007), Event-related potentials and language processing: a brief overview. *Language and Linguistics Compass*, 1(6): 571–591.

Kimura D. (1963), A note on cerebral dominance in hearing. *Acta Otolaryngolica, 56*: 617–618.

Klein D., Mok K., Chen J.K., Watkins K.E. (2014), Age of language learning shapes brain structure: a cortical thickness study of bilingual and monolingual individuals. *Brain and Language, 131*: 20–24.

Kovács A.M., Mehler J. (2009, April 21), Cognitive gains in 7-month-old bilingual infants. *Proceedings of the National Academy of Sciences USA, 106*(16): 6556–60.

Kuhl P. K. (2004), Early language acquisition: cracking the speech code. *Nature Reviews Neuroscience, 5*(11): 831–843.

Lenneberg E.H. (1967), *Biological Foundations of Language*, New York, John Wiley and Sons.

Lewis M.P. (ed) (2009), *Ethnologue: Languages of the World*, (16th edition), Dallas, Sil International.

Li P., Jin Z., Tan L.H. (2004), Neural representations of nouns and verbs in Chinese: an fmri study. *Neuroimage, 21*(4): 1533–1541.

Li P., Legault J., Litcofsky K.A. (2014), Neuroplasticity as a function of second language learning: anatomical changes in the human brain. *Cortex, 58*: 301–324.

Lichtheim L. (1885), On aphasia. *Brain, 7*: 433–448.

Liégeois F., Connelly A., Cross J.H., Boyd S.G., Gadian D.G., Vargha-Khadem F., Baldeweg T. (2004), Language reorganization in children with early-onset lesions of the left hemisphere: an fmri study. *Brain, 127*(6): 1229–1236.

Macsweeney M., Capek C.M., Campbell R., Woll B. (2008), The signing brain: the neurobiology of sign language. *Trends in Cognitive Sciences, 12*(11): 432–440.

Macsweeney M., Woll B., Campbell R., Calvert G.A., Mcguire P.K., David A.S., Simmons A., Brammer M.J. (2002), Neural correlates of British sign language comprehension: spatial processing demands of topographic language. *Journal of Cognitive Neuroscience, 14*(7): 1064–1075.

Mahmoudzadeh M., Dehaene-Lambertz G., Fournier M., Kongolo G., Goudjil S., Dubois J., Grebe R., Wallois F. (2013), Syllabic discrimination in premature human infants prior to complete formation of cortical layers. *Proceedings of the National Academy of Sciences USA, 110*(12): 4846–4851.

Mechelli A., Crinion J.T., Noppeney U., O'Doherty J., Ashburner J., Frackowiak R.S., Price C.J. (2004), Neurolinguistics: structural plasticity in the bilingual brain. *Nature, 431*(7010): 757.

Mehler J., Jusczyk P.W., Lambertz G., Halsted N., Bertoncini J., AMIEL-Tison C. (1988), A precursor of language acquisition in young infants. *Cognition, 29*: 143–178.

Monzalvo K. and Dehaene-Lambertz G. (2013), How reading acquisition changes children's spoken language network. *Brain and Language, 127*(3): 356–365.

Morais J. and Kolinsky R. (2005), Literacy and cognitive change. In: Snowling M. and Hulme C. (eds), *The science of reading: A handbook*, Oxford, Blackwell, 188–203.

Newman S.D., Just M.A., Carpenter P.A. (2002), The synchronization of the human cortical working memory network. *Neuroimage, 15*(4): 810–822.

Newport E.L. (1990), Maturational constraints on language learning. *Cognitive Science, 14*(1): 11–28.

Paradis M. (1989), Bilingual and polyglot aphasia. In: Boiler F. and Grafman J. (eds), *Handbook of neuropsychology*, Amsterdam, Elsevier, 117–140.

Paradis M. (1995), *Aspects of Bilingual Aphasia*, London, Pergamon.

Pascual-Leone A., Torres F. (1993), Plasticity of the sensorimotor cortex representation of the reading finger in Braille readers. *Brain*, 116(1): 39–52.

Paulesu E., Mccrory E., Fazio F., Menoncello L., Brunswick N., Cappa S.F., Cotelli M., Cossu G., Corte F., Lorusso M., Pesenti S., Gallagher A., Perani D., Price C., Frith C.D., Frith U. (2000), A cultural effect on brain function. *Nature Neuroscience*, 3(1): 91–96.

Perani D., Abutalebi J., Paulesu E., Brambati S., Scifo P., Cappa S.F., Fazio F. (2003), The role of age of acquisition and language usage in early, high-proficient bilinguals: an fmri study during verbal fluency. *Human Brain Mapping*, 19(3): 170–182.

Perani D., Dehaene S., Grassi F., Cohen L., Cappa S.F., Dupoux E., Fazio F., Mehler J. (1996), Brain processing of native and foreign languages. *Neuroreport*, 7(15–17): 2439–2444.

Perani D., Saccuman M.C., Scifo P., Anwander A., Spada D., Baldoli C., Poloniato A., Lohmann G., Friederici A.D. (2011), Neural language networks at birth. *Proceedings of the National Academy of Sciences USA*, 108(38): 16056–16061.

Petersen S.E., Fox P.T., Posner M.I., Mintun M., Raichle M.E. (1989), Positron emission tomographic studies of the processing of single words. *Journal of Cognitive Neuroscience*, 1(2): 153–170.

Pitres A. (1895), Aphasia in polyglots. In: Paradis M. (ed) (1983), *Readings on aphasia in bilinguals and polyglots*, Montreal, Marcel-Dieder, 26–49.

Röder B., Stock O., Neville H., Bien S., Rösler F. (2002), Brain activation modulated by the comprehension of normal and pseudo-word sentences of different processing demands: a functional magnetic resonance imaging study. *Neuroimage*, 15(4): 1003–1014.

Stocco A., PRAT, C.S. (2014), Bilingualism trains specific brain circuits involved in flexible rule selection and application. *Brain Lang*, 137: 50–61.

Tan L.H., Spinks J.A., Eden G.F., Perfetti C.A., Siok W.T. (2005), Reading depends on writing, in Chinese. *Proceedings of the National Academy of Sciences USA*, 102(24): 8781–8785.

Thierry G., Vihman M., Roberts M. (2003), Familiar words capture the attention of 11-month-olds in less than 250 ms. *Neuroreport*, 14(18): 2307–2310.

Vanlancker-Sidtis D. (2004), When only the right hemisphere is left: studies in language and communication. *Brain and Language*, 91(2): 199–211.

Vargha-Khadem F., Carr L.J., Isaacs E., Brett E., Adams C., Mishkin M. (1997), Onset of speech after left hemispherectomy in a nine-year-old boy. *Brain*, 120(1): 159–182.

Wartenburger I., Heekeren H.R., Abutalebi J., Cappa S.F., Villringer A., Perani D. (2003), Early setting of grammatical processing in the bilingual brain. *Neuron*, 37(1): 159–170.

Werker J.F. and Curtin S. (2005), PRIMIR: A developmental framework of infant speech processing. *Language Learning and Development*, 1(2): 197–234.

Wernicke C. (1876), Das Urwindungssystem des menschlichen Gehirns. *Archiv für Psychiatrie und Nervenkrankheiten Berlin, 6*: 298–326.

Xu Y., Gandour J., Talavage T., Wong D., Dzemidzic M., Tong Y., LI X., Lowe M. (2006), Activation of the left planum temporale in pitch processing is shaped by language experience. *Human Brain Mapping, 27*: 173–183.

Yakovlev P.I. and Lecours A.R. (1967), The myelogenetic cycles of regional maturation of the brain. In: Minkowski A. (ed), *Regional development of the brain in early life*, Oxford, Blackwell Scientific, 3–70.

5

MEMORY SYSTEMS AND BRAIN PLASTICITY

According to the *Oxford English Dictionary*, memory is "the faculty by which the mind stores and remembers information". However, hidden in this simple definition are different types of memory, mediated by specific, but partially overlapping, brain regions.

Distinctions among memory systems

A basic distinction concerns processes involved in temporary retention versus long-lasting retention. Short term memory (STM) retains a limited amount of material for a short interval of time and must be distinguished from working memory (WM), which refers to structures and processes used for temporarily storing and manipulating information (Baddeley, 1986). This system can be considered a general cognitive capacity, active both in verbal and in non-verbal tasks. Its limited capacity is linked with attention to such a degree that the two functions have been recently integrated in the same system (for a review, see Cowan et al., 2005). Their integrated action is supported by the frontal lobes and, through widespread neural connections, also involves other regions of the brain that support domain-specific modular functions such as language or long term episodic memory.

On the other hand, long term memory capacity is much larger and the memoranda may be held for longer time periods, up to years. The long-term memory system is not a unitary process, as it can be divided into procedural, episodic or autobiographical (AB), and semantic memory (SM). See Figure 5.1.

Memory systems and brain plasticity

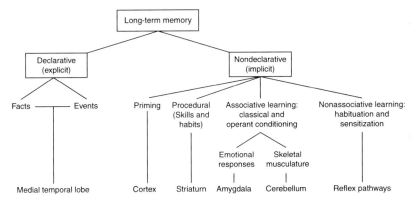

FIGURE 5.1 The organization of long term memory. From Eric R. Kandel, James H. Schwartz, and Thomas M. Jessell (2000) *Principles of Neural Science*, Fourth Edition, with permission from McGraw-Hill Education.

These various forms of memory are thought to fall into two general classes, described as declarative and non-declarative, on the basis of whether learning and retrieval occur consciously or unconsciously. This distinction has been validated by behavioral and neuroimaging experiments in animals and case study reports in humans. Declarative memory is the kind of memory that is referred to when the term *memory* is used in everyday language. The stored representations are flexible, accessible to awareness, and can guide performance in a variety of contexts. Declarative memory provides a way of modeling the external world, and it is either true or false. It encompasses episodic or autobiographic (AB) memory, the memory of events in our own personal past, and semantic memory (SM), the general knowledge about things in the world and their meaning, a distinction proposed by Tulving in 1972. He defined episodic memory as the conscious knowledge of temporally dated, spatially located and personally experienced events or episodes (for example, remembering where and with whom we went to dinner last week). SM, on the other hand, has been conceived by Tulving as a type of mental thesaurus, the organized knowledge a person possesses about words and other verbal symbols, their meaning and referents, and the relations between them. In more recent years, the term SM has assumed a wider meaning, including a system of more generalized knowledge, which includes both the meanings of words and knowledge of the world, such as all the information we possess regarding animals, tools, rules of behavior and so on.

Non-declarative memory is neither true nor false and can be conceived as an assembly of unconscious learning and retrieval capacities that is expressed through performance rather than recollection. Procedural memory (knowing how) is the unconscious memory of skills and how to do things, with particular reference to the use of objects or movements of the body, such as cooking, playing a musical instrument, swimming or cycling.

Processes and plasticity in memory

Memory relies on a set of processes by which information is encoded, consolidated, and retrieved. Through encoding, information is transformed into a memory representation. Encoding efficacy heavily depends on the level of processing performed on a stimulus, with deeper processing producing a stronger, more durable representation and thus increasing the likelihood that the stimulus will be consolidated and further remembered. The last component of the memory, retrieval, refers to the subsequent re-accessing of events or information from the past, which have been previously encoded and stored.

The validation of the multi-componentiality of memory in different components mainly derives from the study of patients with selective deficits of memory, involving defective encoding, storage or retrieval restricted to AB or SM, with a further distinction into different semantic categories (for a review, see Tulving and Craik, 2000).

In addition, experimental studies in animals (electrophysiological studies, tailored brain lesions) and, more recently, neuroimaging studies in healthy humans, converge in assigning to the hippocampal formation (the hippocampus, dentate gyrus and subicular cortex) the main neurological structure related to the long term episodic memory. Following bilateral removal of the medial temporal lobes, including the hippocampal formation, H.M., perhaps the most famous patient in the history of neurology (Corkin, 2013), was left with an inability to form new episodic memory (anterograde amnesia) coupled with a substantial, but not total, loss of old memories (retrograde amnesia). His deficit, however, was not total but limited to expressive, declarative memory. His lexical knowledge was normal, and on most tests of semantic knowledge H.M. performed within the range of control scores (Schmolck et al., 2002). In addition, he was still able to form and retrieve non-declarative memories, such as those related to learning and expressing new motor skills. Finally, his STM was well within normal limits: he had a remarkable capacity for sustained attention, including the ability to retain information for a period of time after it was presented; he could carry on a conversation, and he exhibited an intact digit span (i.e. the ability to repeat back a string of six or seven digits).

The functions of the hippocampus, one of the phylogenetically oldest cortical areas, can be inferred by its pattern of connectivity and neurophysiology.

The primate hippocampal formation is reciprocally connected with all neocortical association areas. Cortical projections provide the hippocampus with highly elaborate information that can be related to episodic memories. The report of single units in the hippocampus, whose firing rate varies as a function of the animal's position in an environment (place cells, for a review see O'Keefe, 1976), with the discovery of the grid cells (place-selective cells that fire at multiple discrete and regularly spaced locations, Fyhn et al., 2004), give experimental support to the notion that the hippocampus can provide a cognitive or spatial map of its environment. According to Rolls and Treves (1994) the wide network of association fibers of the hippocampus allows for building progressively episodic memories based on associations between components of experienced events. Subsequently, connectivity allows for the later retrieval of the entire event, as a result of pattern completion, sometimes originating from the availability of only a fragment of the original event. For consolidation and retrieval, the hippocampus would then retrieve in the neocortex the activation pattern that was present during the original encoding (for a review, see Henke, 2010).

Following the introduction of neuroimaging techniques, many studies in healthy humans have confirmed the fundamental role of the hippocampus in associative memory formation. In a PET study (Henke et al., 1999), regional blood flow was measured in healthy subjects asked to remember pairs of words using different learning strategies: a significant activation was found when subjects were associating items through a semantic strategy, much more evident than in deep, single-item encoding and novelty detection condition. The notion that the hippocampus supports associative memory by interacting with functionally distinct and distributed brain regions has been recently tested in humans. Wang et al. (2014) used targeted non-invasive electromagnetic stimulation to modulate human cortical-hippocampal networks and tested the effects of this manipulation on associative memory (face-cued word recall). Wang et al. submitted a group of healthy adults to trains of repetitive transcranial magnetic stimulation (rTMS) centered on the left dorsal parietal cortex, a component of the cortical-hippocampal network. Multiple-session stimulation increased functional connectivity among distributed cortical-hippocampal network regions and concomitantly improved associative memory performance. These alterations involved localized long-term plasticity because increases were highly selective to the targeted brain regions, and enhancements of connectivity and associative memory persisted for approximately 24 hours after stimulation. Targeted cortical-hippocampal networks can thus be enhanced non-invasively, demonstrating their role in associative memory. At the moment, however, the use of these new techniques for enhancing memory or treating memory deficit by enhancing plasticity in selected brain regions is only a little more than wishful thinking.

The at least partial independence of AB from SM is documented by the dissociation of the two memories following brain damage. As already outlined, patients affected by AB impairment show significantly better performance when tested on SM. On the other hand, SM can be selectively disrupted in semantic dementia, the second most common form of dementia after Alzheimer's disease. Semantic dementia is associated with focal atrophy of the orbito-mesial frontal and anterior temporal lobes. At least three variants of semantic dementia have been described, a temporal variant in which lexical-conceptual disorders prevail and are associated to a left temporal lobe atrophy, a frontal variant characterized by expressive language disorders (primary progressive aphasia) and a behavioral variant that includes changes in personality and interpersonal conduct (for a review, see Piguet et al., 2011).

The effect of sleep deprivation on memory plasticity

Several factors can influence the memory process. Some of them are intrinsic to the memorandum, such as its length, complexity or meaning. Of similar importance is the way of encoding: shallow or deep. Shallow processing focuses on the physical features of an item, rather than its meaning; deep processing is based on semantics and involves forming associations between old and new information, with the effect of a more efficient encoding and subsequent retrieval. In addition, it is undoubtedly proven that attention and motivation can affect memory recall in a surprisingly significant way, their effects having the most noticeable impact during the encoding phase (for a review, see Baddeley et al., 2009).

Memory and its functional and neurological substrate can be heavily influenced by an impaired regulation of other biological systems, such as the wake-sleep system, or by substances acting on the central nervous system, such as ethanol or some commonly used psychoactive drugs (for a review, see White et al., 2000; Beracochea, 2006). In this section we will briefly review some of the more recent data on the effect of sleep deprivation on memory.

Sleep is a physiological condition of partial unconsciousness, characterized by reduced motor activity and responsiveness, from which an individual can be aroused by stimulation. Birds and mammals display two distinct types of sleep, non-rapid eye movement (NREM) sleep and rapid eye movement (REM) sleep, which are most easily distinguished on the basis of their patterns of brain activity (electroencephalogram, EEG) and muscle activity (electromyogram, EMG).

Despite the plethora of experimental and clinical observations, there is no consensus about the purpose of sleep (Siegel, 2005, 2009), but substantial evidence deriving from animal and human studies clearly indicates that sleep benefits proper cognitive functioning; on the contrary, sleep loss or sleep disturbance have the opposite effect, resulting in cognitive deficits such as impaired attention, decision making, learning and various types of memory.

The hippocampus is particularly sensitive to sleep loss, and altered hippocampal plasticity is one of the main effects of sleep deprivation (SD), along with reduced learning and memory deficits (for a review, see Kreutzmann et al., 2015).

SD may have an effect on different phases of memory formation. Human and animal studies show that pre-training SD impairs acquisition and memory encoding in a variety of tasks, pointing toward a particular sensitivity of hippocampus-dependent learning and memory (Abel et al., 2013). In an fMRI study in healthy human subjects, Joo et al. (2007) showed that a full night without sleep before learning produced a significant attenuation of hippocampal activity during episodic memory encoding and resulted in worse retention. The decreased activation of the hippocampal regions during memory encoding was assumed to be responsible for the subsequent memory deficits (Joo et al., 2007). In a more recent fMRI study, Van der Werf et al. (2009) showed that even a mild disruption of sleep without affecting total sleep time is sufficient to affect subsequent hippocampal activity and memory encoding.

On the other side, it is proved that SD following learning can impair memory formation by disrupting the memory consolidation process. Several experimental studies in rats (for a review, see Kreutzmann et al., 2015) have pointed to the hippocampus as particularly sensitive to the SD immediately following acquisition and retention of the memorandum.

The studies reviewed so far concern the effects of short term SD, but animal studies on chronically sleep deprived animals suggest that this condition is associated with shrinkage of the hippocampus.

Several reports of reduced hippocampal volume in human subjects with habitual short sleep or suffering from disorders associated with disrupted sleep have been recently published. A voxel-based morphometry study in healthy humans showed a significant positive correlation between grey matter volume of the bilateral hippocampus and sleep duration during weekdays (Taki et al., 2012). Likewise, a smaller hippocampus has been reported in patients suffering from chronic insomnia (for a review, see Kreutzmann et al., 2015). The potential relevance of this finding was demonstrated by a correlation with poorer cognitive function in a variety of tasks, including verbal and visual memory (e.g., Noh et al., 2012; Joo et al., 2013).

In conclusion, although the precise purpose of sleep remains largely unknown, mounting evidence suggests that sleep plays a decisive role in brain plasticity and memory formation.

Declining memory in aging

Among the memory components susceptible to the effects of aging (see also chapter 3) stand the working memory system and episodic memory. Older people are penalized when the information they have to encode or retrieve is highly specific, including temporal and spatial details of the memorandum. Recent memories are more likely to be lost than more remote memories (Ribot's law). On the other hand, older people are unimpaired when retrieving general information about a topic or on semantic memory tasks. The reason of this dissociation may be found in the 'pyramidal' way knowledge is represented and organized; general commonalities are easily accessible at the top, while increasingly specific pieces of information are less easy to access at the bottom of the hierarchy (Craik, 2008).

According to Hasher and Zacks (1979), the age-related working and episodic memory deficit emerges from a failure of frontal lobe mediated inhibitory mechanisms, preventing irrelevant information from entering the working memory system and deleting no-longer-relevant information. Different mechanisms have been also been proposed, such as an age-related general reduction of processing speed, or reduced processing resources, equally related to a frontal lobe reduced processing ability, as described in chapter 3. A deficit in executive control associated with the changes of prefrontal structures has been proposed by Bories et al. (2013), among others, as a possible critical factor of cognitive decline in healthy older adults. In particular, according to the above theory, older adults have a deficit in the ability to maintain goals of information in the episodic and working memory systems, leading to a decline not only in memory, but also in other cognitive functions.

SUMMARY

Memory, the faculty by which the mind stores and remembers information, is not monolithic, but is composed of subsystems that process specific types of information. In this chapter, definitions, neurological substrates, functions and organization of the memory system are described.

Clinical and experimental studies assign to the hippocampus a major anatomical role in memory functions. This region can be considered the most active brain region for neural plasticity. Neurogenesis is present only in the hippocampus and adjacent regions, while the most-studied model of functional neural plasticity, long term potentiation, and its opposite process, long term depression (see chapter 2), were first identified in the hippocampus.

Different factors can influence the memory process, both at structural and functional levels. Aging, for example, has a deleterious effect on short term and episodic memory, while semantic memory is unaffected. Sleep deprivation reduces learning, affecting the hippocampal activity during the encoding and consolidation processes. In chronic insomnia, regressive structural changes in the hippocampus have been recorded.

Bibliography

Abel T., Havekes R., Saletin J.M., Walker M.P. (2013), Sleep, plasticity and memory from molecules to whole-brain networks. *Current Biology, 23*: R774–788.

Baddeley, A.D. (1986), *Working Memory*, Oxford, Clarendon Press.

Baddeley, A.D., Eysenck M., Anderson M.C. (2009), Memory, Hove (UK), Psychology Press.

Beracochea D. (2006), Anterograde and retrograde effects of benzodiazepines on memory. *Scientific World Journal, 16*(6): 1460–5.

Bories C., Husson Z., Guitton M.J., De Koninck Y. (2013), Differential balance of prefrontal synaptic activity in successful versus unsuccessful cognitive aging. *J Neurosci., 23*: 1344–1356.

Craik F.I. (2008) Memory changes in normal and pathological aging. *Canadian Journal of Psychiatry, 53*(6): 3435.

Corkin S. (2013), *Permanent Present Tense: The Unforgettable Life of the Amnesic Patient, H.M.*, New York, Basic Books.

Cowan N., Elliott E.M., Scott Saults J., Morey C.C., Mattox S., Himsjatullina A., Conway A.R. (2005), On the capacity of attention: its estimation and its role in working memory and cognitive aptitudes. *Cognitive Psychology, 51*(1): 42–100.

Fyhn M., Molden S., Witter M.P., Moser E.I., Moser M.B. (2004), Spatial representation in the entorhinal cortex. *Science, 305*(5688): 1258–1264.

Hasher L., Zacks R.T. (1979). Automatic and effortful processes in memory. *Journal of Experimental Psychology: General, 108*: 356–388.

Henke K. (2010), A model for memory systems based on processing modes rather than consciousness. *Nature Review Neuroscience, 11*(7): 523–532.

Henke K., Weber B., Kneifel S., Wieser H.G., Buck A. (1999), Human hippocampus associates information in memory. *Proceedings of the National Academy of Sciences USA, 96*(10): 5884–5889.

Joo E.Y., Noh H.J., Kim J. S., Koo D.L., Kim D., Hwang K.J., Kim J.Y., Kim S.T., Kim M.R., Hong S.B. (2013), Brain gray matter deficits in patients with chronic primary insomnia. *Sleep, 36*: 999–1007.

Kandel, E.R., Kupferman, I., And Iverson, S. (2000). Learning and memory. In: Kandel E.R., Schwartz J.H., and Jessell T.M. (eds), *Principles of neural science*, New York, McGraw-Hill, 1227–1246.

Kreutzmann J.C. Havekes R., Abel T. and Meerlo P. (2015), Sleep deprivation and hippocampal vulnerability: changes in neuronal plasticity, neurogenesis and cognitive function. *Neuroscience*, Apr 29. doi:10.1016/j.neuroscience.2015.04.053

Noh H.J., Joo E.Y., Kim S.T., Yoon S.M., Koo D.L., Kim D., Lee G.H., Hong S.B. (2012), The relationship between hippocampal volume and cognition in patients with chronic primary insomnia. *Journal of Clinical Neurology, 8*: 130–138.

O'Keefe J. (1976), Place units in the hippocampus of the freely moving rat. *Experimental Neurology, 51*(1): 78–109.

Piguet O., Hornberger M., Miochi E., Hodges J.R. (2011), Behavioural-variant frontotemporal dementia: diagnosis, clinical staging, and management. *Lancet Neurology* 10: 162–72.

Rolls E.T. and Treves A. (1994), Neural networks in the brain involved in memory and recall. *Progress in Brain Research, 102*: 335–341.

Schmolck H., Kensinger E.A., Corkin S., Squire L.R. (2002), Semantic knowledge in patient H.M. and other patients with bilateral medial and lateral temporal lobe lesions. *Hippocampus, 12*(4): 520–533.

Siegel J.M. (2005), Clues to the functions of mammalian sleep. *Nature, 437*: 1264–1271.

Siegel J.M. (2009), Sleep viewed as a state of adaptive inactivity. *Nature Reviews Neuroscience, 10*: 747–753.

Taki Y., Hashizume H., Thyreau B., Sassa Y., Takeuchi H., WU K., Kotozaki Y., Nouchi R., Asano M., Asano K., Fukuda H., Kawashima R. (2012), Sleep duration during weekdays affects hippocampal gray matter volume in healthy children. *NeuroImage, 60*: 471–475.

Treves A., Tashiro A., Witter M.P., Moser E.I. (2008), What is the mammalian dentate gyrus good for? *Neuroscience, 154*(4):1155–72.

Tulving E. (1972), Episodic and semantic memory. In: Tulving E. and Donaldson W. (eds), *Organization of memory*, New York, Academic Press, 381–403.

Tulving E. and Craik F. (eds) (2000), *The Oxford Handbook of Memory*, Oxford, Oxford University Press.

Van Der Werf Y.D., Altena E., Schoonheim M.M., Sanz-Arigita E.J., Vis J.C., De Rijke W., Van Someren E.J. (2009), Sleep benefits subsequent hippocampal functioning. *Nature Neuroscience, 12*: 122–123.

Wang J.X., Rogers L.M., Gross E.Z., Ryals A.J., Dokucu M.E., Brandstatt K.L., Hermiller M.S., Voss J.L. (2014), Targeted enhancement of cortical-hippocampal brain networks and associative memory. *Science, 345*(6200): 1054.

White A.M., Matthews D.B., Best J.P. (2000), Ethanol, memory, and hippocampal function: A review of recent findings. *Hippocampus, 10*(1): 88–93.

Yoo S.S., Hu P.T., Gujar N., Jolesz F.A., Walker M.P. (2007), A deficit in the ability to form new human memories without sleep, *Nature Neuroscience, 10*: 385–392.

6
THE SELF AND ITS BRAIN

The sense of body ownership ("having the same old body," James, 1890) constitutes a fundamental aspect of self-awareness. This feeling has been related to a cognitive function subserving conscious awareness of the body and provided with its own neurological substrate; the sensations normally occurring with perception of the body and their orientation in respect both to the internal or external space has been considered due to the presence and constant activation of the body schema or body image (for a review, see Denes, 1999; Berlucchi and Aglioti, 2001). According to Head and Holmes (1911–12), body orientation occurs by means of two mechanisms. The first, a lower level representation, concerns the appreciation of the posture and passive movement by measuring every change of body posture against the preceding posture or movement (the postural body schema). A higher-level representation allows the precise localization, identification and naming of the body parts (the superficial body schema). The construction of these processes depends on the processing and integration of somatosensory (proprioceptive, tactile, and vestibular) and visual stimuli, leading to a dynamic organization of one's own body and its relations to other bodies. These processes develop in the earliest phases of infancy, newborns reproducing elementary gestures they see an adult perform (Meltzoff, 1990).

Bodily self-consciousness, however, does not depend only on body orientation processes but involves imaginative and mnestic processes, as shown by its resilience to traumatic bodily changes, such as limb amputation, or by its loss following acquired brain lesions, sometimes with some opposite counter-intuitive effects, such as the phantom limb phenomenon or anosognosia for hemiplegia.

Left parietal lobe lesions are sometimes characterized by a selective difficulty pointing, either on verbal command or on imitation, to body parts, that can be, however, identified and named once they have been singled out by the examiner. The nature of this deficit seems to depend on an impaired conceptual, mainly linguistic, representation of the body parts (Semenza and Goodglass, 1985). On the other side, a loss of awareness of the left part of the body, hemiasomatognosia, can be observed following right parietal lesion. Often hemiasomatognosia is a part of a wider deficit of attention, awareness and representation (neglect) of the left hemispace. In some cases, however, the deficit is more evident in body centered representation, up to denial of the motor and sensory deficit of the left body (anosognosia, for a review, see Bisiach, 1999: 179–196).

> Sense of body ownership constitutes a fundamental aspect of self-awareness. It is through this function that we perceive the position of the body in space and can localize the position of the body parts both in respect to the external space and to the whole body. Some lesions, mostly centered in the right hemisphere, can impair this skill, up to the point of denial that a body part belongs to its owner. Here we focus on the persistence or change of body representations that have been described following loss of one body part or surgery-induced body modifications.

The strange case of the phantom limb

The phenomenon of the phantom limb was first described by a sixteenth-century French barber-surgeon, Ambroise Paré, as the vivid perception of an amputated limb. This phenomenon is frequent, appearing in over 80% of patients undergoing limb amputation in the acute phase and lasting a few days or weeks. In the post-acute and chronic stage, it often gradually fades. In up to 30% of cases, however, it can persist for the entire lifespan (for a review, see Ramachandran and Hirstein, 1998). The phenomenon of the 'phantom' does not occur only following amputation of a limb: phantoms have been described following amputation of other organs, such as male genitalia and female breasts, or following spinal cord transaction or brachial plexus deafferentation. Phantoms have been described in cases of congenital absence of a limb (phocomelia, for a review, see Ramachandran and Rogers-Ramachandran, 2000). Phantoms may appear in two different forms, which often occur together: a real phantom, in the perception of the missing body part, including its spatial relationship to the rest of the body, and phantom sensations, such as paresthesias, pain, and so on. These sensations can be spontaneous or evoked by sensory, mostly tactile, stimulation. In arm amputees, sensations can be elicited by stimuli delivered not only to the stump and contiguous regions, but often following stimulations distant from the amputated body part: phantom sensations in lower limb and breast amputees can be elicited following facial stimulation.

A first hypothesis, that phantom sensations arise from the irritation of severed axon terminals in the stump caused by the presence of scar tissue and neuromas, has been discarded, among other reasons, because of the presence of phantoms in subjects with congenital absence of the limbs (phocomelia). According to Melzack (1990), phantom phenomena originate from the persisting activity of the somatosensory neural network, or neuromatrix components, that have been deprived of their normal inputs because of the loss of a body part and the brain's interpretation of this activity as originating from the lost part. An experimental support for this hypothesis comes from reports of patients in whom the 'phantom' disappears following a cerebral lesion, usually centered in the contralateral posterior parietal lobe affecting the neural representation of the missing part. In addition, different mechanisms are thought to contribute to the process of somatosensory reorganization in phantom limb patients. Deafferented cortical regions can react to previously ineffective inputs from intact body regions; contiguous cortical maps may take over the deafferented cortical area through an increase of new or normally silent synaptic connections. Alternatively, the reorganization process could be explained by a process of sprouting of new axon terminals from neurons supplying anatomically adjacent cortical areas.

Using magnetoencephalography (MEG), Yang et al. (1993) recorded the somatosensory map in the left hemisphere of a patient whose right arm had been amputated and compared it with the corresponding somatosensory map of the normal limb in the right hemisphere. The maps showed a striking asymmetry: the hand area in the left hemisphere could no longer be discerned, but this area could be activated by touching either the lower face or the map of his upper arm 10 cm above the line of amputation. In addition, electrical and magnetic cortical stimulations (TMS) and brain-imaging studies have revealed expansions of sensory and motor central representations of intact body segments at the expense of deafferented adjacent representations (for a review, see Berlucchi and Aglioti, 2001).

134 Specific skills

In conclusion, the investigation of phantoms represents an experimental opportunity to investigate how the functional architecture of the brain is able to reorganize itself, even in adulthood, through a process of the emergence of new neural connections, updating based on the changes in sensory inputs.

> Phantom limb phenomenon consists of the vivid perception of an amputated limb. This phenomenon, also observed following amputations of other body parts, has been interpreted as the effect of the persisting activity of the somatosensory neural network deprived of its normal inputs. Recent neuroimaging studies have revealed expansions of sensory and motor central representations of intact body segments at the expense of deafferented adjacent representations.

The changing-body representation

Body representation is not constant; body changes are age dependent and multisensory stimulation can temporarily modify body representation, as in the Pinocchio illusion (the feeling that one's nose is growing longer). Lackner (1988) described a phantom nose illusion (Pinocchio illusion) in subjects, mostly men (Burrack and Brugger, 2005), who had their biceps tendon vibrated while the fingers of the vibrated arm touched the tip of their nose. Apparently, the brain bridges the gap between fingers felt at a distance in front of one's face and the tip of one's nose by filling in the illusory gap with a prolongation of the nose (or, alternatively, of the fingers, as reported by some subjects).

A particular example of the plasticity of the body representation derives from the (few) studies of patients who underwent a gradual, long-lasting modification of the body, following body elongation through a surgical technique (Ilizarof and Deviatov, 1971). Applied mostly to achondroplasic subjects without brain lesions, this technique induces surgical lengthening of the arm, but leaves the afferent and efferent connections between the arm and the somatosensory cortices intact. Cimmino et al. (2013) explored the effect of arm lengthening in an achondroplasic woman, without brain lesions, who at the age of 29, was submitted to bilateral arm elongation of about 10 cm. Shortly after the surgery, and again one year later, the patient was submitted to a series of tests exploring tactile perception, implicit perceptual measure of body size (tactile distance judgment) and body representation. While no changes were found in primary tactile perception, the patient's arm neural representation was significantly modified in tactile distance and body image tests, supporting the view that cerebral body representation is a plastic, dynamic construct, modeled and remodeled by experience throughout the life.

> A particular example of the plasticity of the body representation derives from the (few) studies of patients who underwent a gradual, long-lasting modification of the body, following body elongation through a surgical technique. Following this procedure, a patient's arm neural representation was found to be significantly modified in tactile distance and body image tests.

Xenomelia

The robustness of the body integrity concept has been, however, challenged by the findings of some healthy persons affected by a disorder of body identity called xenomelia or aptomelia. Affected individuals feel the continuous experience of being 'overcomplete' in possessing four limbs and the resulting request is for surgical removal of the unwanted 'foreign' extremity (Brugger et al., 2013; Hilti et al., 2013). Neither neurological or neuropsychological deficits are found in these patients. Similarly, the presence of psychotic disorders has been ruled out. The availability of neuroimaging techniques has recently shifted the pendulum toward a brain-based theory of this disorder. McGeoch et al. (2011), in a MEG study in xenomelic patients, showed the superior parietal lobule unresponsive to tactile stimulation of specifically 'undesired' parts of the body. In a magnetic resonance imaging study by Hilti et al. (2013), xenomelic subjects showed reduced cortical thickness in the right superior parietal lobule and reduced cortical surface area in the primary and secondary somatosensory cortices in the inferior parietal lobule, as well as in the anterior insular cortex. According to Brugger et al. (2013) the insular abnormalities could be meaningful, since the right insular cortex is not only a key region for integrating interoceptive bodily feelings, but it is a critical region for the convergence of somesthesis and sexual arousal.

> Xenomelia consists in the continuous experience of being 'overcomplete' in possessing four limbs. The affected persons require surgical removal of the unwanted 'foreign' extremity. Neither neurological nor neuropsychological deficits are found in these patients. Similarly, the

presence of psychotic disorders has been ruled out. Neuroimaging studies report a reduced cortical surface area in the primary and secondary somatosensory cortices in the inferior parietal lobule, as well as in the anterior insular cortex.

SUMMARY

Through a dynamic process, the brain is able to build up and change a representation of the body and its relations to the external space. This representation, body schema, is supported by a specific neural substrate and can be altered following focal brain lesion. Once formed, a complete body representation can persist, despite loss of a body part, as in the phantom limb phenomenon. On the other hand, body representation can change following surgically induced body part modifications.

Bibliography

Berlucchi G. and Aglioti S.M. (2001), The body in the brain revisited. *Experimental Brain Research*, *200*(1): 25–35.

Bisiach E. (1999), Unilateral neglect and related disorders. In: Denes G. and Pizzamiglio L. (eds), *Handbook of clinical and experimental neuropsychology*, Hove (UK), Psychology Press, 479-496.

Brugger P., Lenggenhager B., Giummarra M.J. (2013), Xenomelia: a social neuroscience view of altered bodily self-consciousness. *Frontiers in Psychology*, *4*: 204.

Burrack A. and Brugger P. (2005), Individual differences in susceptibility to experimentally induced phantom sensations. *Body Image*, *2*(3): 307–313.

Cimmino R.L., Spitoni G., Serino A., Antonucci G., Catagni M., Camagni M., Haggard P., Pizzamiglio L. (2013), Plasticity of body representations after surgical arm elongation in an achondroplasic patient. *Restorative Neurology and Neuroscience*, *31*(3): 287–298.

Denes G. (ed) (1999), Disorders of Body Awawreness and Body Schema in : Denes G. and Pizzamiglio L. (eds), Handbook of clinical and experimental neuropsychology, pages 497-508. Hove (UK), Psychology Press.

Head H. and Holmes G. (1911–1912), Sensory disturbances in cerebral lesions. *Brain*, *34*: 102–254.

Hilti L.M., Hänggi J., Vitacco D.A., Kraemer B., Palla A., Luechinger R., Jäncke L., Brugger P. (2013), The desire for healthy limb amputation: structural brain correlates and clinical features of xenomelia. *Brain*, *136*(1): 318–329.

Ilizarov G.A. and Deviatov A.A. (1971), Surgical elongation of the leg. *Ortopediia travmatologiia i protezirovanie*, *32*(8): 20–25.

James W. (1890), *The Principles of Psychology*, New York, Holt.
Lackner J.R. (1988), Some proprioceptive influences on the perceptual representation of body shape and orientation. *Brain, 111*(2): 281–297.
McGeoch P.D., Brang D., Song T., Lee R.R., Huang M., Ramachandran V.S. (2011), Xenomelia: a new right parietal lobe syndrome. *Journal of Neurology Neurosurgery and Psychiatry, 82*(12): 1314–1349.
Meltzoff A.N. (1990), Towards a developmental cognitive science. The implications of cross-modal matching and imitation for the development of representation and memory in infancy. *Annals of the New York Academy of Sciences, 608*: 1–31.
Melzack R. (1990), Phantom limbs and the concept of a neuromatrix. *Trends in Neuroscience, 13*(3): 88–92.
Ramachandran V.S. and Hirstein W. (1998), The perception of phantom limbs. The D.O. Hebb lecture. *Brain, 121*(9): 1603–1630.
Ramachandran V.S. and Rogers-Ramachandran D. (2000), Phantom limbs and neural plasticity. *Archives of Neurology, 57*(3): 317–320.
Semenza C. and Goodglass H. (1985), Localization of body parts in brain injured subjects. *Neuropsychologia, 23*(2): 161–175.
Yang T.T., Gallen C.C., Schwartz B., Bloom F.E. (1993), Noninvasive somatosensory homunculus mapping in humans by using a large-array biomagnetometer. *Proceedings of the National Academy of Sciences USA, 90*: 3098–3102.

SECTION 4
The mechanisms of repair

7
SENSORY DEPRIVATION AND NEURAL PLASTICITY

The studies on capacity to overcome a severe, often total, inborn or very early acquired deficit of processing sensory information in one (visual or auditory) or many modalities have a long history and can be traced back to the seventeenth century to Molyneux (quoted by Sacks, 1993). The philosopher, whose wife was blind, questioned whether a man born blind would, after having his sight restored, be able to visually recognize shapes that he would have been able to discriminate previously by touch. The question rose a high debate, both among philosophers and biologists. Based on, however, scarce and feeble evidence, the experimenters concluded that the answer to Molyneux's problem, in short, was 'no'.

Much more fruitful was the search for how individuals deprived of one sensory modality could rely more efficiently on the remaining modalities to compensate for their deficit. Until a few years ago, the evidence was essentially anecdotal. The most often-quoted examples are congenital or early blind people who, like Louis Braille (1829), develop a heightened tactile sensibility in the finger tips, used for reading and writing in embossed paper (sensory compensation hypothesis). Often individuals who lack vision from birth develop enhanced functional and processing capabilities in the unimpaired sensory modalities (enhanced compensation, Röder and Neville, 2003), up to a level similar or even higher than that shown by typically developed subjects. If the process of compensation fails, sensory deprived individuals not only are inefficient in the deprived modality tasks, but perform at lower levels even in tasks not involved in the deprived modality (perceptual deficiency hypothesis, Voss et al., 2010).

The knowledge of the mechanisms of adjusting and recovering the lost sensory functions has greatly improved in the last few years, thanks to the advancement of biotechnology, allowing a deeper knowledge of brain mechanisms at the base of compensatory plasticity. At the same time, the possibility of restoring, sometimes at surprising levels, the lost sensory function through the application of sensory substitution devices (SSDs) such as cochlear implants (CI) or visual-auditory devices has greatly influenced our knowledge of restorative plasticity.

In the following section, we will review the anatomo-functional basis of compensatory plasticity and sensory substitution.

Cross-modal and unimodal plasticity in sensory impaired subjects

Neural plastic changes following sensory deprivation can impinge on sensory areas of impaired or spared modalities (unimodal plasticity) or on polymodal association areas (polymodal plasticity).

Unimodal plasticity

The neural implications of unimodal plasticity can manifest in two ways. According to the sensory compensation hypothesis, the brain areas serving the impaired sensory modality may develop the ability to process perceptual inputs from one or more of the intact sensory systems (reallocation account). Sensory cortices associated with the deprived modality can be 'colonized' by the remaining modalities, as found in experimental animals (see Bavelier and Neville, 2002, for review) and human subjects. Based on a number of studies comparing brain activity of congenitally blind (CB) and sighted individuals (SI), the current prevailing view is that visual deafferentation results in a reliable recruitment of the occipital cortex for non-visual sensory processing to compensate for the challenging condition secondary to visual deprivation. Collignon et al. (2011), in an fMRI study, compared the brain activity of CB and SI in processing either the spatial or the pitch properties of sounds carrying information in both domains. In comparison to SI, CB showed a substantial recruitment of the occipital cortex for sound processing, involving either auditory or spatial analysis. In addition, the study found that the regions activated by auditory spatial tasks in CB subjects were the same ones activated by SI by visuo-spatial processing. On this basis, the authors suggest that plasticity in CB may be constrained by the innate disposition of a specific cortical area to selectively serve a particular function; alternatively, the cortical areas of the remaining senses may acquire enhanced functional and processing capabilities (remaining senses hypertrophy account).

According to the sensory compensation hypothesis (for a review, see Pavani and Bottari, 2012), a hypertrophy of the spared sensory cortices can occur following unimodal deprivation. An increase of the number of neurons that respond to somato-sensory and auditory information has been found in rats, cats and monkeys visually deprived at birth (Bavelier and Neville, 2002). Similarly, a hypertrophy of the facial vibrissae, and a corresponding expansion of their central representation in the somatosensory cortex of binocularly deprived kittens, enhancing their processing capabilities, has been reported by Rauschecker (1995).

Multimodal restorative plasticity

Integration of information from multiple senses is fundamental to perception and cognition. The primate and human brains contain some anatomically restricted areas whose neurons, in contrast to primary sensory areas, receive and integrate inputs from multiple sensory modalities (visual, tactile and auditory). These polisensory or multimodal areas have been located in the mammalian brain at cortical and subcortical levels. Experimental evidence suggests that these areas are involved in representing visual, tactile and auditory space near the body and in controlling defensive movements (see Graziano and Gross, 1993, 1998, for a review).

A crucial role of these multimodal brain areas has been furthermore implied in the development and enhancement of the remaining sensory modalities following deprivation of a single modality capability through a process of functional reorganization. This process implies a reorganization of the brain functions that varies across neural systems and according to the nature and time of occurrence of altered experience.

Several studies convincingly show that higher-order auditory areas process non-auditory stimuli in deaf animals. For example, it has been demonstrated that recruitment of auditory areas, normally involved in sound localization, underlies enhanced peripheral localization of visual stimuli in deaf animals (Butler and Lomber, 2013). As with that observed in congenital deaf cats (Lomber et al., 2010), early deafened humans show some visual abilities that exceed those reported in normal hearing subjects, mainly expressed as enhanced reactivity to visual events and spatial attention skills (Bavelier et al. 2006; Dye and Bavelier, 2010). Similarly, congenitally blind people are able to navigate independently in space, to recognize objects, to learn how to use utensils, to catch other people's intentions and feelings; very often they make sighted people notice some specific sensorial aspects that they are unable to detect, such as a specific timbre of the voice that conveys information of one's feeling or a sudden mild change of temperature (Ricciardi and Pietrini, 2011).

Mechanisms of multimodal plasticity

Research on the mechanisms that are involved in the process of cross-modal plasticity not only can be central to understanding the differentiation and role of specific sensory systems, but can have important clinical applications, such as predicting the success of sensory implants (including cochlear). The process of reorganization of cross-modal plasticity can involve changes of connectivity at different levels, subcortical and cortical (see Figure 7.1).

The process is not, however, uniform across species and ages: some mechanisms are available only in developing organisms, such as changes in long-range subcortical connections: blind mole rats from the inferior colliculus[1] instead of projecting only to the auditory center of the thalamus, it

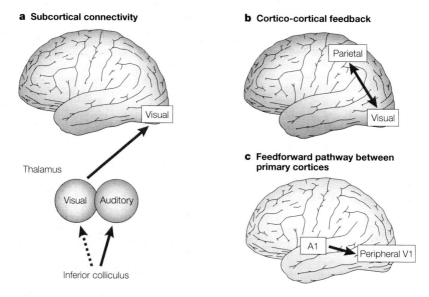

FIGURE 7.1 Possible mechanisms at the system level for cross-modal plasticity; see text. Reprinted by permission from Macmillan Publishers Ltd: Daphne Bavelier and Helen J. Neville (2002). Cross-modal plasticity: where and how? *Nature Reviews Neuroscience 3*, 443–452.

also project to the visual thalamus resulting in the recruitment of the visual cortex by auditory stimuli.(see Figure 7.1a) (see Neville and Bavelier, 2002, for a review). Other mechanisms are available at all times, even in the adults (as in mature primates), such as stabilization of long-range cortico-cortical connections between sensory modalities (see Figure 7.1b). Finally, Falchier et al. (2002) have found the presence of direct projections from the auditory cortex to peripheral visual area 17, suggesting important consequences for higher visual functions of area 17, including multimodal integration at early stages of the visual cortical pathway (see Figure 7.1c).

> Neural plastic changes following sensory deprivation can impinge on sensory areas of impaired or spared modality through a process of unimodal or polymodal plasticity. Unimodal plasticity refers to the process by which the brain areas serving the impaired sensory modality may develop the ability to process perceptual inputs from one or more of the intact sensory systems. Alternatively, a complex process of functional reorganization of multimodal sensory areas can enhance the remaining sensory modalities following deprivation of a single modality. Reorganization varies across neural systems and according to the nature and time of occurrence of altered experience.

Preverbal deafness, cochlear implants and speech and language development

Preverbal deafness

Congenital or preverbal deafness (PVD) is defined as the hearing loss that is present at birth and, consequently, before speech development. It is the most prevalent sensory-neural disorder in developed countries and its incidence is estimated between 1 and 3 children per 1,000 newborns, of which 20 to 30% have profound hearing loss. About 50% of the cases are of genetic origin. Infectious or prenatal diseases and other causes account for the remaining 50% (see Kral and O'Donoghue, 2010, for a review).

PVD can result from a defective transmission at any point between the outer ear and the auditory cortex (see Figure 7.2), and it is now possible to detect whether the damage affects the cochlea or the auditory nerve.

The great majority of congenital deafness is a consequence of a sensory-neural loss caused by abnormalities in the hair cells of the organ of Corti[2] in the cochlea.

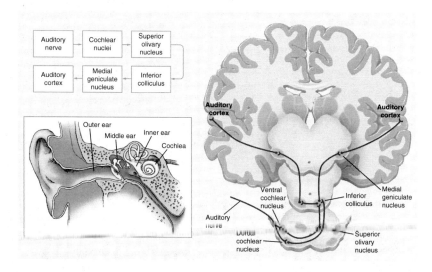

FIGURE 7.2 General picture of the auditory route (from Denes, 2011). (Adapted from Bear, Connors & Paradiso, Bear, M. F., Connors, B. W., & Paradiso, M. A. (1996). Neuroscience: Exploring the brain. Baltimore: Williams & Wilkins.1996 in Denes Talking Heads, Psychology Press 2011.)

PVD has a profound impact on the anatomical and functional properties of the auditory system, impairing the cortical development of auditory areas and leading to atypical organization of the auditory nervous system and its interaction with other sensory areas (visual and somatosensory). At the level of Heschl's gyrus,[3] shorter dendrites bearing fewer synaptic spines were found in animals deafened at birth (McMullen and Glaser, 1988; McMullen et al., 1988). In humans, recent neuroimaging studies showed that early auditory deprivation can change the neural pattern of auditory cortex. In an MRI study, Smith et al. (2011) found that PVD subjects show increased grey matter and decreased white matter volumes in anterior Heschl's gyrus compared with the normal hearing subjects. In addition, the PVD group do not exhibit the typical L > R *planum temporale*[4] asymmetry pattern that the hearing subjects show. This pattern may represent a sign of abnormal cortical development in primary sensory cortex, similar to that found in animal models of sensory deprivation. After critical maturation and language development steps, the auditory cortex of PVD subjects is colonized by visual cells. In addition, cross-modal pathways stabilize, and the auditory association areas in superior temporal regions can no longer be recruited by auditory stimulation, even though primary regions usually respond to electrical stimulation of the auditory nerve (Nishimura et al. 1999).

If not rehabilitated, PVD can have a profound negative impact that extends beyond the hearing loss. No sign of visual hyper-compensation has been found in performing basic visual tasks such as color discrimination, brightness and contrast sensitivity (for a review, see Pavani and Röder, 2012). The impairment is not, however, limited to basic visual tasks, but extends to more complex skills such as a deficit of short term memory, leading to a difficulty in visual attention and visual sequence learning tasks (see Möller et al., 2007).

The deleterious effect of PVD can be alleviated, bypassing the anatomical damage through the insertion of cochlear implants or through the development of language modalities not involving the auditory modality, such as sign language (see chapter 4). Both processes involve a reorganization of innate language networks through a process of neural plasticity.

Cochlear implants and auditory plasticity

Cochlear implants (CI) are small, surgically implanted, electronic devices, about the size of a cardiac pacemaker, that are designed to restore a sense of sound to individuals with severe to profound deafness. Although the first cochlear implants, developed more than 30 years ago, did little more than provide a sense of awareness of sounds and cadence, modern cochlear implant systems have become highly effective at providing the ability for patients to perceive and understand speech at such a level that they are now considered to be standard of care in the treatment of children with severe to total sensory-neural hearing loss (for a review, see Kral and O' Donoughe, 2010).

CI can restore hearing, bypassing the non-functional organ of Corti. They electrically stimulate the undamaged auditory nerve fibers that survive the loss of hair cells and contain several speech-encoding algorithms that transform sound into electrical stimuli (Dorman and Dahlstrom, 2004). CI can be inserted into one or both ears, but bilateral implants can substantially improve sound localization and ability to hear speech against background noise (Lovett et al., 2010).

Following implantation, early (before the development of language) cochlear-implanted children can reorganize their auditory cortex similar to hearing children: recording of auditory evoked potentials[5] revealed principal activity from the auditory cortex in normal hearing and early implanted children. In addition, longer cochlear implant experience has been related to enhanced recruitment of the auditory cortex (Pantev et al., 2006; Sandmann et al., 2009) and higher functional specialization of the auditory system. On the contrary, in PVD children implanted at later age (around 7 year old)) ,auditory stimulation activated the parieto-temporal cortex demonstrating reorganized cortical pathways (Gilley et al., 2008). Reorganization of central auditory pathways is thus limited by the age at which implantation occurs, and may help explain the benefits and limitations of implantation in congenitally deaf children. Early implanted children reach a remarkable success in acquiring spoken language, especially if exposed to enriched language environments and supported by committed parents and caregivers. On the other side, implantation in later childhood results in successively less benefit and implantation at the elementary school age or later, does not lead to good speech understanding. Late-implanted subjects can detect the auditory stimulus but the majority of them are not able to discriminate the complex sounds of language appropriately in everyday situations, even after many years of implant use. The consequence is substantially compromised speech understanding and oral language learning (for a review, see Kral and Sharma, 2012).

The time of restoring hearing in early infancy coincides with the period during which language develops, independent of the modality of experience (including the visual modality, Mayberry et al., 2002) and thus the contemporary availability of visual and auditory inputs could be essential, as in normal developing children, to form a modality independent neural network, specific for language processing (Leonard et al., 2012).

Age is not, however, the only predictor of the success of implants; the availability of neuroimaging techniques has considerably enriched the chances of assessing the benefit of the procedure. Lee et al. (2007) correlated preoperative glucose metabolism, as measured by F-18 fluorodeoxyglucose positron emission tomography (PET), with individual speech perception performance assessed 3 years after implantation, in 22 PVD children between 1 and 11 years. They reported that speech scores were selectively associated with enhanced metabolic activity in the left prefrontal cortex and decreased metabolic activity in right Heschl's gyrus and in the posterior superior temporal sulcus. These results reinforce the notion that implantation should be performed as early as possible to prevent cross-modal takeover of auditory regions and suggest that rehabilitation strategies may be more efficient if they capitalize on general cognitive functions supported by supramodal cognitive areas, like the frontal ones. Similarly, Strelnikov et al. (2013) found that rate of auditory recovery 6 months after unilateral implant in the adult post-lingually deaf could be predicted shortly after implantation by the amount of neural activity induced by a speech processing task. A positive correlation was found between activation of areas of visual cortex and in the postero-temporal cortex, crucial for audio-visual integration and auditory speech recovery.

Preverbal deafness (PVD) affects 1–3 children per 1,000 newborns. Its origin is mostly genetic and it is the consequence of an impaired neural transmission at any point between the outer ear and the auditory cortex. PVD has a profound impact on the anatomical and functional properties of the auditory system, impairing the cortical development of auditory areas and leading to atypical organization of the auditory nervous system and its interaction with other sensory areas.

Early implantation of electronic devices (cochlear implants) can restore a sense of sound to individuals with severe to profound deafness, leading to a reorganization of the auditory cortex that is similar to hearing children's. Success of implant depends on the year of implantation: early implanted children reach a remarkable success in acquiring spoken language, while Implantation in later childhood results in successively less benefit. Late-implanted subjects can detect the auditory stimulus, but the majority of them are not able to discriminate and identify the complex sounds of language.

The mechanisms of neural plasticity in congenitally blind subjects

The primary visual cortex (area 17 or visual striate cortex) of primates receives a unique thalamic input from the lateral geniculate nucleus, and its maturation requires constant interactions with visual inputs. Since the seminal work of Wiesel and Hubel (1963), it has been known that there is a critical period early in life during which visual input is necessary for normal development. In kittens deprived of normal visual experience in one eye (suturation of one eyelid) during the first 3 months of the cat's life, the circuitry of the neurons in the visual cortex is irreversibly altered: when the kitten reaches adulthood and the eyelid is opened again, recordings of the electrophysiological activity of cells in layers of lateral geniculate bodies fed by the deprived eye was diminished and marked histological changes were present in layers fed by the deprived eye.

A similar pattern has been found in humans: lack of visual input leads to significant structural and functional changes in the visual pathways of blind subjects, including grey and white matter atrophy of the cortical visual areas (for a review, see Kupers and Ptito, 2011). These changes are massive, with volume reductions ranging from 20% in extrastriate visual areas up to 25% in the primary visual cortex (Ptito et al., 2008). Veraart et al. (1990), in a PET study, found that glucose utilization was decreased in the visual cortex of blind human subjects who became blind after completion of visual development ('late blindness'). In contrast, in subjects who became blind early in life ('early blindness'), metabolism in the visual cortex was elevated, comparable to that of normal subjects studied with the eyes open. This difference between early and late blind subjects might reflect, according to Veraart et al., the persistence, in early blindness, of supranumerary synapses which would escape the normal developmental decrease in synaptic density during infancy and facilitate the involvement of the visual cortex in non-visual tasks.

Despite their anatomical reduction, the visual areas of blind individuals can be engaged in several non-visual tasks, ranging from auditory-spatial processing (Collignon et al., 2011) to reading, through connections with auditory and somatosensory systems. Sadato et al. (1996), in a PET study, measured the activation of occipital cortex during tactile discrimination tasks in sighted subjects and in Braille readers blinded in early life. While normal controls showed a deactivation of primary and secondary visual areas, an activation of these areas was found in blind subjects during tactile tasks. In particular, CB subjects showed an activation in Braille reading tasks of the VWFA (Cohen et al., 2000), a visual area that in sighted people is selectively activated for letters over other complex visual categories (e.g. faces).

> Congenital blindness leads to significant structural and functional changes in the visual pathways, including grey and white matter atrophy of the cortical visual areas. These areas, however, can be engaged in several non-visual tasks, ranging from auditory-spatial processing to tactile processing, as in Braille reading.

Visual substitution sensory devices in blindness

At odds with PVD, whose deleterious effects can be alleviated by CI, the availability of sensory aids that can aid in developing visual processing in blind persons is, at present, scarce.

Visual neuroprostheses are invasive and their applicability is restricted to particular etiologies. In addition, the cost-benefit ratio is poor, given their extremely high cost in comparison to their poor resolution and visual field. Finally, a number of technical problems limit their value; the resulting visual acuity is lower than predicted because the translation from technical resolution to functional acuity is highly complex (for a review, see Striem-Amit, Guendelman and Amedi, 2012).

Visual rehabilitation may alternatively be, at least in part, aided by the use of sensory substitution devices (SSDs), which enable the blind to see through tactile or auditory modality.

More than 40 years ago, Bach-y-Rita (for a review, see Bach-y-Rita and Kercel, 2003) developed tactile vision substitution systems (TVSS) to deliver visual information from a TV camera to arrays of stimulators in contact with the skin of one of several parts of the body. Mediated by the skin receptors, energy transduced from any of a variety of artificial sensors (e.g. camera, pressure sensor, displacement) is encoded as neural pulse trains. In this manner, the brain is able to perceive environmental information as 'visual' images that originate in a TV camera. Indeed, after sufficient training, blind subjects reported experiencing the images in space, instead of on the skin.

In an fMRI study, Striem-Amit et al. (2012) trained a group of CB adult Braille expert readers to read through a visual-to-auditory SSD by which high resolution visual information is extracted from complex soundscapes (Bach-y-Rita and Kercel, 2003). After a brief training, CB subjects learned to 'read' through this novel modality. Reading was concomitant to a specific activation of the visual word form area (VWFA) These findings are particularly important in the present context, since they not only show a supramodal activity of the VWFA, irrespective of the modality of presentation, but suggest that a process of neural plasticity can occur well beyond the end of critical period and following a short (two-hour) training.

In conclusion, the above findings show that the visual areas of early blind subjects are widely cross-modally reorganized, becoming part of a network wired to serve specific functions, from auditory localization to reading.

SUMMARY

Early sensory deprivation in visual or auditory modality involves a process of neural reorganization through a process of unimodal or multimodal restorative plasticity. The process can be characterized by enhancing the activity of intact sensory areas or by a changing the pattern of connectivity between different sensory modalities.

Application of cochlear implants to pre-verbally deaf children can significantly improve their language development. The success is, however, age-dependent, with early implanted children reaching a normal language processing ability.

Notes

1 The inferior colliculus is a part of the midbrain that serves as a principal auditory center for the body, projecting to the medial geniculate body of the thalamus.
2 The organ of Corti is part of the cochlea of the inner ear and is provided with hair cells or auditory sensory cells.
3 Heschl's gyrus or Heschl's convolution, located in transverse temporal gyri, is the area of the primary auditory cortex.
4 The human planum temporale is a roughly triangular region located posteriorly to the primary auditory area. It is, on average, larger in the left hemisphere, suggesting it may have a special role in language processing and cerebral dominance (Geschwind and Levitsky, 1968).
5 Recording of cortical auditory evoked potential provides information about maturation of auditory pathways terminating in the auditory cortex, and reflects the cortical activity mediated by cortico-thalamic connections.

Bibliography

Bach-Y-Rita P. and Kercel S.W. (2003), Sensory substitution and the human-machine interface. *Trends in Cognitive Sciences*, 7(12): 541–546.
Bavelier D., Dye M.W., Hauser P.C. (2006), Do deaf individuals see better? *Trends in Cognitive Sciences*, 10(11): 512–518.
Bavelier D. and Neville H.J. (2002), Cross-modal plasticity: where and how? *Nature Reviews Neuroscience*, 3(6): 443–452.
Braille L. (1829), *Procédé pour écrire les paroles, la musique et le plain-chant au moyen de points, à l'usage des aveugles et disposé pour eux*. Paris.
Butler B.E. and Lomber S.G. (2013), Functional and structural changes throughout the auditory system following congenital and early-onset deafness: implications for hearing restoration. *Frontiers in Systems Neuroscience*, 7: 92.
Cohen L., Dehaene S., Naccache L., Lehéricy S., Dehaene-Lambertz G., Hénaff M.A., Michel F. (2000), The visual word form area: spatial and temporal characterization of an initial stage of reading in normal subjects and posterior split-brain patients. *Brain*, 123(2): 291–307.
Collignon O., Vandewalle G., Voss P., Albouy G., Charbonneau G., Lassonde M., Lepore F. (2011), Functional specialization for auditory-spatial processing in the occipital cortex of congenitally blind humans. *Proceedings of the National Academy of Sciences USA*, 108(11): 4435–4440.
Dorman M.F. and Dahlstrom L. (2004), Speech understanding by cochlear-implant patients with different left- and right-ear electrode arrays. *Ear and Hearing*, 25(2): 191–194.
Dye M.W. and Bavelier D. (2010), Attentional enhancements and deficits in deaf populations: an integrative review. *Restorative Neurology and Neuroscience*, 28(2): 181–192.
Falchier A., Clavagnier S., Barone P., Kennedy H. (2002), Anatomical evidence of multimodal integration in primate striate cortex. *Journal of Neuroscience*, 22(13): 5749–5759.

Geschwind N. and Levitsky W. (1968), Human brain: left-right asymmetries in temporal speech region. *Science, 161*(3837): 186–187.

Gilley P.M., Sharma A., Dorman M.F. (2008), Cortical reorganization in children with cochlear implants. *Brain Reseach, 1239*: 56–65.

Graziano M.S. and Gross C.G. (1993), A bimodal map of space: somatosensory receptive fields in the macaque putamen with corresponding visual receptive fields. *Experimental Brain Research, 97*(1): 96–109.

Graziano M.S. and Gross C.G. (1998), Spatial maps for the control of movement. *Current Opinion in Neurobiology, 8*(2): 195–201.

Kral A. and O'Donoghue G.M. (2010), Profound deafness in childhood. *New England Journal of Medicine, 363*(15): 1438–1450.

Kral A. and Sharma A. (2012), Developmental neuroplasticity after cochlear implantation. *Trends in Neurosciences, 35*(2): 111–122.

Kupers R. and Ptito M. (2011), Insights from darkness: what the study of blindness has taught us about brain structure and function. *Progress in Brain Research, 192*: 17–31.

Lee H.J., Giraud A.L., Kang E., Oh S.H., Kang H., Kim C.S., Lee D.S. (2007), Cortical activity at rest predicts cochlear implantation outcome. *Cerebral Cortex, 17*(4): 909–917.

Leonard M.K., Ferjan Ramirez N., Torres C., Travis K.E., Hatrak M., Mayberry R.I., Halgren E. (2012), Signed words in the congenitally deaf evoke typical late lexicosemantic responses with no early visual responses in left superior temporal cortex. *Journal of Neuroscience, 32*(28): 9700–9705.

Lomber S.G., Meredith M.A., Kral A. (2010), Cross-modal plasticity in specific auditory cortices underlies visual compensations in the deaf. *Nature Neuroscience, 13*(11): 1421–1427.

Lovett R.E., Kitterick P.T., Hewitt C.E., Summerfield A.Q. (2010), Bilateral or unilateral cochlear implantation for deaf children: an observational study. *Archives of Disease in Childhood, 95*(2): 107–112.

Mayberry R.I., Lock E., Kazmi H. (2002), Linguistic ability and early language exposure. *Nature, 417*(6884): 38.

Mcmullen N.T. and Glaser E.M. (1988), Auditory cortical responses to neonatal deafening: pyramidal neuron spine loss without changes in growth or orientation. *Experimental Brain Research, 72*(1): 195–200.

Mcmullen N.T., Goldberger B., Suter C.M., Glaser E.M. (1988), Neonatal deafening alters nonpyramidal dendrite orientation in auditory cortex: a computer microscope study in the rabbit. *Journal of Comparative Neurology, 267*(1): 92–106.

Möller M.P., Tomblin J.B., Yoshinaga-Itano C., Mcdonald Connor C., Jerger S. (2007), Current state of knowledge: language and literacy of children with hearing impairment. *Ear & Hearing, 28*: 740–753.

Neville and Bavelier D. (2002), Human brain plasticity: evidence from sensory deprivation and altered language experience. *Progress in Brain Research, 138*: 177–188.

Nishimura H., Hashikawa K., Doi K., Iwaki T., Watanabe Y., Kusuoka H., Nishimura T., Kubo T. (1999), Sign language 'heard' in the auditory cortex. *Nature, 397*(6715): 116.

Pantev C., Dinnesen A., Ross B., Wollbrink A., Knief A. (2006), Dynamics of auditory plasticity after cochlear implantation: a longitudinal study. *Cerebral Cortex, 16*(1): 31–36.

Pavani F. and Bottari D. (2012), Visual abilities in individuals with profound deafness: a critical review. In: Murray M.M. and Wallace M.T. (eds), *The neural bases of multisensory processes – frontiers in neuroscience*, Boca Raton (FL), Crc Press, 22.

Pavani F. and Röder B. (2012), Crossmodal plasticity as a consequence of sensory loss: insights from blindness and deafness. In: Stein B.E. (ed), *The new handbook of multisensory processes*, Cambridge (MA), Mit Press, 737–759.

Ptito M., Schneider F.C., Paulson O.B., Kupers R. (2008), Alterations of the visual pathways in congenital blindness. *Experimental Brain Research, 187*(1): 41–49.

Rauschecker J.P. (1995), Compensatory plasticity and sensory substitution in the cerebral cortex. *Trends in Neurosciences, 18*(1): 36–43.

Ricciardi E and Pietrini P. (2011), New light from the dark: what blindness can teach us about brain function. *Current Opinion in Neurology, 24*(4): 357–363.

Röder B. and Neville H.J., (2003), Developmental functional plasticity. In: Grafman J. and Robertson I.H. (eds), *Handbook of neuropsychology*, (2nd edition), Oxford, Elsevier Science, 9: 231–270.

Sacks O. (1993), To see and not see: a neurologist's notebook. *New Yorker*, May 10, 1993, 59–73.

Sadato N., Pascual-Leone A., Grafman J., Ibañez V., Deiber M.P., Dold G., Hallett M. (1996), Activation of the primary visual cortex by Braille reading in blind subjects. *Nature, 380*(6574): 526–528.

Sandmann P., Eichele T., Buechler M., Debener S., Jäncke L., Dillier N., Hugdahl K., Meyer M. (2009), Evaluation of evoked potentials to dyadic tones after cochlear implantation. *Brain, 132*(7): 1967–1979.

Smith K.M., Mecoli M.D., Altaye M., Komlos M., Maitra R., Eaton K.P., Egelhoff J.C., Holland S.K. (2011), Morphometric differences in the Heschl's gyrus of hearing impaired and normal hearing infants. *Cerebral Cortex, 21*: 991–998.

Strelnikov K., Rouger J., Demonet J.F., Lagleyre S., Fraysse B., Deguine O., Barone P. (2013), Visual activity predicts auditory recovery from deafness after adult cochlear implantation. *Brain, 136*(12): 3682–3695.

Striem-Amit E., Guendelman M., Amedi A. (2012), 'Visual' acuity of the congenitally blind using visual-to-auditory sensory substitution. *PLoS One, 7*(3): e33136.

Veraart C., De Volder A.G., Wanet-Defalque M.C., Bol A., Michel C., Goffinet A.M. (1990), Glucose utilization in human visual cortex is abnormally elevated in blindness of early onset but decreased in blindness of late onset. *Brain Research, 510*(1): 115–121.

Voss P., Collignon O., Lassonde M., Lepore F. (2010), Adaptation to sensory loss. *Wiley Interdisciplinary Reviews Cognitive Science, 1*(3): 308–328.

Wiesel T.N. and Hubel D.H. (1963), Single-cell responses in striate cortex of kittens deprived of vision in one eye. *Journal of Neurophysiology, 26*: 1003–1017.

8
PLASTICITY AND RECOVERY OF BRAIN DAMAGE

Despite its anatomical complexity and the innumerable functions it carries out, the brain is relatively resistant to noxious factors of different origin and, when damaged, capable of recovery – sometimes of considerable degree. This latter process could be considered, *prima facie*, counterintuitive, because, as detailed in the preceding chapters, the process of anatomical regeneration is, unlike other biological tissues, at best, limited.

On the contrary, work in animal models and observations in brain damaged persons have unequivocally demonstrated that the process of recovery of neurological functions, following a diffuse or, more often, focal damage, is possible not only in the developmental period, whose plasticity is higher, but also along the entire lifespan. This later-in-life recovery occurs by way of changing structure and function in response to afferent signals in a way previously observed only in the developing brain (Ward and Cohen, 2004).

While the outcome of behavioral changes represents the golden standard for assessing the efficacy of any spontaneous or treatment-guided neural recovery process, different levels can be applied to the analysis of brain mechanisms involved in post-lesional brain plasticity. Some methods are invasive, ranging from *in vivo* cellular recording or examination of synaptic changes (Kolb and Gibb, 2010), to the study of the reorganization of cortical topography following retinal lesion in adult animals (for a review, see Gilbert and Li, 2012). When, however, the analysis is applied to humans, the level must be forcefully limited to non-invasive methods, such as brain imaging or electrophysiological techniques. In addition, while in animals the details of brain damage (extent, site and age at which the cerebral damage has been inflicted) can be exactly mapped, in humans the process of recovery can be studied only following ischemic, traumatic or neoplastic damage, whose extent and boundaries can be only loosely defined. In addition, while in animals the recovery process can be observed in different skills, ranging from motor improvement to spatial orientation and learning, using *ad hoc* tests that are administered before and following the onset of damage, the pattern is different in humans. Most often, the pre-lesional level of the impaired skill is not available and the study of the recovery is, in practice, limited to few skills – mostly motor functions and language, which show the most disabling and frequent symptoms – following the onset of a stroke (also known as a cerebro-vascular accident, CVA). Only a tiny minority of studies has been devoted to the plastic changes following different pathologies, mostly affecting sensory input impairment (see chapter 7). Finally, while the details of treatment (number of sessions, amount of stimuli) can be easily recorded in animals, the details of treatment and the interaction with other tasks performed in humans are often unclear and difficult to quantify.

Factors influencing recovery

Recovery after an acquired brain lesion is not a uniform process, but is subjected to the influence of several factors. In particular, the process of neural plasticity cannot be fully understood without taking into consideration different factors, often interacting, such as the age at which the damage occurs or the nature, extent and temporal pattern (sudden or slow growing) of the injury.

> Despite the process of anatomical regeneration being limited, the brain, when damaged, can show considerable capacities for recovering its lost functions. Several factors influence the recovery process, whose mechanisms are, however, not fully clarified. Research in the human species limits itself to the contribution of clinical observations supplemented by the results of neuroimaging studies.

Age

The issue of the effect of age on cerebral recovery is heavily influenced by at least two interacting factors: vulnerability versus enhanced plasticity in the immature or developing brain and equipotentiality versus innate cerebral specialization. Woods and Carey (1979) reported that damage in the first year of life is followed by a better neural and functional reorganization than a late-acquired damage. In contrast, several studies (for a review, see Pavlovic et al., 2006; Keenan et al., 2007) examining the outcome of focal and diffuse lesions in infancy suggest that damage during this time may be particularly detrimental, given its high degree of vulnerability.

As far as the second issue, a first view posits that the young brain is 'equipotential', with both hemispheres capable of carrying out functions that in the adult brain have a neurological basis mostly restricted to one hemisphere. This hypothesis has been supported by the lack of gross language impairment in children submitted to hemispherectomy for the treatment of intractable epilepsy, irrespective of the hemisphere removal (Basser, 1962). On the other side, the innate specialization position argues that cognitive functions, language *par excellence*, have a predetermined innate localization, critical for their acquisition and representation. Accordingly, language impairment should be expected following damage to specific, predetermined areas, irrespective of the time of lesion onset. A compromise position suggests that brain development is characterized by increasing age-dependent specialization (Johnson, 2001, 2005). Experimental support of this view derives from the results of neuroimaging studies demonstrating increasing lateralization of language function with age (Szaflarski et al., 2006). Along the same lines, Vargha-Khadem et al. (1994), among others, have reported that in some instances of early left brain insult, the non-dominant hemisphere can mediate language, albeit with high risk of delayed emergence and imperfect recovery (see chapter 4).

Anderson and colleagues (2011), in their careful review on neural plasticity after early brain insult, suggest that the outcome is underpinned by a range of complex neural processes, which interact with predetermined mechanisms and environmental influences. They conclude that neither enhanced infant neural plasticity nor early vulnerability are able to predict, in isolation, the consequences of the brain damage and the mechanisms and amount of recovery.

> It is widely held that the outcome of the recovery process following a brain lesion in the first years of life is better in comparison to that following damage in adult life. This peculiarity could be the consequence of two interacting factors: a higher degree of plasticity in the developing brain coupled with a lesser degree of cortical specialization, with both hemispheres capable of carrying out functions that in the adult brain have a neurological basis mostly restricted to one hemisphere.

Nature, extent and site of lesion

The initial severity of the lesion (in adult men, mostly of cerebrovascular origin) and the size and extent of the lesion are considered, in general, the most reliable indicators of prognosis following spontaneous or therapy-induced recovery (Maas et al., 2012; Plowman et al., 2012). However, there are some important exceptions. Riley et al. (2011), for example, found that, in subjects with chronic stroke, the amount of damage of the white matter tracts descending from the primary motor cortex and dorsal pre-motor cortex to the spinal cord correlated better with motor gains than lesion volume or baseline clinical status.

The contribution of demographic factors, such as gender or handedness, as explanatory variables for prognosis appears to contribute less to the prediction of final outcome (for a review, see Geranmayeh et al., 2014).

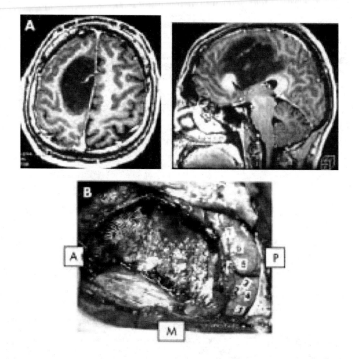

FIGURE 8.1 (A) Preoperative T1-weighted axial and sagittal MRI showing a left temporal low-grade gliomas. (B) Post-operative axial and sagittal. Reproduced from Duffau H., Capelle L., Denvil D., Sichez N., Gatignol P., Lopes M., et al. (2003), Functional recovery after surgical resection of low grade gliomas in eloquent brain: hypothesis of brain compensation. *Journal of Neurology, Neurosurgery & Psychiatry*, 74: 901–7 with permission from BMJ Publishing Group Ltd.

While acute ischemic or hemorrhagic focal cerebrovascular events give rise to immediately detectable deficits, followed, in most of the cases, only by a limited recovery (see sections 8.3.1 and 8.3.2), some slow cerebral lesions of neoplastic origin (low-grade gliomas, LGG) show a different impact on the type and extent of cerebral damage. While the onset of an acute, focal vascular lesion is followed by elementary or cognitive deficits congruent with the site and extent of the anatomical damage, some LGG patients appear normal or only slightly impaired both preoperatively and after tumor resection (see Figures 8.1 and 8.2), even in the presence of large cortical lesions involving highly specialized, 'eloquent' areas. These data, which *prima facie* seem counterintuitive, show that different plastic processes can compensate

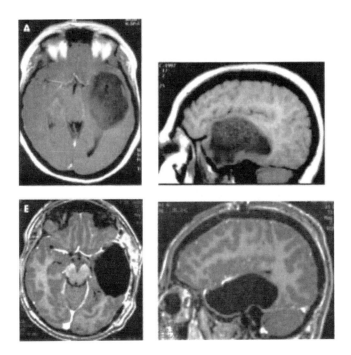

FIGURE 8.2 (A) Preoperative T1 weighted axial and sagittal MRI showing a left (dominant hemisphere) temporal low grade glioma in a patient without any neurological deficit. (E) Postoperative axial and sagittal MRI, after the second operation, showing a total glioma resection. The patient was not clinically worse. Reproduced from Duffau H., Denvil D., Capelle L. (2002), Long term reshaping of language, sensory, and motor maps after glioma resection: a new parameter to integrate in the surgical strategy. *Journal of Neurology, Neurosurgery & Psychiatry*, 72: 511–6 with permission from BMJ Publishing Group Ltd.

for the effect of a slow-growing cerebral lesion in comparison to the effects of sudden CVA damage. According to Desmurget et al. (2007), this pattern can be explained by a process of preoperative cerebral reorganization: given the slow, infiltrative character of the lesion, a redistribution of functions in the areas adjacent to the tumor or a recruitment of a new neural network in the same or contralateral hemisphere can take place, limiting the effects of the primary damage.

> The recovery of functions is negatively correlated to the size of the lesion. Slow-growing lesions of neoplastic origin allow a better process of cerebral reorganization than vascular lesions of sudden onset.

The mechanisms of recovery

It is widely held that two types of recovery following acute non-progressive brain damage can occur: a spontaneous recovery, limited to the first months after the injury, and a long-term process, spontaneous and/or therapy guided, that can extend for years. These processes are not mutually exclusive, since the times of spontaneous and therapy-guided recovery often interact, both at anatomical and efficacy levels.

Spontaneous recovery

The early phase of recovery following the onset of a non-progressive brain lesion, usually of vascular origin, is considered the effect of two interacting factors. The first is anatomical, linked to the disappearance of cerebral edema and intracranial hypertension, the reabsorption of blood, the normalization of hemodynamics in ischemic penumbra areas and the resolution of local inflammation (Baldwin et al., 2010). The second factor, of functional nature, is, according to Von Monakow (1914, for a review, see Feeney and Baron, 1986; Carrera and Tononi, 2014), the resolution of diaschisis (from the Greek word σκισεις, interruption). He proposed that after the onset of acute focal cortical and subcortical region damage, the following sequence of neural events occurs: a first aspect, defined by a cessation of functions in regions adjacent to, or remote from but connected to, the primary site of damage; a second aspect, consisting of a temporary interruption of the intra- and inter-hemispheric connection between the lesion and remote areas. These events usually occur simultaneously, but one form may predominate, depending upon the 'injured connections' and the degree of cortical development in the species under study. The third key aspect of the process is its resolution. Diaschisis, according to Von Monakow, is not stable, but is subject to 'gradual resolution', with resumption of function of the cerebral areas temporally disconnected and recruitment of perilesional spared areas (Heiss et al., 1999; Warburton et al., 1999; Croquelois et al., 2003). Although Von Monakow's theory was not supported by experimental data, it not only enjoyed a large diffusion among clinicians, but in more recent times, gave rise, both in animals and humans, to a number of studies aimed to clarify the remote functional effects of a focal brain lesion, mostly of vascular origin. Reductions in cerebral blood flow on both hemispheres, mostly in the first week after the onset, have been reported in unilateral hemisphere damaged stroke patients, since Kempinsky et al.'s (1961) seminal report. In addition to changes in metabolism and blood flow, diaschisis is also reflected by direct changes in neuronal activity in regions of the brain remote to the ischemic infarct. For example, in patients with stroke affecting the striate or visual cortex, visual activation (evidenced by fMRI changes in blood-oxygenation-level-dependent signals) was found to be reduced or absent in extra striate cortex in the first 10 days after stroke, but restored in the same regions 6 months after infarction (Brodtmann et al., 2007).

Finally, thanks to the progress of functional neuroimaging methods, Carrera and Tononi (2014) added an important contribution to the understanding of the mechanisms of diaschisis: they distinguished a diaschisis at rest and a functional diaschisis. Diaschisis 'at rest' is defined as the focal decrease in energy metabolism without stimulation or activation in anatomically intact brain regions distant from the lesion. By contrast, functional diaschisis refers to the alteration of functional responsiveness of a neural system remote from a lesion when challenged by physiological activation.

A word of caution is, however, needed before accepting a causal relation between the clinical transient deficits attributed to the effect of diaschisis and the neuroimaging data. Crossed cerebellar diaschisis (CCD) describes a pattern of hypo-metabolism in a cerebellar hemisphere secondary to a lesion in the contralateral cerebral hemisphere and present in ~50% of the cases. It is thought to be the consequence of the destruction or inactivation of the cortico-ponto-cerebellar tract. It was first described by Baron et al. (1981), who, using positron emission technology (PET), showed a marked reduction in blood flow and metabolism in the contralesional cerebellar hemisphere of stroke subjects. Unfortunately, up to now, there has been no well-established clinical expression of CCD. For example, Pappata et al. (1990) found no obvious association between CCD and cerebellar deficits in a group of patients with pure capsular infarct.

> Spontaneous recovery of functions after brain damage can occur in the early or late stage. The main factor in the acute stage is the gradual resolution of diaschisis, a sudden loss of function in regions adjacent or connected to, but at a distance away from, the damaged area.

Late stage recovery

Once the acute stage of a non-progressive brain lesion (stroke) is over (usually within 6 months), the process of recovery, either spontaneous or therapy guided, can extend for months and years, although at a slower pace.

The results of the many neuroimaging studies in stroke patients have supported three hypotheses at the base of the process of late-stage recovery, which are not, however, mutually exclusive. According to the first hypothesis, the recovery pattern is mediated by a process of reconstitution of specific neural systems in tissues around the lesion, leading to a new functional and neural pattern lesion (the 'perilesional' hypothesis). A second hypothesis postulates that recovery is mediated by the contralateral hemisphere taking over the damaged hemisphere (the 'laterality-shift' hypothesis). This ability to compensate the lost function can be similar to the experience of a right-handed person, unable to temporarily use his right hand, who can easily learn to write with a little training of the left hand, although often not at the same level. In other words, the goal is attained, but employing different motor plans, muscles and forces. The compensatory effect on motor improvement after focal ischemia was experimentally shown by Metz et al. (2005): some laboratory rats developed a compensatory movement strategy following unilateral cerebral ischemia that was more successful than the one used prior to the lesion and supported by the intact hemisphere (Biernaskie et al., 2005). A similar mechanism had been shown in a subset of unilaterally brain damaged patients; activation in a contralesional homologous region, induced by acute lesions after stroke (Saur et al., 2006) or by slow-growing lesions (see section 8.1.2) such as gliomas (Desmurget et al., 2007) had been observed through fMRI studies.

The third, the 'disinhibition' hypothesis, is mainly based on the results of fMRI and rTMS studies. It claims that the activity of the corresponding intact regions of the contralateral hemisphere is the product of loss of transcallosal inhibition. Transcallosal inhibition refers to suppression of one hemisphere by the opposite hemisphere, which may help to maintain hemispheric dominance in cognitive and motor tasks (Li, Lai and Chen, 2013). This 'abnormal' influence contributes little to or may even hinder the process of recovery that is normally possible thanks to the contribution of undamaged tissue of the lesioned hemisphere.

Functional neuroimaging experiments using PET or fMRI have demonstrated abnormal cortical activation patterns in the subacute to chronic phase after stroke during movements of the paretic hand. The interested areas can be located in the damaged (ipsilateral) as well in the contralateral hemisphere (for a revision, see Grefkes and Fink, 2011). Similarly, an altered pattern of the visual attention network has been reported by Corbetta et al. (2005) in patients affected by unilateral spatial agnosia,[1] following right hemisphere lesion or in aphasia. In a longitudinal functional MRI study, Ward et al. (2003) have reported that the pattern of neural reorganization following acute cortical or subcortical lesion is not stable: while in the acute phase neural activity is often enhanced in both hemispheres, in the chronic phase it tends to return to levels similar to those observed in healthy subjects, in particular in subjects with good recovery. Along the same line, Grefkes and Fink (2011) suggest that the persistence of abnormal activation patterns can represent a negative factor, a sort of maladaptive functional reorganization.

Three hypotheses at the base of the process of late-stage recovery following unilateral brain damage have been formulated. The first, most probable, hypothesis postulates that the recovery pattern is mediated by a process of reconstitution of specific neural systems in tissues around the lesion (the 'perilesional' hypothesis). A second hypothesis postulates that recovery is mediated by the contralateral hemisphere taking over the damaged hemisphere (the 'laterality-shift' hypothesis). The third, the 'disinhibition' hypothesis, claims that the activity of the corresponding intact regions of the contralateral hemisphere is the product of the loss of transcallosal inhibition. This 'abnormal' influence may hinder the process of recovery carried out by intact regions contiguous to the anatomical damage. The pattern of neural reorganization following acute lesion is not stable: while in the acute phase neural activity is often enhanced in both hemispheres, in the chronic phase it tends to return to levels similar to those observed in healthy subjects.

The restoration of lost functions: the effect of therapy

Pharmacological and replacement therapies for stroke-induced motor deficits are at present under experimental investigation; their basis and their possible use in humans are far from established (for a review, see Dimyan and Cohen, 2011). We will instead focus on non-invasive therapies, such as task-oriented models of motor learning and, in the following section, non-invasive brain stimulation (NIBS) techniques, such as repetitive transcranial magnetic stimulation (rTMS) and transcranial direct current stimulation (tDCS). Motor and language deficits are the most prominent and disabling symptoms following a stroke, and it is not surprising that the search for new therapeutic methods, the testing of their efficacy and the effort to clarify the processes underpinning the therapy-guided process of recovery represent a continuous and evolving field of research. From the beginning, however, it must be stated that clear-cut conclusions are far from reached, since prognosis and efficacy of therapeutic interventions interact over and above the process of 'natural' recovery.

Neural plasticity underlying rehabilitation of motor function after stroke

The motor system consists of cortical (primary and secondary motor areas, the Pyramidal Tract) and extra-cortical areas (basal ganglia and cerebellum, the Extrapyramidal System). Furthermore, a close interaction with sensory systems (e.g. the primary somatosensory cortex, S1) is a prerequisite for proper movement execution and motor learning. An acquired damage to the system following CVA can damage either the cortical representation of muscles and movements or the connecting tracts.

As in language deficits, the process of motor recovery can be carried out by an increased activation of secondary areas or by a process of reactivation of task-specific neural systems involved in motor learning and execution.

The first mechanism is more active in the acute stage and seems to reflect a process of contigous or distant cortical hyper-excitability of limited functional advantage (Ward et al., 2003). In the chronic stage, a 'good' recovery, as reflected by the degree of movement reacquisition, seems to be related to a process of reorganization of the normal motor network. Patients with no residual impairment have relatively normal activation maps compared with controls, while patients with more marked residual impairment recruit larger portions of secondary motor areas and homologous areas of the contralateral hemisphere. This additional recruitment, concomitant to the poor functional recovery, seems far from being beneficial, but rather interferes with the process of neural reorganization of the specific neural circuits. In a longitudinal fMRI study of stroke patients, Ward et al. (2003) found an initial over-activation in many primary and secondary motor regions, followed by a focusing toward a normal activation pattern that parallels recovery. The degree to which mechanisms underlying cerebral reorganization are successful is likely to depend on the functional integrity of the surviving elements of specific neural systems.

The effect of training and physical activity to restore motor function after neural injury has long been appreciated. A recent Cochrane Stroke Group study (Pollock et al., 2014) reported that physical rehabilitation was found to have a beneficial effect, as compared with no treatment, on functional recovery after stroke, with persistence of effect beyond the length of the intervention period. While the dose of intervention (length of treatment) proved to be significant, no one physical rehabilitation approach was more (or less) effective than any other approach in improving independence in activities of daily living and motor independence.

One of the most investigated rehabilitation techniques is constrain induced (CI) movement therapy, based on 'forced' use of the paretic limb in activities of daily living and intensive functional training, associated with restraint of the non-paretic limb (Taub et al., 2002). This approach encourages use of the paretic upper extremity in daily life and is thought to help overcome what Taub first described in a deafferented monkey model as 'learned nonuse' (Taub, 1980). Several meta-analyses have shown that this therapy is associated with an immediate decrease in disability rating scores (Sirtori et al., 2009). According to its proponents (for a review, see Mark et al., 2006), CI induces a large change in brain organization and function related to the improvement of motor function. Liepert et al. (1998) showed that CI therapy leads to an enlarged representation on the cortical lesioned hemisphere of the abductor digiti pollicis brevis muscle (mapped using focal transcranial magnetic stimulation, see section 8.4) as compared with the contralateral hemisphere, thus indicating the recruitment of motor areas adjacent to the original location.

The effects of speech therapy

A recent Cochrane review on the efficacy of speech and language therapy (Brady et al., 2012) presented evidence of the effectiveness of treatment for people with aphasia following stroke in terms of improved functional communication, receptive and expressive language. The AA, however, were unable to report sufficient evidence to draw any conclusion regarding the effectiveness of any one specific therapeutic approach over another. One possible reason for this latter datum could be due to the polymorphic aspect of aphasia. Aphasia is not a uniform and stable disorder: certain linguistic deficits (lexical, syntactic, phonological, and semantic) can characterize the language impairment, being the consequence of a specific damage within the language network; in addition, the process of recovery can be limited to a specific linguistic parameter. The reorganization of linguistic functions after damage of the specific areas may take place ipsilaterally, within the spared regions of the dominant hemisphere language areas, or contralaterally, in homologous regions of the right hemisphere.

Several functional fMRI studies indicated that re-activation of spared left hemispheric areas is frequently observed in recovered aphasics (Warburton et al., 1999; Perani et al., 2003). For example, Meinzer et al. (2008) found a correlation between training-induced improvement in picture naming and reactivation of perilesional areas in the left hemisphere. In a more recent study, the same group (Menke et al., 2009) reported that a stable linguistic improvement was associated with activation in the undamaged language areas contiguous to the left hemisphere lesion and in the homologous right hemispheric regions. Similarly, Marcotte et al. (2012) in a group analysis of recovered aphasic patients, found that a therapy based on Semantic Feature Analysis[2] induced recovery that was characterized by (a) a significant correlation between improvement and activation in the left precentral gyrus before therapy and (b) the recruitment of the left inferior parietal lobule, an area known for its role in semantic integration.

On the other hand, a substantial number of neuroimaging studies (for a review, see Cappa, 2011) support the idea that recovery of impaired linguistic functions, such as naming or syntactic processing, depends on the linguistic properties of the right hemisphere. This hypothesis stems from the evidence of considerable right-hemispheric linguistic abilities, especially at the lexical-semantic level, in split-brain subjects (Gazzaniga, 1983). The presence of increased right hemispheric activity in recovered aphasics during language tasks has been replicated by many studies, starting from the early PET investigation of the correlates of word generation in recovered Wernicke's aphasics (Weiller et al., 1995). More recently, Forkel et al. (2014), in a tractographic study, hypothesized that the process of recovery of aphasia following left hemisphere lesion was more efficient in those patients showing a more developed right hemisphere language network, as guessed by the length of the arcuate fasciculus, a white matter tract in the left hemisphere connects the Broca's and Wernicke's areas.

From a correlation of the quality of improvement with the hemisphere involved in the process, it seems that a 'good' recovery is mediated by a reorganization process of the left language-dominant hemisphere, the role of the opposite hemisphere being of lesser degree or even counterproductive. According to Postman-Caucheteux et al. (2010), the right-sided activation might reflect a 'maladaptive' functional reorganization, due to the presence of the left lesion itself, while effective recovery mediated by therapy, such as Melodic Intonation Therapy, a music-based treatment (Sparks et al., 1974), might be associated with the reactivation of left-hemispheric undamaged structures.

A recent work by Abel et al. (2014) examined the effects of the therapy methods over type of impairment (phonological versus semantic) and related to the fRMI pattern of activation. In general, left hemisphere, perisylvian brain areas were involved in successful therapy-induced recovery of aphasic word production. In addition, they found a specific activation related to the type of therapy. Phonologically oriented rehabilitation tasks activated only the left hemisphere. On the contrary, and in accordance with previous studies (Fridriksson et al., 2012), they found a right hemisphere activation in semantic guided therapy, pointing to the right hemisphere capacity in compensating for lexical-semantic processing. In conclusion, the process of neural plasticity in therapy-guided aphasia treatment is, at least in part, dependent on the type of linguistic impairment, calling for different neural substrates.

Non-invasive methods for enhancing plasticity in the human cortex: uses and limitations

A promising approach to enhance recovery in the injured, mostly post-stroke, brain has been considered in the application of non-invasive brain stimulation (NIBS) techniques that should be capable of enhancing cortical plasticity. There are three basic forms of NIBS methods. The first two are repetitive transcranial magnetic stimulation (rTMS) and paired associative stimulation (PAS). The third NIBS technique is that of transcranial direct current stimulation (tDCS).

rTMS involves the application of trains of transcranial magnetic stimuli at various frequencies to targeted cortical regions. The method features the application of rapidly changing magnetic field pulses to the scalp via a copper wire coil connected to a magnetic stimulator. These brief, pulsed magnetic fields painlessly pass through the skull and create electric currents of sufficient magnitude in discrete brain regions to depolarize neurons. Trains of rTMS pulses at various stimulation frequencies and patterns can induce modification of activity in the targeted brain region, which can outlast the effects of the stimulation. rTMS protocols decrease or increase the critical excitability on the basis on the intensity of stimulation, coil orientation and frequency. In general, low frequency rTMS protocols (<1 Hz) decrease cortical excitability, while high frequency rTMS protocols (>5 Hz) increase cortical excitability (Di Lazzaro et al., 2011; Ridding and Rothwell, 2007). In more recent time, 'patterned' stimulation has been developed, involving the application of high frequency bursts of theta frequency. Continuous application of bursts (3 stimuli at 50 Hz every 200 msec) for 20–40 seconds can induce a lasting reduction in cortical excitability. In contrast, intermittent TBS (iTBS), which involves the application of bursts for 2 sec every 10 sec for a total duration of 190 sec, can increase cortical excitability.

Since its introduction (Barker et al., 1985), rTMS has been used for the evaluation of the motor system, for the functional study of several cerebral regions, and for the physiological study of several neuropsychiatric illnesses. In addition, it has been postulated that rTMS could represent a valid therapeutic tool in modulating plastic changes in different psychiatric and neurological pathologies, ranging from severe depression to focal epilepsy (with the aim to modulate the activity in the targeted cortex) to Parkinson's disease (modulation of activity in a dysfunctional cortico-subcortical network) to the process of restoring the functional organization of the neurological network following stroke and finally to the suppression of maladaptive plasticity in chronic pain (for a review, see Fregni and Pascual-Leone, 2007; Rodriguez-Martin et al., 2009; Hao et al., 2013). It is clearly out of the focus of the present book to review all the relevant literature on the therapeutic use of rTMS (see recent Cochrane reviews). We will then limit this review to the effects of rTMS treatment on the two most frequent and disabling effects of the stroke: motor impairment and aphasia.

According to its proponents, **PAS** can modulate cortical excitability and connectivity within cortico-cortical pathways by inducing changes in the synaptic strength in the stimulated pathways (for a review, see Vallence and Ridding, 2014). PAS technique consists of the repeated application of a peripheral nerve stimulus paired with an appropriately timed TMS pulse to a target region of the cortex (Stefan et al., 2000): a single electrical stimulus is directed to a peripheral nerve in advance of TMS delivered to the contralateral primary motor cortex (M1). Repeated pairing of the stimuli (i.e. association) over an extended period may increase or decrease the excitability of corticospinal projections from M1, in a manner that depends on the interstimulus interval (Carson and Kennedy, 2013).

Transcranial direct current stimulation (tDCS) requires the application of weak direct currents, delivered between two surface electrodes placed over the scalp (Nitsche et al., 2008). Anodal stimulation acts to excite neuronal activity while cathodal stimulation inhibits or reduces neuronal activity (Paulus, 2011).

The use of NIBS to promote functional recovery after stroke

In the past years, NIBS, together with other innovative non-invasive methods (for a review, see Faralli et al., 2013) have flanked standard physical therapy as rehabilitative intervention of the motor deficit following stroke.

The rationale of the interventions is twofold: decreasing the cortical excitability of the unaffected hemisphere in regions that are presumed to hinder optimal recovery by low-frequency rTMS and increasing the cortical excitability of the affected hemisphere by high-frequency rTMS trains. The exact mechanisms of how rTMS works in motor rehabilitation are, however, still under investigation. Similarly, no definite conclusions about the efficacy of this treatment can be offered. According to Hsu et al.'s (2012) review, rTMS has a positive effect on motor recovery in patients with stroke. On the contrary, however, a recent Cochrane review (Hao et al., 2013), failed to show a statistically significant effect on motor function recovery after stroke Much more promising are the results of rTMS application in treat-ing aphasic symptoms, mostly lexical access disorders (anomia). The ratio-nale of the therapy, applied to the unaffected hemisphere, is to decrease the post-stroke, unusually high activation in the RH, related to transcallosal dis-inhibition (see section 8.2.2), leading to a re-activation of some areas within the damaged LH. From the results of the studies reviewed by Cappa (2011) and Naeser et al. (2012), rTMS treatments result in significant improvement in naming and often in phrase length during propositional speech. Theseare long lasting, up to 2 months, or even as long as 2 years, post-rTMS treatment. A correlation between the clinical improvement and fRMI studies report significant improvement in naming in those cases with new LH activation or a shift to overall LH lateralization.

Transcranial direct current stimulation (tDCS) has been used in relatively few studies as an adjunct to further improve the efficiency of standard therapies for motor deficits and aphasia after stroke. A recent Cochrane review (Elsner et al., 2013) failed to show any evidence for the effectiveness of this technique for improving aphasia after stroke. Similarly, no evidence is at present available on the effectiveness of tDCS (anodal/cathodal/dual) versus control for improving ADL performance and function after stroke (Elsner et al., 2013). In addition to its potential use to improve neurological functions supported by the cerebral, tDCS has been applied to the cerebellum (transcranial cerebellar direct current stimulation, tcDCS). According to its proponents (for a review, see Priori et al., 2014) tcDCS can induce prolonged functional changes consistent with a direct influence on the human cerebellum. It may modulate cerebellar motor cortical inhibition, gait adaptation, motor behavior, and cognition (learning, language, memory, attention). The experimental evidence is, however, too weak to draw any conclusion on its potential therapeutic use. In conclusion, at the moment, no solid evidence is available on the effectiveness of tDCS for improving performance and function after stroke.

In conclusion, although advances have been made, further efforts must be made for a clearer understanding of the mechanisms underlying spontaneous or therapy-induced cerebral reorganization following acute brain injury in order to develop therapeutic strategies.

Three non-invasive brain stimulation techniques that should be able to enhance cortical plasticity have been used to enhance the recovery process of motor and language deficits following stroke: repetitive transcranial magnetic stimulation (rTMS), paired associative stimulation (PAS), and transcranial direct current stimulation (tDCS). No definite conclusions about their efficacy can be at present drawn: rTMS has been found in some studies to show a positive effect on motor recovery in patients with stroke, while others failed to show a statistically significant positive effect. Much more promising are the results of rTMS application in treating lexical disorders in aphasic patients. The recovery is statistically significant and long lasting, beyond the end of treatment. No definite conclusions have been drawn about the efficacy of PAS and tDCS in treating motor and language disorders following stroke.

SUMMARY

The human brain shows a remarkable degree of recovery of its functions following postnatal damage. The degree and quality of recovery are dependent upon three main factors: the age of the subject and the size and type of the lesion. Recovery can be spontaneous and/or therapy guided.

Early spontaneous recovery following stroke is mostly due to the resolution of diaschisis, a sudden loss of function in regions adjacent or connected to, but at a distance from, the damaged area. Late-stage recovery, either spontaneous or therapy guided, is, most probably, mediated by a process of reconstitution of specific neural systems in tissues around the lesion. Results of the application of non-invasive brain stimulation techniques in treating motor and language disorders following stroke are, at present, promising, but no definite conclusions can be drawn.

Notes

1. A failure to report, respond to or orient to novel stimuli presented to the side opposite a brain lesion (usually in the right hemisphere), when this failure cannot be attributed to either sensory or motor defects.
2. Semantic Feature Analysis is thought to improve retrieval of conceptual information by accessing the semantic network (Massaro and Tompkins, 1992).

Bibliography

Abel S., Weiller C., Huber W., Willmes K. (2014), Neural underpinnings for model-oriented therapy of aphasic word production. *Neuropsychologia*, 57: 154–165.

Anderson V., Spencer-Smith M., Wood A. (2011), Do children really recover better? Neurobehavioural plasticity after early brain insult. *Brain*, 134(8): 2197–2221.

Baldwin, K., Orr, S., Briand, M., Piazza, C., Veydt, A., Mccoy, S. (2010), Acute ischemic stroke update. *Pharmacotherapy*, 30: 493–514.

Barker A.T., Jalinous R., Freeston I.L. (1985), Non-invasive magnetic stimulation of human motor cortex. *Lancet*, 1(8437): 1106–1107.

Baron J.C., Bousser M.G., Comar D., Castaigne P. (1981), Crossed cerebellar diaschisis in human supratentorial brain infarction. *Transactions of American Neurological Association*, 105: 459–461.

Basser L.S. (1962), Hemiplegia of early onset and the faculty of speech with special reference to the effects of hemispherectomy. *Brain*, 85: 427–460.

Biernaskie J., Szymanska A., Windle V., Corbett D. (2005), Bi-hemispheric contribution to functional motor recovery of the affected forelimb following focal ischemic brain injury in rats. *European Journal of Neuroscience*, 21(4): 989–999.

Brady M.C., Kelly H., Godwin J., Enderby P. (2012), Speech and language therapy for aphasia following stroke. *Cochrane Database of Systematic Reviews*, 5: CD000425.

Brodtmann A., Puce A., Darby D., Donnan G. (2007), fMRI demonstrates diaschisis in the extrastriate visual cortex. *Stroke*, 38(8): 2360–2363.

Cappa S.F. (2011), The neural basis of aphasia rehabilitation: evidence from neuroimaging and neurostimulation. *Neuropsychological Rehabilitation*, 21(5): 742–754.

Carrera E. and Tononi G. (2014), Diaschisis: past, present, future. *Brain*, 137(9): 2408–2422.

Carson R.G. and Kennedy N.C. (2013), Modulation of human corticospinal excitability by paired associative stimulation. *Frontiers in Human Neuroscience*, 7: 823.

Corbetta M., Kincade M.J., Lewis C., Snyder A.Z., Sapir A. (2005), Neural basis and recovery of spatial attention deficits in spatial neglect. *Nature Neuroscience*, 8: 1603–1610.

Croquelois A., Wintermark M., Reichhart M., Meuli R., Bogousslavsky J. (2003), Aphasia in hyperacute stroke: language follows brain penumbra dynamics. *Annals of Neurology*, 54(3): 321–329.

Desmurget M., Bonnetblanc F., Duffau H. (2007), Contrasting acute and slow-growing lesions: a new door to brain plasticity. *Brain*, 130(4): 898–914.

Di Lazzaro V., Dileone M., Pilato F., Capone F., Musumeci G., Ranieri F., Ricci V., Bria P., Di Iorio R., De Waure C., Pasqualetti P., Profice P. (2011), Modulation of motor cortex neuronal networks by rTMS: comparison of local and remote effects of six different protocols of stimulation. *Journal of Neurophysiology, 105*(5): 2150–2156.

Dimyan M.A. and Cohen L.G. (2011), Neuroplasticity in the context of motor rehabilitation after stroke. *Nature Reviews Neurology, 7*(2): 76–85.

Duffau H., Capelle L., Denvil D., Sichez N., Gatignol P., Lopes M., Mitchell M.C., Sichez J.P., Van Effenterre R. (2003), Functional recovery after surgical resection of low grade gliomas in eloquent brain: hypothesis of brain compensation. *Journal of Neurology Neurosurgery and Psychiatry, 74*(7): 901–907.

Duffau H., Denvil D., Capelle L. (2002), Long term reshaping of language, sensory, and motor maps after glioma resection: a new parameter to integrate in the surgical strategy. *Journal of Neurology Neurosurgery and Psychiatry, 72*(4): 511–516.

Elsner B., Kugler J., Pohl M., Mehrholz J. (2013), Transcranial direct current stimulation (tDCS) for improving aphasia in patients after stroke. *Cochrane Database Systematic Reviews, 6*: CD009760.

Faralli A., Bigoni M., Mauro A., Rossi F., Carulli D. (2013), Noninvasive strategies to promote functional recovery after stroke. *Neural Plasticity, 2013*: 854597.

Feeney D.M. and Baron J.C. (1986), Diaschisis. *Stroke, 17*(5): 817–830.

Forkel S.J., Thiebaut De Schotten M., Dell'Acqua F., Kalra L., Murphy D.G., Williams S.C., Catani M. (2014), Anatomical predictors of aphasia recovery: a tractography study of bilateral perisylvian language networks. *Brain, 137*(7): 2027–2039.

Fregni F. and Pascual-Leone A. (2007), Technology insight: noninvasive brain stimulation in neurology-perspectives on the therapeutic potential of rTMS and tDCS. *Nature Clinical Practice Neurology, 3*(7): 383–393.

Fridriksson J., Richardson J.D., Fillmore P., Cai B. (2012), Left hemisphere plasticity and aphasia recovery. *NeuroImage, 60*(2): 854–863.

Gazzaniga M.S. (1983), Right hemisphere language following brain bisection. A 20-year perspective. *American Psychologist, 38*(5): 525–537.

Geranmayeh F., Brownsett S.L., Wise R.J. (2014), Task-induced brain activity in aphasic stroke patients: what is driving recovery? *Brain, 137*(10): 2632–2648.

Gilbert C.D. and Li W. (2012), Adult visual cortical plasticity. *Neuron, 75*(2): 250–264.

Grefkes C. and Fink G.R. (2011), Reorganization of cerebral networks after stroke: new insights from neuroimaging with connectivity approaches. *Brain, 134*(5): 1264–1276.

Hao Z., Liu M., Wang D., Wu B., Tao W., Chang X. (2013), Etiologic subtype predicts outcome in mild stroke: prospective data from a hospital stroke registry. *Bmc Neurology, 13*: 154.

Hao Z., Wang D., Zeng Y., Liu M. (2013), Repetitive transcranial magnetic stimulation for improving function after stroke. *Cochrane Database of Systematic Reviews, 5*: CD008862.

Heiss W.D., Thiel A., Grond M., Graf R. (1999), Contribution of immediate and delayed ischaemic damage to the volume of final infarcts. *Lancet, 353*(9165): 1677–1678.

Hsu W.Y., Cheng C.H., Liao K.K., Lee I.H., Lin Y.Y. (2012), Effects of repetitive transcranial magnetic stimulation on motor functions in patients with stroke: a meta-analysis. *Stroke, 43*(7): 1849–1857.

Johnson M.H. (2001), Functional brain development in humans. *Nature Reviews Neuroscience, 2*: 475–483.

Johnson M.H. (2005), *Developmental Cognitive Neuroscience*, Malden (MA), Blackwell Publishing.

Keenan H.T., Hooper S.R., Wetherington C.E., Nocera M., Runyan D.K. (2007), Neurodevelopmental consequences of early traumatic brain injury in 3-year-old children. *Pediatrics, 119*(3): e616–623.

Kempinsky W.H., Boniface W.R., Keating J.B., Morgan P.P. (1961), Serial hemodynamic study of cerebral infarction in man. *Circulation Research, 9*: 1051–1058.

Kolb B. and Gibb R. (2010), Tactile stimulation after frontal or parietal cortical injury in infant rats facilitates functional recovery and produces synaptic changes in adjacent cortex. *Behavioural Brain Research, 214*(1): 115–120.

Li J.-Y., Lai P.-H., Chen R. (2013), Transcallosal inhibition in patients with callosal infarction. *Journal of Neurophysiology 109*(3):659–665.

Liepert J., Miltner W.H., Bauder H., Sommer M., Dettmers C., Taub E., Weiller C. (1998), Motor cortex plasticity during constraint induced movement therapy in stroke patients. *Neuroscience Letters, 250*(1): 5–8.

Maas A.I., Menon D.K., Lingsma H.F., Pineda J.A., Sandel M.E., Manley G.T. (2012), Re-orientation of clinical research in traumatic brain injury: report of an international workshop on comparative effectiveness research. *Journals of Neurotrauma, 29*(1): 32–46.

Marcotte K., Adrover-Roig D., Damien B., De Préaumont M., Généreux S., Hubert M., Ansaldo A.I. (2012), Therapy-induced neuroplasticity in chronic aphasia. *Neuropsychologia, 50*(8): 1776–1786.

Mark V.W., Taub E., Morris D.M. (2006), Neuroplasticity and constraint-induced movement therapy. *Europa Medicophysica, 42*(3): 269–284.

Massaro, M., Tompkins, C.A. (1992), Feature analysis for treatment of communication disorders in traumatically brain-injured patients: An efficacy study. *Clinical Aphasiology, 22*, 245–256.

Meinzer M., Flaisch T., Breitenstein C., Wienbruch C., Elbert T., Rockstroh B. (2008), Functional re-recruitment of dysfunctional brain areas predicts language recovery in chronic aphasia. *Neuroimage, 39*(4): 2038–2046.

Menke R., Meinzer M., Kugel H., Deppe M., Baumgärtner A., Schiffbauer H., Thomas M., Kramer K., Lohmann H., FLÖEL A., Knecht S., Breitenstein C. (2009), Imaging short- and long-term training success in chronic aphasia. *BMC Neuroscience, 10*: 118.

Metz G.A., Antonow-Schlorke I., Witte O.W. (2005), Motor improvements after focal cortical ischemia in adult rats are mediated by compensatory mechanisms. *Behavioural Brain Research, 162*(1): 71–82.

Naeser M.A., Martin P.I., Ho M., Treglia E., Kaplan E., Bashir S., Pascual-Leone A. (2012), Transcranial magnetic stimulation and aphasia rehabilitation. *Archives of Physical Medicine and Rehabilitation, 93*(1): S26–34.

Nitsche M.A., Cohen L.G., Wassermann E.M., Priori A., Lang N., Antal A., Paulus W., Hummel F., Boggio P.S., Fregni F., Pascual-Leone A. (2008), Transcranial direct current stimulation: State of the art 2008. *Brain Stimulation, 1*(3): 206–223.

Pappata S., Mazoyer B., Tran Dinh S., Cambon H., Levasseur M., Baron J.C. (1990), Effects of capsular or thalamic stroke on metabolism in the cortex and cerebellum: a positron tomography study. *Stroke, 21*(4): 519–524.

Paulus W. (2011), Transcranial electrical stimulation (tES–tDCS; tRNS, tACS) methods. *Neuropsychological Rehabilitation, 21*(5): 602–617.

Pavlovic J., Kaufmann F., Boltshauser E., Capone Mori A., Gubser Mercati D., Haenggeli C.A., Keller E., Lütschg J., Marcoz J.P., Ramelli G.P., Roulet Perez E., Schmitt-Mechelke T., Weissert M., Steinlin M. (2006), Neuropsychological problems after paediatric stroke: two year follow-up of Swiss children. *Neuropediatrics, 37*(1): 13–19.

Perani D., Cappa S.F., Tettamanti M., Rosa M., Scifo P., Miozzo A., Basso A., Fazio F. (2003), A fMRI study of word retrieval in aphasia. *Brain and Language, 85*(3): 357–368.

Plowman E., Hentz B., Ellis C. Jr. (2012), Post-stroke aphasia prognosis: a review of patient-related and stroke-related factors. *Journal of Evaluation in Clinical Practice, 18*(3): 689–694.

Pollock A., Baer G., Campbell P., Choo P.L., Forster A., Morris J., Pomeroy V.M., Langhorne P. (2014), Physical rehabilitation approaches for the recovery of function and mobility following stroke. *Cochrane Database of Systematic Reviews, 4*: CD001920.

Postman-Caucheteux W.A., Birn R.M., Pursley R.H., Butman J.A., Solomon J.M., Picchioni D., Mcardle J., Braun A.R. (2010), Single-trial fMRI shows contralesional activity linked to overt naming errors in chronic aphasic patients. *Journal of Cognitive Neuroscience, 22*(6): 1299–1318.

Priori A., Ciocca M., Parazzini M., Vergari M., Ferrucci R. (2014), Transcranial cerebellar direct current stimulation and transcutaneous spinal cord direct current stimulation as innovative tools for neuroscientists. *Journal of Physiology, 592*(16): 3345–3369.

Ridding M.C. and Rothwell J.C. (2007), Is there a future for therapeutic use of transcranial magnetic stimulation? *Nature Reviews Neuroscience, 8*(7): 559–567.

Riley J.D., Le V., Der-Yeghiaian L., See J., Newton J.M., Ward N.S., Cramer S.C. (2011), Anatomy of stroke injury predicts gains from therapy. *Stroke, 42*(2): 421–426.

Rodriguez-Martin J.L., Barbanoj J.M., Schlaepfer T., Clos S., Pérez V., Kulisevsky J., Gironelli A. (2009), Transcranial magnetic stimulation for treating depression. *Cochrane Database of Systematic Reviews, 2*: CD003493.

Saur D., Lange R., Baumgaertner A., Schraknepper V., Willmes K., Rijntjes M., Weiller C. (2006), Dynamics of language reorganization after stroke. *Brain, 129*(6): 1371–1384.

Sirtori V., Corbetta D., Moja L., Gatti R. (2009), Constraint-induced movement therapy for upper extremities in stroke patients. *Cochrane Database of Systematic Reviews, 4*: CD004433.

Sparks R., Helm N., Albert M. (1974), Aphasia rehabilitation resulting from melodic intonation therapy. *Cortex, 10*(4): 303–316.

Stefan K., Kunesch E., Cohen L.G., Benecke R., Classen J. (2000), Induction of plasticity in the human motor cortex by paired associative stimulation. *Brain, 123*(3): 572–584.

Szaflarski J.P., Holland S.K., Schmithorst V.J., Byars A.W. (2006), fMRI study of language lateralization in children and adults. *Human Brain Mapping, 27*(3): 202–212.

Taub E. (1980), Somatosensory deafferentation research with monkeys: Implications for rehabilitation medicine. In: Ince L.P. (ed), *Behavioral psychology in rehabilitation medicine: Clinical applications*, New York, Williams & Wilkins, 371–401.

Taub E., Uswatte G., Elbert T. (2002), New treatments in neurorehabilitation founded on basic research. *Nature Reviews Neuroscience, 3*(3):228–236.

Vallence A.M. and Ridding M.C. (2014), Non-invasive induction of plasticity in the human cortex: Uses and limitations. *Cortex, 58C*: 261–271.

Vargha-Khadem F., Isaacs E., Muter V. (1994), A review of cognitive outcome after unilateral lesions sustained during childhood. *Journal of Child Neurology, 9*(2): 67–73.

Von Monakow C. (1914), *Die Lokalisation im Grosshirn und Abbau der Funktion durch kortikale Herde*, Wiesbaden, Bergmann.

Warburton E., Price C.J., Swinburn K., Wise R.J. (1999), Mechanisms of recovery from aphasia: evidence from positron emission tomography studies. *Journal of Neurology Neurosurgery and Psychiatry, 66*(2): 155–161.

Ward N.S., Brown M.M., Thompson A.J., Frackowiak R.S. (2003), Neural correlates of motor recovery after stroke: a longitudinal fmri study. *Brain, 126*(11): 2476–2496.

Ward N.S. and Cohen L.G. (2004), Mechanisms underlying recovery of motor function after stroke. *Archives of Neurology, 61*(12): 1844–1848.

Weiller C., Isensee C., Rijntjes M., Huber W., Müller S., Bier D., Dutschka K., Woods R.P., Noth J., Diener H.C. (1995), Recovery from Wernicke's aphasia: a positron emission tomographic study. *Annals of Neurology, 37*(6): 723–732.

Woods B.T. and Carey S. (1979), Language deficits after apparent clinical recovery from childhood aphasia. *Annals of Neurology, 6*(5): 405–409.

GLOSSARY

Agraphia. Acquired impairment of writing, following a deficit of the lexical or sublexical route (central agraphias) or damage to the orthographic representations of letters and words (peripheral agraphias).

Alexia. Total or partial loss of reading ability following cerebral lesion. Developmental dyslexia is a specific learning disorder of reading that cannot be attributed to a more generalized learning disorder.

Alzheimer's Dementia. See Dementia.

Anomia. Difficulty accessing the lexicon with consequent impossibility in recalling the phonology or orthography of a word.

Aphasia. A disorder of verbal communication due to an acquired lesion of the central nervous system (usually specific zones of the left hemisphere) involving one or more aspects of comprehending and producing verbal messages.

Autism Spectrum Disorder (ASD). ASD is a lifelong development disability characterized by difficulties in social interaction, communication, restricted and repetitive interests and behavior. It includes autism, Asperger syndrome, pervasive developmental disorder not otherwise specified (PDD-NOS), childhood disintegrative disorder, and Rett syndrome.

Basal Ganglia. A group of four subcortical nuclei: (1) the corpus striatum (divided into the caudate nucleus, the putamen, and the ventral striatum); (2) the globus pallidus; (3) the substantia nigra; and (4) the subthalamic nucleus.

Cerebral Cortex. The most phylogenetically recent part of the cerebral nervous system. It is composed of two cerebral hemispheres. It can be divided into the primary cortex and the association cortex.

Cerebral Dominance. A characteristic peculiar to the human species, consisting of a functional asymmetry between the two cerebral hemispheres, so that a cognitive function has its anatomical and functional base exclusively or prevalently in one hemisphere. Moreover, for 90% of the human population, the left hemisphere dominates for language and manual preference.

Cognitive Reserve. In most cases, there does not appear to be a direct relationship between the degree of brain pathology and the clinical manifestation. From this observation emerged the idea of a sort of reserve that can act as moderator between pathology and clinical outcome.

Computerized Axial Tomography (CT). CT or CAT scan is a neuroimaging method that allows investigation of the brain to reveal the structures of the central nervous system and possible lesions *in vivo*. The formation of a CT image depends on the transmission of an x-ray beam through a section of the brain. The transmission results in an attenuation of the radiation beam, which depends on the tissue absorption coefficient and is measured by external detectors. These measurements are repeated for multiple entry points and at different angles.

Corpus Callosum. A band of fibers that connects the two cerebral cortices, allowing exchange and integration of information.

Dementia. Dementia describes a group of symptoms affecting thinking and social abilities severely enough to interfere with daily functioning. The most common causes of dementia are neurodegenerative diseases such as Alzheimer's disease. Dementia can also be of vascular or infectious origin. Memory loss generally occurs in dementia. However, memory loss alone is not compatible with a diagnosis of dementia. Dementia can be suspected when at least two cognitive functions, including memory, are affected.

Dendrite. Dendrites are the branched projections of a neuron that act to propagate the electrochemical stimulation received from other neural cells to the cell body, or soma, of the neuron from which the dendrites project. Electrical stimulation is transmitted onto dendrites by the axons of the neurons via synapses.

Dendritic Spines. Dendritic spines are protrusions of the dendritic membrane that serve as primary recipients of excitatory synaptic input in the mammalian central nervous system. Many studies indicate that a mutual relationship exists between spine morphology and function of synapses. Dendritic spines can be stable, but they are also dynamic structures that undergo morphological remodeling during development and in adaptation to sensory stimuli or in learning and memory.

Diffusion Tensor Imaging (DTI). Diffusion tensor imaging (DTI) provides measures of white matter integrity in the brain. A more elaborate method of probabilistic tractography with DTI can be used to estimate the strength of the structural connection between two regions of interest, such as thalamus and cortex. Strengths of tract connectivity estimated for individuals can then be linked with inter-individual differences in human behavior.

Electroencephalography (EEG). Electroencephalography is the neurophysiological measurement of electrical activity in the brain, as recorded by electrodes placed on the scalp or, in special cases, subdurally or in the cerebral cortex. The resulting pattern represents a summation of post-synaptic potentials from a large number of neurons. This pattern is composed of different frequencies, Hertz varying from 0.1 cycles per second (delta frequency, as in sleep), to 13 to 60 pulses per second, when the subject is fully alert. EEG pattern is not constant, but varies according to the site of registration, age, state of consciousness and presence of pathology.

Epigenetics. The stably heritable phenotype traits resulting from changes in a chromosome without alterations in the DNA sequence.

Event-Related Potentials (ERP). ERPs are voltage fluctuations in the electroencephalogram (EEG) induced within the brain that are time locked to sensory (auditory, visual), motor, or cognitive events. They provide a direct, non-invasive measure of the temporal course of the voltage changes that are extremely sensitive to manipulations of the cognitive context within which the eliciting stimuli are embedded. By contrast, the spatial resolution for identification of the neural sources generating these signals has been poor relative to the newer brain imaging techniques. Electrical brain activity can be recorded by placing electrodes on a person's scalp. ERPs are obtained by presenting the participant with stimuli and/or a certain task, and recording the electrical potentials from the start of the stimulus or other event of interest. These potentials are then averaged over a large number of trials of the same type, yielding the ERP. Averaging will enhance the brain potentials that are related to the onset of the event, and will reduce brain potentials that are not tied to the onset of the event and are assumed to be random. The ERP is a sequence of positive and negative deflections. Several waveforms, such as the N1, P2, and N400, have been distinguished on the basis of their polarity, timing (latency) of the onset or the peak, their duration, and/or distribution across the scalp – that is, at which positions on the scalp a waveform is smallest or largest.

fMRI. See Magnetic Resonance Imaging.

Glia. Glial cells are the most abundant cells within the central nervous system. Unlike neurons, glial cells do not conduct electrical impulses. The glial cells surround neurons and provide support for and insulation between them.

Left-Handedness. The preferential use of the left hand in skilled movements, a particularity shared by around 10% of the world population. While in left-handers the right hemisphere is 'dominant' for the manual dexterity, the language representation is mostly located in the left hemisphere.

Limbic System. The limbic system is a complex set of brain structures that are located in the telencephalon and diencephalon. It includes the olfactory bulbs, hippocampus, amygdala, anterior thalamic nuclei, fornix, columns of fornix, mammillary body, septum pellucidum, habenular commissure, cingulate gyrus, parahippocampal gyrus, limbic cortex, and limbic midbrain areas. The limbic system supports a variety of functions, including adrenaline flow, emotion, behavior, motivation, long-term memory, and olfaction.

Long Term Depression And Potentiation. In neurophysiology, long term potentiation and long term depression are enduring changes in synaptic strength, induced by specific patterns of synaptic activity. These phenomena occur in many areas of the central nervous system with varying mechanisms, depending upon brain region and developmental progress.

Magnetic Resonance Imaging (MRI). MRI is a cerebral neuroimaging technique that allows visualization of the structures of the central nervous system in both normal and pathological conditions without the use of x-ray. Functional MRI (fMRI) derives its signal from deoxyhemoglobin concentrations in response to neuronal firing (blood-oxygen-level dependent, BOLD contrast imaging). Similar to PET, but without injection or inhalation of exogenous substances, it allows measurement of variation of cerebral blood flow in areas of the brain during different states of cerebral activity (control condition versus experimental conditions).

Magnetoencephalography (MEG). MEG refers to a non-invasive technique of directly recording the magnetic fields generated by post-synaptic currents associated with synchronous neural firing in the brain. It allows the mapping of sensory motor and motor cortices in both the healthy and damaged brain.

Memory. The process by which information is encoded, stored, and retrieved. Short term memory allows accurate recall of a limited amount of information for a limited time. Long term memory includes episodic or autobiographical memory and semantic memory. Episodic memory concerns events connoted in space and time that make up an individual's personal memory. Semantic memory is long term declarative memory that includes the general knowledge common to a specific society (for example, the meanings of words).

Myelin. Myelin is an electrically insulating membrane composed of fatty lipids and proteins that forms a layer, the myelin sheath or white matter, around the axon of a neuron; its integrity is essential for efficient neural transmission . The production of the myelin, myelination, begins in the 14th week of fetal development and occurs quickly in infancy and adolescence. Myelination continues through the adolescent and early adulthood stages of life.

Neuron. A neuron is an electrically excitable nerve cell that processes and transmits information through electrical and chemical signals. A typical neuron possesses a cell body (soma), dendrites, and an axon.

Parkinson's Disease. Chronic neurological disease arising in adults and resulting from a deterioration of the basal nuclei, characterized by tremor, rigidity and slowness in the execution of voluntary movements.

Phantom Limb. The vivid impression that an amputated (or sometimes congenitally missing) limb is not only still present, but in some cases, painful. Usually present in the majority of patients in the early days after amputation, it gradually fades or shrinks in the chronic stage, but with some remarkable exceptions.

Positron Emission Tomography (PET). PET is a relatively non-invasive neuroimaging technique that allows the display of quantitative maps of brain activity, via tracer modeling of previously injected or inhaled radioactive components (for example, ^{18}F-fluorodeoxyglucose). Cerebral activation can be monitored at rest and during the execution of specific tasks by recording changes of the cerebral blood flow, a marker of synaptic activity. The anatomic location can be determined by mapping the signal changes into a standardized coordinate system and superimposing onto an MRI or CT brain image. Spatial resolution is good, while temporal resolution is poor.

Sign Language. Sign language is a language, mostly used by preverbal deaf populations, that uses manual communication and body language to convey meaning, as opposed to acoustically conveyed sound patterns. In comparison to spoken language, it is more iconic and conveys information more directly. Its neurological bases largely coincide with those of auditory-oral language.

Sprouting. Sprouting refers to any phenomena invoking axonal growth in the central and peripheral nervous system. The changes are usually represented by modifications to synapses, evidenced as either alterations in synapse number or junctional area. Such alterations can occur in response to normal and pathological stimuli as part of neural plasticity.

Synapse. A synapse is a structure that permits a neuron to pass an electrical or chemical signal to another cell (neural or otherwise). The synapse consists of a presynaptic ending that contains neurotransmitters, a postsynaptic ending that contains receptor sites for neurotransmitters, and a space between the presynaptic and postsynaptic endings.

Thalamus. The thalamus is a midline symmetrical structure of two halves situated between the cerebral cortex and the midbrain. Some of its functions are the relaying of sensory and motor signals to the cerebral cortex and the regulation of consciousness, sleep, and alertness.

Transcranial Direct Current Stimulation (TDCS). Transcranial direct current stimulation is a non-invasive, painless brain stimulation treatment that uses direct electrical currents to stimulate specific parts of the brain. A constant, low intensity current is passed through two electrodes placed over the head that modulate neuronal activity. There are two types of stimulation with tDCS: anodal and cathodal stimulation. Anodal stimulation acts to excite neuronal activity, while cathodal stimulation inhibits or reduces neuronal activity.

Transcranial Magnetic Stimulation (TMS). TMS is based on the principle of electromagnetic induction. When an electrical current is passed through a wire, it generates a time-varying magnetic field. If a second wire is placed nearby, the magnetic field induces electrical current flow in that second wire. In TMS, the 'first wire' is the stimulating coil and the 'second wire' is a targeted region of the brain. The most common coil in use in TMS is a figure-eight shape in which electrical current flows in opposite directions. The coil is placed on the scalp, and the resulting magnetic field passes through the skull and induces an electrical field in the underlying cortex. Since its introduction in clinical practice, TMS has been applied in many fields, from the study of cortical maps to the treatment of a variety of neurologic disorders, ranging from motor and language deficits to depression. Pulses of TMS can be applied at varying intensities, and in single pulses or in repetitive trains (rTMS) of low or high frequency. The choice of stimulation parameters determines whether the effects of stimulation are excitatory or inhibitory.

Voxel. A voxel represents a value on a regular grid in three-dimensional space. Voxel is a combination of *volume* and *pixel*; *pixel* is a combination of *picture* and *element*.

Voxel-Based Morphometry. Voxel-based morphometry (VBM) involves a voxel-wise comparison of the local concentration of grey matter between two groups of subjects. Voxel-based morphometry of MRI data involves spatially normalizing all the images to the same stereotactic space, extracting the grey matter from the normalized images, smoothing, and finally performing a statistical analysis to localize and make inferences about individual and group differences. The output from the method is a statistical parametric map showing regions where grey matter concentration differs significantly between individual and groups.

Xenomelia. Xenomelia, or the "foreign limb syndrome," is characterized by the non-acceptance of one or more of one's own extremities and the resulting desire for elective limb amputation.

AUTHOR INDEX

Abel, S. 167
Abel, T. 127
Aglioti, S. M. 131, 133
Agosta, F. 42
Akers, K. G. 29
Albert, M. L. 109
Alivisatos, A. P. 10
Altenmüller, E. 44
Altman, J. 29
Amedi, A. 115, 150
Amunts, K. 33
Ances, B. M. 68
Anderson, C. T. 63
Anderson, V. 157
Andreano, J. M. 77, 78
Andres, R. H. 30
Angeletti, P. U. 28
Annett, M. 80, 81
Arenas-Mena, C. 4
Ashburner, J. 85n7
Augustine of Hippo 65

Bach-y-Rita, P. 151
Baddeley, A. D. 69, 122, 126
Baillargeon, R. 18
Baldwin, K. 160
Bao, A. M. 79
Barker, A. T. 168

Barnes, C. A. 67
Baron, J. C. 160, 161
Bashir, Z. I. 35
Basser, L. S. 157
Basso, A. 82
Bates, E. 41
Bateson, P. 3, 4, 10, 62
Baumeister, R. F. 21
Bavelier, D. 42
Bavelier, Daphne 113, 142, 143, 144, 145
Bear, M. F. 35, 41
Benali, H. 39
Beracochea, D. 126
Berlingeri, M. 70
Berlucchi, G. 22, 24, 131, 133
Bielsky, I. F. 78
Biernaskie, J. 162
Bisiach, E. 132
Bliss, T. V. 28
Bolger, D. J. 106
Bories, C. 128
Borod, J.C. 82
Bottari, D. 143
Bourgeois, J. P. 16
Brady, M. C. 165
Braille, Louis 114, 141
Brauer, J. 98

Broca, P. 96
Brodtmann, A. 161
Brugger, P. 134, 135
Büchel, C. 114
Buchtel, H. A. 22, 24
Burke, S. N. 67
Burrack, A. 134
Burton, H. 115
Butler, B. E. 143
Butz, M. 35
Byl, N. N. 44
Byrd, M. 68

Cabeza, R. 68, 71
Cahill, L. 77, 78
Capelle, L., 158, 159
Cappa, S. F. 166, 169
Cappell, K. A. 71
Carey, S. 65, 157
Carrera, E. 160, 161
Carrol, J. 76
Carruthers, P. 18
Carson, R. G. 168
Cashmore, A. R. 3, 9
Cattell, R. B. 85n8
Caviezel, F. 116n3
Chaieb, L. 29
Chang, F. F. 10
Changeux, J. P. 15
Charrier, C. 11
Chen, C. 107
Chen, F. C. 11
Chen, R. 162
Chomsky, N. 47n5, 95
Chugani, H. T. 64
Cimmino, R. L. 134
Cohen, L. G. 19, 26, 38, 106, 150, 155, 164
Cole, M. W. 75, 76
Collignon, O. 142, 150
Collingridge, G. L. 28
Cona, G. 69
Conti, A. M. 44
Corballis, M. C. 80
Corbetta, M. 163
Corina, D. 113
Corkin, S. 124
Cowan, N. 122
Craik, F.I.M. 28, 68, 124, 128
Crick, F. 20, 69

Croquelois, A. 161
Crow, T. J. 83
Curtin, S. 99
Curtiss, S. 100

Dabholkar, A. S. 12, 15, 17, 64, 98
Daffner, K. R. 69
Dahlstrom, L. 147
Danchin, A. 15
Danelli, L. 36, 103
Davis, S. W. 71
Daw, N. W. 62
Dayan, E. 38
Deahene, S. 106
Deary, I. J. 74
Deep-Soboslay, A. 83
DeFelipo, J. 93
De Haan, M. 41
Dehaene, S. 19, 26
Dehaene-Lambertz, G. 106
Déjerine, J. 104, 105
Denes, G. 16, 98, 99, 105, 109, 116n3, 131, 146
Denvil, D. 158, 159
De Renzi, E. 81, 82
Desmurget, M. 160, 162
Deviatov, A. A. 134
Di Lazzaro, V. 168
Dimyan, M. A. 164
Domielöff, E. 81
Dorman, M. F. 147
Doyon, J. 39
Draganski, B. 33
Dragovic, M. 83
Driemeyer, J. 32
Duffau, H. 158, 159
Dworkin, R. H. 45
Dye, M. W. 143

Elsner, B. 169
Epel, D. 4
Ericsson, K. A. 40
Eriksson, P. S. 16

Fabbro, F. 110
Fabiani, M. 69, 84n4
Fagiolini, M. 13
Faglioni, P. 81, 82
Falchier, A. 145
Falk, D. 74

Faralli, A. 169
Farné, A. 35
Feeney, D. M. 160
Feng, J. 79
Field, D. T. 47n7
Fink, G. R. 42, 163
Fitch, W. T. 47n5
Fliers, E. 78
Floyer-Lea, A. 39
Fodor, J. A. 18, 74
Forkel, S. J. 166
Fox, S. E. 65
Franceschini, M. A. 13
Freeman, R. D. 63
Fregni, F. 168
Fridriksson, J. 167
Friederici, A. D. 97, 98
Friedrich, M. 99
Friston, K. J. 85n7
Fromkin, V. 100
Fusco, G. 4
Fyhn, M. 125

Gabrieli, J. D. 68
Gall, Franz Josef 74
Galton, F. 73
Gandour, J. 97, 107
Ganguly, K. 27, 63
Garavan, H. 39
Gardner, H. 74
Garland, T., Jr. 4
Gaser, C., 32
Gatignol, P. 158
Gazzaniga, M. S. 166
Geranmayeh, F. 158
Gervain, J. 47n2
Geschwind, D. H. 11
Geschwind, N. 16, 152n4
Gibb, R. 62, 64, 155
Giedd, D. H. 33
Giedd, J. N. 17, 78
Gilbert, C. D. 155
Gilbert, D. T. 72
Gilbert, S. E. 4
Gilley, P. M. 148
Glaser 146
Gluckman, P. 3, 10
Goel, A. 41
Goldenberg, G. G. 82, 83
Goldstein, J. M. 78

Golestani, N. 98, 112
Golgi, Camillo 23
Goodglass, H. 132
Gordon, K. A. 64
Gori, M. 42, 43
Gottfredson, L. S. 73
Gould, S. J. 12, 18, 19
Gratton, G. 69
Graziano, M. S. 143
Greenough, W. T. 10
Grefkes, C. 42, 163
Grosjean, F. 109
Gross, C. G. 143
Guendelman, M. 150
Gundersen, H. J. 67
Gur, R. C. 78

Haier, R. J. 75
Hamilton, R. 115
Hammond, G. 83
Han, Y. 40
Hansel, C. 35
Hao, Z. 168, 169
Hardy, J. D. 45
Harris, L. J. 81
Harvey, T. 74
Hasher, L. 128
Hauser, M. D. 19, 47n5, 96
He, K. 41
Head, H. 131
Heatherton, T. F. 79
Hebb, Donald 25, 26, 27
Hebden, J. C. 47n2
Hedden, T. 68
Heiss, W. D. 161
Helt, M. 79
Henke, K. 125
Hensch, T. K. 61
Herculano-Houzel, S. 15
Hickock, G. 97
Hihara, S. 28
Hilti, L. M. 135
Hirstein, W. 132
Holmaat, A. 28
Holmes, G. 131
Hopkins, W. D. 47n3
Hoshi, Y. 47n2
Houghton, G. 21
Hsu, W. Y. 169
Hubel, D. H. 6, 27, 62, 63, 84n1, 149

Author Index

Hübener, M. 62
Huttenlocher, P. R. 12, 15, 17, 64, 98
Hyde, J. S. 78

Ilizarof, G. A. 134
Imfeld, A. 40
Ingalhalikar, M. 78
Inman, L. A. 47n7
Innocenti, G. M. 10, 16, 62
Iriki, A. 35
Itard, J. M. G. 100

Jacobs, E. 79
James, William 22, 23, 24, 131
Jäncke, L. 40
Jenkins, I. H. 36
Jessell, Thomas M. 123
Johnson, Mark H. 13, 14, 15, 157
Johnson, W. 74
Joo, E. Y. 127
Jordan-Young, R. 79
Jost, A. 77
Jung, R. E. 75

Kaan, E. 107
Kanai, R. 77
Kandel, Eric R. 123
Karmiloff-Smith, A. 19
Karni, A. 36, 39,
Kasai, H. 28
Katzman, R. 70
Kauffman, A. S. 78
Keenan, H. T. 157
Kelley, W. M. 79
Kelly, A. M. 39
Kelly, S. A. 4
Kempermann, G. 29
Kempinsky, W. H. 161
Kennedy, N. C. 168
Kercel, S. W. 151
Khaitovich, P. 12
Kigar, D. L. 74
Kimura, D. 101
Kinzler, K. 19
Klein, D. 110
Knecht, S. 82, 83
Kolb, B. 62, 64, 155
Kolinsky, R. 20, 106
Konopka, G. 11
Konorski, J. 25

Kovács, A. M. 111
Kral, A. 145, 147, 148
Krendl, A. C. 79
Kreutzmann, J. C. 127
Kupers, R. 149

Lackner, J. R. 134
Lai, P.-H. 162
Lashley, K. S. 24
Lecours, A. R. 99
Lee, H. J. 148
Lee, H. K. 41
Legault, J. 110
Lehmann, A. C. 40
Lenneberg, Eric H. 95, 100
Lenroot, R. K. 17
Leonard, M. K. 148
Lepore, F. E. 74
Levay, S. 6
Levelt, C. N. 62
Levi-Montalcini, R. 28
Levitsky, W. 16, 152n4
Lewis, M. P. 107
Li, J.-Y. 162
Li, P. 108, 109, 110
Li, W. 155
Li, W. H. 11
Lichtheim, L. 96
Liégeois, F. 103
Liepert, J. 165
Liepmann, H. 82
Litcofsky, K. A. 110
Liu, X. 12
Loggia, M. L. 45
Lomber, S. G. 143
Longo, F. M. 29
Lopes, M. 158
Lopez-Muñoz, F. 23
Lövden, M. 69
Lovett, R. E. 147
Lugaro, Ernesto 24

Maas, A. I. 158
Macagno, E. R. 22
MacSweeney, M. 114
Maguire, E. A. 31, 32
Mahmoudzadeh, M. 98
Malenka, R. C. 35, 41
Marcotte, K. 166
Mark, V. W. 165

Martin, J. H. 63
Martin, P. 4
Masel, J. 4
Massa, S. M. 29
Massey, P. V. 35
Matthews, P. M. 39
Mayberry, R. I. 148
McGeoch, P. D. 135
McManus, I. C. 81
McMullen, N. T. 146
McWilliams, L. A. 45
Mechelli, A. 110, 112
Mehler, J. 98, 111
Meinzer, M. 166
Meltzoff, A. N. 131
Melzack, R. 45, 133
Menke, R. 166
Merabet, L. B. 42
Merskey, H. 45
Metz, G. A. 162
Minelli, A. 4
Möller, M. P. 147
Molyneux, William 141
Monzalvo, K. 106
Morais, J. 20, 106
Moscovitch, M. 19
Mosso, Angelo 23, 47n7
Mower, G. D. 63
Mueller, S. 76
Müller, G. B. 11
Münte, T. F. 44

Naeser, M. A. 82, 169
Nagai, M. 5
Negash, S. 72
Nelson, C. A. 64
Neville, Helen J. 42, 141, 142, 143, 144, 145
Newcombe, N. S. 19
Newman, S. D. 113
Newport, E. L. 62, 95
Nishimura, H. 146
Nitsche, M. A. 168
Noe, A. 74
Noh, H. J. 127
Nulty, B. 63

Obler, L. K. 109
O'Donoghue, G. M. 145, 147
O'Keefe, J. 125

Paillard, J. 37, 47n8
Pakkenberg, B. 67
Pallier, C. 112
Pantev, C. 147
Pappata, S. 161
Paradis, M. 110
Park, D. C. 68
Pascual-Leone, A. 25, 36, 39, 62, 65, 114, 168
Paulesu, E. 108
Paulus, W. 168
Paus, T. 78
Pavani, F. 143, 147
Pavlovic, J. 157
Payton, A. 74
Pekna, M. 45
Pekny, M. 45
Penke, L. 74
Perani, D. 98, 110, 111, 166
Petanjek, Z. 17
Petersen, R. C. 85n6
Petersen, S. E. 108
Phoenix, C. H. 77
Piaget, Jean 18
Pietrini, P. 144
Piguet, O. 126
Pitres, A. 109
Pizzamiglio, L. 16
Plowman, E. 158
Poeppel, D. 97
Poldrack, R. A. 39
Pollock, A. 165
Poo, M. M. 27, 63
Postman-Caucheteux, W. A. 166
Prat, C. S. 111
Pratt, J. 79
Preuss, T. M. 13
Price, D. J. 10, 16, 62
Price, T. D. 6
Priori, A. 169
Ptito, M. 149

Qi, H. X. 42
Quoidbach, J. 72

Rabaglia, C. D. 76
Rakic, P. 16, 17
Ramachandran, V. S. 132, 133
Ramón y Cajal, Santiago 23, 24, 25, 27, 29

Author Index

Rauschecker, J. P. 143
Rees, G. 77
Reuter-Lorenz, P. A. 70
Ricciardi, E. 144
Richeson, J. A. 79
Rickard, T. C. 40
Ridding, M. C. 168
Riley, J. D. 158
Rizzolatti, G. 35
Röder, B. 115, 141, 147
Rodriguez-Martin, J. L. 168
Rogers-Ramachandran, D. 133
Rolls, E. T. 125
Rosenkranz, K. 44
Roe, K. 41
Rossini, P. M. 27
Rothwell, J. C. 168
Rubenstein, J. L. 15
Rumelhart, D. E. 21
Rumiati, R. 79
Rutherford, M. D. 5

Saab, C. 45
Sacks, O. 141
Sadato, N. 42, 150
Salthouse, T. A. 68, 69
Sandkühler, J. 45
Sandmann, P. 147
Saur, D. 162
Sawada, M. 29
Sawamoto, K. 29
Schaechter, J. D. 37
Schlaug, G. 32, 33
Schmolck, H. 124
Schneider-Garces, N. J. 70
Scholz, J. 33, 34
Schwartz, James H. 123
Seitz, R. J. 27, 36
Semenza, C. 132
Shallice, T. 68
Sharma, A. 148
Sherrington, C. S. 23
Sichez, N. 158
Siegal, M. L. 4
Siegel, J. M. 127
Simion, F. 63
Simon, L. 79
Sirtori, V. 165
Smith, K. M. 146

Somel, M. 11, 12
Sparks, R. 167
Spelke, E. 19
Spence, I. 79
Sperling, R. A. 72
Sporns, O. 27, 78
Spurzheim, Johann 74
Stefan, K. 168
Stern, Y. 70
Stocco, A. 111
Streim-Amit, E. 150, 151
Strelnikov, K. 148
Sullivan, K. 79
Sur, M. 15
Svoboda, K. 28
Swaab, D. F. 78, 79
Swain, P. A. 37
Szaflarski, J. P. 157

Taki, Y. 127
Tan, L. H. 108
Tanzi, Eugenio 24
Taub, E. 165
Taylor, M. J. 62
Tees, R. C. 63
Teskey, G. C. 64
Teuber, H. L. 65
Thierry, G. 99
Toldi, J. 42
Tononi, G. 160, 161
Tornero, D. 30
Torres, F. 114
Treves, A. 125
Tulving, E. 123, 124
Twyman, A. D. 19

Umiltà, C. 19
Ungerlieder, L. G. 39

Vallence, A. M. 168
Vallender, E. J. 11
Vallortigara, G. 19
van den Honert, D. 83
Van der Werf, Y. D. 127
Vanlancker-Sidtis, D. 102
Vargha-Khadem, F. 36, 65, 102, 103, 157
Vauclair, J. 47n3
Veraart, C. 149, 150
Verhaak, P. F. 45

Von Monakow, C. 160, 161
Voss, P. 141
Vrba, E. S. 18, 19

Wainwright, P. C. 6
Walker, M. P. 40
Wang, J. X. 125
Warburton, E. 161, 166
Ward, N. S. 37, 155, 163, 164
Wartenburger, I. 110
Weeks, R. 42
Weiller, C. 166
Werker, J. F. 63, 99
Wernicke, C. 96
West, R. L. 67, 69
West-Eberhard, M. J. 4, 5
White, A. M. 126

Wiesel, T. N. 6, 10, 27, 62, 63, 84n1, 149
Will, B. 47n8
Wilson, T. D. 72
Windsor, J. 64
Witelson, S. F. 74, 78
Wittmann, B. C. 40
Woods, B. T. 65, 157
Wraga, M. 79

Xu, Y. 107

Yakovlev, P. I. 99
Yang, T. T. 133
Yoo, S. S. 127

Zacks, R. T. 128
Zorzi, M. 21

SUBJECT INDEX

achondroplasia 134
acute ischemic events 159; *see* cerebro-vascular accident, CVA (stroke)
adaptation 4, 6, 22, 29, 32, 72
age: and cochlear implants 148; effect on cerebral organization 26; as factor in language acquisition 110; and neural plasticity 46; and recovery from brain injury 156–7; *see also* aging
aging: anatomical changes in the brain 65–7; changes in hemodynamic response 67; cognitive decline 71–2; cognitive functions in the aging brain 68–9; cognitive reserve 70, 73; compensatory strategies 68–71; declining memory 128–9; definition 66; frontal lobe hypothesis of 68; inter-individual differences 69–70, 84; living 72; neuronal changes 67–8; and neuroplasticity 6, 61–73; normal vs. pathological 66, 71–2; subjective vs. objective 72; *see also* age
agraphia 104
agnosia, unilateral spatial 163
alexia 104, 115
allodynia 45

Alzheimer's disease (AD) 66, 67, 70, 71–2, 73, 84, 126; *see also* dementia
amblyopia 63
amnesia 124
amygdala 78
anosognosia, retrograde and anterograde 132 *see also* memory
aphasia 41, 82–3, 96, 113, 116n3, 165, 166; polyglot 109; primary progressive 126
apraxia 82–3
aptomelia 135
Aristotle 9
astrocytes 45
asymmetries: cerebral 112; hemispheric 16, 47n3
auditory cortex 98, 147, 152n5
auditory localization 151
auditory plasticity 147–9
auditory-motor mapping 97
Australopithecus 15
Autism Spectrum Disorders (ASD) 5
autobiographical (AB) memory 122, 124, 126 *see also* memory
axonal sprouting 32, 34
axons 15, 16, 22, 29

Subject Index

basal ganglia 110, 164
bilingualism 109–11; *see also* second language (L2) acquisition
blindness: congenital (CB) 142–3, 149; 'late' vs. 'early' 150'; and the use of visual substitution sensory devices 150–1
body elongation 134
body ownership 131–2
body schema, superficial 131
body self-consciousness 131
Braille system 42, 114–15, 141, 150, 151
brain anatomy *see* neuroanatomy
brain changes, morphological 27, 29
brain damage 27, 29, 30, 38, 42, 46; factors influencing recovery 156–60; mechanisms of recovery 160–3; and memory 126; nature, extent and site of lesion 158–9; and neural plasticity 46; recovery from 155–70; in the sensitive period 64–5; *see also* recovery
brain development: and the behavioral abilities of infants 14; cerebral cortex 15–17; effect of hormones on 77; and epigenetics 12–13; evolution and 10–17; microscopic vs. macroscopic exuberance 16; process of 13–15; *see also* development
brain imaging *see* neuroimaging
brain plasticity *see* neuroplasticity; plasticity
brain remapping *see* neuroplasticity
brain stimulation, non-invasive *see* non-invasive brain stimulation (NIBS)
brain-derived neurotrophic factor (BDNF) gene 29
Broca rule 81
Broca's area 98–9, 108, 110, 113, 166
Brodmann areas (BAs) 75

cerebral asymmetry 16, 47n3, 112
cerebral blood volume (CBV) 13
cerebral cortex: age-related changes in 67; development of 15–17, 28; functions of 24, 73; occipital 115; prefrontal frontal 111
cerebral dominance, for language 81, 82

cerebro-vascular accident, CVA (stroke) 156, 160, 164; rehabilitation after 164–5; *see also* acute ischemic events
changing-body representation 134–5
Chinese language 107–8
circuit-related utilization of neural circuit hypothesis (CRUNCH) 70–1
cochlear implants (CI) 64, 141, 147–9, 151
Cochrane Stroke Group 165
cognitive enrichment 65
cognitive modularity 76
cognitive reserve (CR) 70
cognitive skills, human-specific 12
communication, and language development 96
congenital deafness *see* deafness
congenital blindness *see* blindness
connectionist models 20
connectivity: between-hemispheric 78; cortical and subcortical 45–6; inter-neural 27; within-hemispheric 78
constrain induced (CI) movement therapy 165
corpus callosum 33, 40, 71, 78, 105
cortical maps, cultural recycling of 19–21
cortical motor area, mapping of 25
cortical plasticity *see* neuroplasticity
cortical progenitor zone 15
cortical space, remapping of 35–6, 38
cortical visual areas 149
cortico-spinal fibers (CSF) 40
corticospinal tract (CST) 63
cortico-subcortical connectivity 45
critical period: and language development 95, 100
crossed cerebellar diaschisis (CCD) 161
cross-modal plasticity 41–3, 144
cross-sectional studies 31, 34
cultural variability 19–20
CVA *see* cerebro-vascular accident (stroke)

Darwin, Charles 19
Darwinism 24
deafness: in humans 143; preverbal/congenital (PVD) 145–7, 148–9

Subject Index 193

dementia 66, 67, 63, 73, 126; semantic 126; *see also* Alzheimer's disease
dendrites 15, 17, 22, 29, 146
dendritic arborizations 64, 76
dendritic spines 27–8; effect of aging on 67; formation of 33, 34
dentate gyrus (DG) 29, 124
development 10; critical period 61–64, 84; postnatal 13, 15, 17, 29, 33, 46, 61–3; prenatal 12, 77, 79; sensitive period 62, 64; *see also* brain development; language development
diaschisis 160–2, 170
dichotic listening testing 101
diffusion tensor imaging (DTI) 75, 78
disinhibition hypothesis 162, 163
DNA, and evolution 11
domain specificity 18–19, 21, 41, 43, 75–6, 122
dorsal pathway 98
dorsolateral prefrontal cortex 75
Down syndrome 116n1
DTI (diffusion tensor imaging) 75
dyslexia 83, 105, 106

education, effect on neural reserve 70
EEG (electroencephalogram) 126
Einstein, Albert 74
elasticity 4
electroencephalogram (EEG) 126
electromyogram (EMG) 126
electrophysiological techniques 155
embouchure dystonia 44
EMG (electromyogram) 126
empiricism 9, 18
encoding 124, 126, 127
'End of History Illusion' 72
environmental changes 4, 6
environmental enrichment (EE) 13
environmental hypoxia 6
epigenetics 12–13
episodic memory 68, 122, 128, 129; *see also* autobiographical (AB) memory
Equipotentiality theory 24
event-related optical signals (EROS) 68
event-related potential (ERP) 99, 68
evo-devo (evolutionary developmental biology) 11

evolution 10; and brain development 10–17
evolutionary developmental biology 11
exaptation 19
executive function 72; age-related changes in 68–9
experience: brain changes due to 26, 27; and learning 18, 19, 21, 22, 25, 26, 30, 34, 35, 37, 46, 61–3, 65, 70, 76–7, 84, 85n8, 100, 111–12, 135
expressive language disorders 126

FA (fractional anisotropy) 40, 47n11
face-processing strategies 5, 41, 63
faculty psychology 74
FD-NIRS *see* frequency-domain near-infrared spectroscopy
flexibility, vs. plasticity 47n8
fluid intelligence 85n8
fMRI (functional MRI) studies 25, 30, 34, 36, 37, 39, 42, 46, 68, 70, 71, 77, 79, 98, 103, 110, 111, 112, 115, 127, 142, 151, 161, 162, 163, 166, 167; on blindness 142
fNIRS (functional NIRS) 47n2
FOXP2 gene 11
fractional anisotropy (FA) 40, 47n11, 71
frequency-domain near-infrared spectroscopy (FD-NIRS) 13
frontal lobe development 74
frontal lobe hypothesis of aging 68
frontotemporal dementia (FTD) 42
functional MRI (fMRI) studies 25, 30, 34, 36, 37, 39, 42, 46, 68, 70, 71, 77, 79, 98, 103, 110, 111, 112, 115, 127, 142, 151, 161, 162, 163, 166, 167; on blindness 142
functional NIRS (fNIRS) 47n2
functional neuroimaging 161, 163; *see also* functional MRI; functional NIRS
functional trans-cranial Doppler ultrasonography 82

gender, and recovery from stroke 158
gender identity disorders (GID) 79–80
gene expression 11–12
genetics 9, 74; and brain development 11–12; effect on neural reserve 70

Subject Index

genomes, human and primate 11
genotypes 18
g factor 73
glial activation 45
glial cell genesis 32
glial cell processes 15
glioma resection 158, 159
global connectivity 75–6
grapheme 108
grey matter: atrophy of 149; changes in 27, 31–4, 40

handedness 80–2, 83; and cerebral dominance 82; left 80–4, 99, 101; and praxis 82–4; and recovery from stroke 158; right 33, 36, 44, 80–4, 99, 101, 104, 116n3, 162
hemiasomatognosia 132
hemiplegia 132
hemodynamic response, changes due to aging 67
hemorrahagic focal cerebrovascular events 159
Heschl's gyrus (Heschl's convolution) 146, 147, 148, 152n3
heterochrony 12
hippocampus 67, 78, 124–5, 127, 129; changes in 31–2
hormones, and brain development 77, 79
human genome 11
hyperalgesia 45
hypothalamus 78
hypoxia, environmental 6

ILPG (intrasulcal length of the precentral gyrus) 33
inductive reasoning, age-related changes in 68
infants, advance in behavioral abilities of 14
inferior colliculus 144, 152n1
inferior parietal lobule 75
informational encapsulation 18
insomnia, chronic 127, 129
intelligence 73; fluid 76, 85n8
interactionism 18
inter-hemispheric connection 33
inter-neural connectivity 27

intrasulcal length of the precentral gyrus (ILPG) 33

knowledge: 'inborn' 19; nature of 9; pre-existing 18

language: anatomo-functional basis of 96–7; Chinese 107–8; cross-linguistic differences 107–8; cross-linguistic differences in processing 108–9; European 107; neural representation of 112; neurological model of 96; sign language 96; tonal vs. atonal 107; written 96; *see also* language acquisition; language development
language acquisition 63–4, 65; age as factor in 110; beyond the critical period 99–104; and the bilingual brain 109–13; the case of Alex 102–3; the case of Genie 100–1; and cochlear implants 148; individual differences in L2 learning 111–13; and left hemisphere dominance 99; and social isolation 100–2; *see also* second language (L2) acquisition
language development 18–21, 41, 95–6; in the critical period 100; neurological basis of 98–9
language impairment 41, 165–6
language modalities, culturally acquired 104–7
lateral prefrontal cortex (LPFC) 75–6
laterality-shift hypothesis 162m 163
learning: and experience 18, 19, 21, 22, 25, 26, 30, 34, 35, 37, 46, 61–3, 65, 70, 76–7, 84, 85n8, 100, 111–12, 135; fast motor skill 39; habituation of 24; motor skill 38; oral language 148; process of 21; slow motor skill 39–40; theories of 25; *see also* language acquisition
left angular gyrus 105
left handedness 80–4, 99, 101
left hemisphere: activation of 170; and language development 99–104
left inferior frontal gyrus 98, 111
left inferior parietal lobe 112
left parietal lobe 105, 114, 132
left superior temporal gyrus 108

leisure activities, effect on neural reserve 70
Lenneberg hypothesis 100
lexical tones 107
lexical-semantic tasks 110
lexicon 97
linguistic competence 110
logographic systems 108
London taxi drivers, study of 31–2
long term memory, organization of 123
long term potentiation (LTP) 29
longitudinal studies 31, 34
low-grade gliomas (LGG) 159

Magnetic Resonance Imaging (MRI) 25, 30, 31–4, 37, 46, 77, 79
magnetic resonance spectroscopy 75
magnetoencephalography (MEG) 27, 133
malleability 4, 6; see also plasticity
Maradona, Diego 81
Mass Theory 24
medial temporal lobe (MTL) neurons 67
MEG (magnetoencephalography) 27, 133
Melodic Intonation Therapy 167
memory: associative 125; autobiographical 122; declarative vs. non-declarative 123; effect of aging on 128–9; effect of sleep deprivation on 126–8; episodic 68, 122, 128, 129; long term 123; procedural 122; processes and plasticity in 124–6; semantic 68, 122; short term 106, 122, 124, 129; systems, distinctions among 122–4; verbal 20, 115; working 122, 128
memory systems, distinctions among 122–4
mental gymnastics 22–3
microcephalia 11
microglia 45
mild cognitive impairment 72, 85n6
mind, making of 18–21
modular components 19
modularity 18
molecular biology 3
morphology 102

morphometry see voxel-based morphometry (VBM)
motor skill learning 38; see also learning
motor system 164
MRI (Magnetic Resonance Imaging) 25, 30, 31–4, 37, 46, 77, 79
mRNA 12
multiple intelligence theory 74
musician's dystonia (MD) 43–4, 46
musicians: brain analysis of 33, 38–9; brain changes in 41; practice required by 40
myelin 17
myelination 17, 33, 71; delayed 98

nativism 9, 18, 19
nature-versus-nurture 9–10
near-infrared spectroscopy (NIRS) 47n2
neural architecture, fixed 18
neural compensation 70
neural networks 20, 25
neural plasticity see neuroplasticity
neural reserve 70
neural stem cells 29–30, 47n9
neuroanatomy: comparative 9; developmental 9; inter-individual differences 75; of language 97; see also *specific brain regions/components by name*
neurochemistry 78
neurodegenerative disorders 71
neurogenesis 17, 29–30, 32, 34, 129; brain injury during 65; following brain injury 64
neuroimaging methods and studies 3, 9, 38, 74–5, 78, 100, 101, 104, 105, 106, 112, 125, 135, 155, 163; on aging 67; on chronic pain 45; functional 161, 163; on memory 124; in stroke patients 162, 166; see also diffusion tensor imaging (DTI); electroencephalogram (EEG); electromyogram (EMG); fractional anisotropy (FA); frequency-domain near-infrared spectroscopy (FD-NIRS); functional MRI (fMRI) studies; functional NIRS (fNIRS); Magnetic Resonance Imaging (MRI); magnetic resonance spectroscopy;

Subject Index

magnetoencephalography (MEG); near-infrared spectroscopy (NIRS); positron emitting tomography (PET) studies
neurons: activation of 63, 84n1, 161, 168; age-related changes in 67–8; depolarization of 167; excitability of 35; in the human cortex 15, 16, 28, 32, 35; hypertrophy of 24; loss due to aging 67–8; sensory 45; systems of 32; *see also* dendritic spines; neurogenesis; synapses
neuropeptidergic systems 78
neuropil 15
neuroplasticity: defining 21–30; and the dynamics of dendritic spines 27–8; effect of age on 61–73; genetic factors 10; historical notions of 22–6; inter-individual differences 73–7, 84; and neurogenesis 29; and neurotrophins 28–9; and sensory deprivation 141–2; sex/gender differences, 77–80, 84; spatial and temporal characteristics of 38–40; structural and functional 26–7, 34; unimodal and cross-modal 41–3; *see also* plasticity
neuropsychiatric disorders 17
neurotrophins 28–9
NIRS (near-infrared spectroscopy) 47n2
non-invasive brain stimulation (NIBS) 38, 164, 167–8; *see also* PAS (paired associative stimulation); transcranial direct current stimulation (tDCS); transcranial magnetic stimulation (TMS)
nutritional factors 12

obligatory firing 18
occipital cortex 42, 104, 105, 115, 142, 150
occipital lobes 75
ocular dominance (OD) plasticity 63
oral language learning 148
organ of Corti 145, 147, 152n2
orthographic representations 105

pain, chronic, 44–6
paired associative stimulation (PAS) 168, 170

paracingulate gyrus 78
Paré, Ambroise 132
Parieto-Frontal Integration Theory (P-FIT) 75
parieto-temporal cortex 147
Parkinson's disease 66, 71, 73, 168
pars opercularis 98; *see also* Broca's area
PAS (paired associative stimulation) 168, 170
perilesional hypothesis 162, 163
PET (positron emitting tomography) studies 27, 36, 39, 68, 70, 75, 110, 148, 150, 161, 163; on blindness 149; on Braille reading 114; on memory 125
phantom limb phenomenon 132–4
phantom nose illusion 134
pharmacological therapy 163
phenotypes 18, 108, 112
phonemic awareness (PA) 20, 47n6
phonemic contrast 97, 99
phonemic segmentation 106
phonetics 97
phonological processing 167
phonology 97, 108
phonological processing 167
phrenology 74
Pinocchio illusion 134
planum temporale 152n4; hemispheric differences 16
plasticity: auditory 147–9; classifications of 5; cross-modal 41–3, 144; defined 3–7; vs. elasticity 4; enhancement of 167–70; and epigenetics 12; experience-dependent 62; experience-expectant 62; experience-independent 62; vs. flexibility 47n8; functional 26–7, 35, 37–8; limitations on 5–6; long-term 125; maladaptive 6, 43–6; mechanisms of multimodal 144–5; multimodal restorative 143–4; ocular dominance (OD) 63; and recovery of brain damage 155–70; reduction in 6; in sensory impaired subjects 142–5; structural 26–7, 37–8, 40; synaptic functional 35; unimodal 142–3; *see also* neuroplasticity
Plato 9
polyglot aphasia 109

Subject Index

positron emitting tomography (PET) studies 27, 36, 39, 68, 70, 75, 110, 148, 150, 161, 163; on blindness 149; on Braille reading 114; on memory 125
postero-temporal cortex 148
preadaptation 18, 19
prefrontal cortex (PFC) 12, 15, 67–9, 71
preverbal deafness (PVD) 145–7, 148–9
primary motor cortex 168
primary progressive aphasia 126; *see also* aphasia
primary sensory cortex 146
primary visual cortex 63, 84n1, 149
primates, genomes of 11
procedural memory 122; *see also* autobiographical (AB) memory
processing speed, age-related changes in 68
prosody 97, 99
psychodynamic theories 24
pyramidal tract 63

Rapid Instructed Task Learning 111
reading 104–7; dual route models for 105; neurological model of 104–5
recovery: auditory 148; and the disinhibition hypothesis 162, 163; language recovery 165–7; and the laterality-shift hypothesis 162, 163; late stage 162–3; motor recovery 164–5; and the perilesional hypothesis 162, 163; and the restoration of lost functions 163–7; spontaneous 160–2
rehabilitation: after stroke 164–5; visual 151; *see also* recovery
remapping, of cortical space 35–6, 38
repetitive transcranial stimulation (rTMS) 125
replacement therapies 163
reticular theory 22
retrograde amnesia 124
Ribot's law 128
right handedness 33, 36, 44, 80–4, 99, 101, 104, 116n3, 162
right insular cortex 135
right parietal lobe 114
Right Shift Theory 81
RNA transcription 12

robustness 3–4
rTMS (repetitive transcranial stimulation) 125, 162, 164

schizophrenia 83
Schumann, Robert 44
second language (L2) acquisition 109, 110–11; age of acquisition 109, 110, 112; *see also* bilingualism
self-awareness 131–2
semantic dementia 126
semantic feature analysis 171n2
semantic memory (SM) 68, 122, 124, 126
sensitive period, brain changes following injury in 64–5
sensory compensation hypothesis 142–3
sensory cortex 42, 146; *see also* somatosensory cortex
sensory enrichment 65
sensory substitution devices (SSDs) 141, 151
short term memory (STM) 106, 122, 124, 129; *see also* memory
sighted individuals (SI) 142
sign language 96; neural basis of 113–14
skills, domain-specific 21
sleep: non-rapid eye movement (NREM) 126; rapid eye movement (REM) 126
sleep deprivation (SD) 127; effect on memory plasticity 126–8
social isolation, and language acquisition 100–2
somatosensory cortex 36, 143, 164; *see also* sensory cortex
somatosensory neural network 133
speech and language disorders 65
speech therapy 165–7
speech understanding 148
SRGAP2 gene 11
stem cells *see* neural stem cells
stochasticism 22
stroke *see* acute ischemic events; cerebro-vascular accident (CVA)
studies: cross-sectional 31, 34; gender-related 79; of London bus drivers (LBD) 32; of London taxi drivers (LTD) 31–2; longitudinal 31, 34

Sturge-Weber syndrome 36, 47n10, 102, 116n4
subicular cortex 124
subventricular zone (SVZ) 29
superior parietal lobule 75
supra marginal cortex 108
synapses 12, 16, 17, 25; density of 98; and synaptic functional plasticity 35
synaptic connections 15–16
synaptic pruning 16–17, 28
synaptic spines 146
synaptogenesis 12, 64, 76; postnatal 15
syntactic contrast 102
syntactic processing 110
syntax 97

tactile vision substitution system (TVSS) 151
tDCS (transcranial direct current stimulation) 164, 167–8, 168–9, 170
temporal lobes 75
thalamic afferent axons 15
therapy: physical rehabilitation 165; speech 165–7
TMS (Transcranial Magnetic Stimulation) 25, 39, 115, 133, 167–8, 169–70
traits 3–6, 10, 22, 80, 83–4
transcallosal inhibition 162
transcranial direct current stimulation (tDCS) 164, 167–8, 168–9, 170
transcranial magnetic stimulation (TMS) 25, 39, 115, 133, 167–8, 169–70
transsexual individuals 79

TVSS (tactile vision substitution system) 151

ultrasonography, functional trans-cranial Doppler 82
unilateral spatial agnosia 163

VBM (voxel-based morphometry) 75, 85n7, 127
ventral pathway 97
ventral post-central gyrus 37–8
verbal memory 20, 115
visual cortical areas 115, 145
visual neuroprostheses 150
visual word form area (VWFA) 106, 151
visual-auditory devices 142
visual-to-auditory sensory substitution device (SSD) 151
visuo-spatial processing 142
voxel-based morphometry (VBM) 75, 85n7, 127

Wechsler IQ test 103
Wernicke's area 16, 113, 166
white matter 71, 146; atrophy of 149; changes in 27, 33–4, 40; in men's brains 78
working memory (WM) 76, 122, 128; age-related changes in 68–9; *see also* memory
writing 104–7; *see also* language

xenomelia 135–6